A YEAR

IN THE

SADDLE

365 stories from the world of cycle sport

Written by Giles Belbin
Illustrated by Daniel Seex

Aurum
Press

First published in Great Britain
2015 by Aurum Press Ltd
74—77 White Lion Street
Islington
London N1 9PF
www.aurumpress.co.uk

A catalogue record for this book is available from the British Library.

ISBN 978 1 78131 443 2

1 3 5 7 9 10 8 6 4 2
2015 2017 2019 2018 2016

Interior design by: Neal Cobourne

Printed in China

CONTENTS

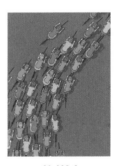

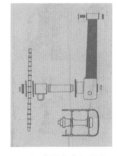

JANUARY

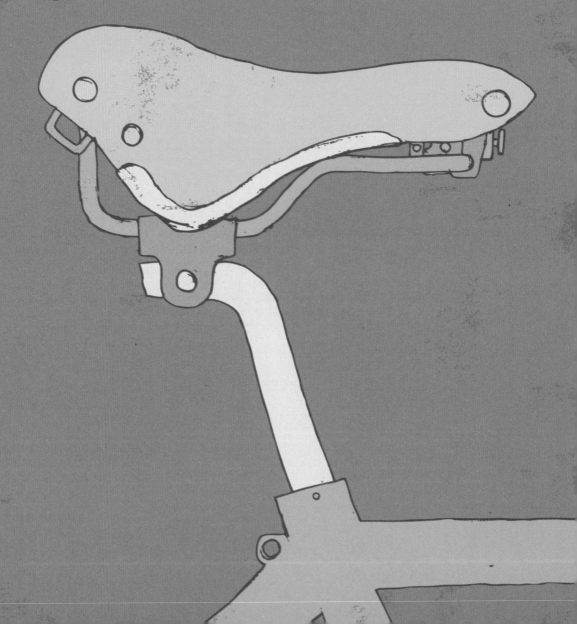

1 January

The first GP Sven Nys is won by .... Sven Nys
(2000)

For the uninitiated cyclo-cross essentially involves riding a bike as fast as you can around a circuit, through tyre-deep sludge, in the depths of a northern Europe winter. Races can be raucous affairs, often with the smell of beer and French fries pervading the frozen air as people in coats and hats watch people in Lycra riding bikes in mud, even though it is minus five.

Sometimes conditions mean that riding is impossible. When that happens, instead of giving up and going home to a nice fire, racers are forced to shoulder their mud-splattered bike and run, normally up a murderously steep hill, before remounting and resuming their furious pedalling. Yep, that's cyclo-cross. In short, it is tough. And Sven Nys is one of the best there has ever been at it.

Nys was born in 1976, in the Belgian town of Bonheiden. An Under-23 world champion in 1997 and 1998, he turned professional in September 1998 with the Dutch Rabobank team. Victory in the Superprestige, a renowned season-long competition that has been held since 1983,

came in that first season. In the years that were to follow Nys would claim that same title a further twelve times, a record haul and one that could yet grow still further.

Just fifteen months after turning professional, Nys had a race named after him. Organised by his fan club in his home town of Baal, the Grand Prix Sven Nys was first held on New Year's Day in 2000. Nys won it. Given the dominance that was to come, perhaps that should have been expected. The race has been held every year since, attracting a world-class field to race over the 2.7km circuit. Nys must feel protective over his race: out of the now sixteen editions there have been, he has won twelve of them.

But, then, winning is what Nys does. So far he's claimed two world championships, nine national titles, thirteen Superprestige wins, seven world cup victories and eight Trophée GVA wins. And that's just cyclo-cross – he's no slouch in mountain bike either, with four national titles to his name so far. All of which makes Sven Nys one of Belgium's best ever bike racers.

2 January

The death of Fausto Coppi
(1960)

To this day Fausto Coppi remains one of cycling's greatest riders. He rode with grace and panache, a silky, smooth pedalling action belying the effort he put into cycling. His appeal was best summed up by fellow rider André Leducq, who described Coppi as riding like 'a great artist painting a watercolour'.

Coppi was born in 1919, in Castellania, north-west Italy. He developed his cycling legs early in life, working as a delivery boy for a butcher. His first race win came in 1938 in the Castelletto d'Orba-Alessandria. His breakthrough year was 1940, with a national title on the track, followed by a stage win and the overall victory in the Giro d'Italia; the first of five wins in Italy's national tour.

Despite losing some of his prime years to the Second World War, Coppi's palmares (list of races won) place him at the top table of cycling's greats. The early part of his career was defined by his intense rivalry with Gino Bartali, which divided both cycling and Italy. Coppi won the Tour de France twice; holds the record for most wins in the Tour of Lombardy, triumphing on five occasions, four of them in succession; won Milan–Sanremo three times; and became world champion in 1953. He also held the hour record from 1942 until 1956.

Away from the bike his life was beset by tragedy. Fausto's younger brother Serse – a fellow cyclist who had won the Paris–Roubaix classic – died in 1951, after falling while sprinting to the finish line of the Giro del Piemonte. Later, Coppi faced the wrath of the Catholic Church for his affair with Giulia Occhini. Nicknamed Coppi's 'White Lady', Occhini had met the cyclist at a race and, despite both being married, they became lovers. When the story broke the two became embroiled in a national scandal. Even the Pope got involved, first telling Coppi to return to his wife and then later refusing to bless the Giro's peloton because of Coppi's presence.

In December 1959, having retired earlier that year, Coppi travelled to Upper Volta in Africa for an exhibition race. He returned complaining of feeling unwell and was diagnosed as having pneumonia. In fact, Coppi had contracted malaria. He died on the morning of 2 January 1960. Ten thousand mourners attended his funeral.

3 January

Ale Jet is born
(1974)

At the height of his powers Alessandro Petacchi, aka Ale Jet, was one of the fastest men in the peloton. After turning professional with the Italian Scrigno team in 1996, Ale Jet signed for Fassa Bortolo in 2000 and the wins soon followed. To date Petacchi has taken more than 175 professional victories over the course of his twenty-one-year-and-still-going career. That haul includes forty-eight stage wins in Grand Tours.

The first time he spread his arms wide in victory at a Grand Tour was at the 2000 Vuelta a España, where he claimed stage eight's bunch gallop into Salou. Three years later, he added stages at the Giro d'Italia and the Tour, where he would continue to triumph through the 2000s. Ale Jet is one of only five riders to have won the points jersey at all three Grand Tours.

But three-week stage racing wasn't the only string to Petacchi's bow and he also fared well in one-day classics. Perhaps his greatest win of all was in the 2005 Milan–Sanremo, where he claimed his sole Monument.

4 January

Thomas Stevens arrives home after cycling the world
(1887)

San Francisco. Four days into 1887 and a steamer arrives in port. It had set out some seventeen days earlier from Yokohama. On board was Thomas Stevens. Among his belongings was a penny-farthing.

Stevens was an Englishman who had emigrated to the United States. Living in California, the adventurer within got the better of him and he hatched a plan to cycle across America. He departed San Francisco on 22 April 1884 and rode to Boston.

But that wasn't enough for Stevens. Encouraged by *Outing* magazine, on he went. After taking a ship to Liverpool, Stevens rode through Europe and into Asia.

There he cycled across India before travelling to Singapore and on to Hong Kong. After traversing the southern reaches of China he finally reached Japan to record the first bike ride around the world. It had been 13,500 miles and over three and a half years since he'd left San Francisco. Described as an 'impracticable scheme of a visionary', his dream had been realised.

Stevens documented his travels but didn't really touch on the reaction to his arrival back home, of which he wrote simply, but tellingly: '... the daily press of the time contains ample record'.

5 January

Alfred Dreyfus is stripped of his military rank
(1895)

The roots of the Tour de France can be traced to a seemingly unrelated event some nine years before that first loop of France was completed.

In 1894 Alfred Dreyfus, a Jewish officer in the French army, was accused of spying for Germany. He was found guilty and on 5 January 1895 was publicly stripped of his military rank. He was later jailed for life. His case, however, was controversial and divided France. Half the country thought him a traitor, the other a victim of a miscarriage of justice and of anti-Semitism. The case raged for years.

Firmly in the pro-Dreyfus camp was Pierre Giffard, founder of a daily sports newspaper called *Vélo*. Giffard publicly backed the officer much to the disquiet of some of his financial backers, including one Albert de Dion.

Dion opted to withdraw his backing and, in 1900, set up a rival sports paper – *L'Auto-Vélo*. The paper would later become *L'Auto* (see 16 January) and would go on to organise the Tour de France.

In 1906 Dreyfus was acquitted, a miscarriage of justice that, in a roundabout way, would help lead to the creation of the world's greatest bicycle race.

6 January

Antonio Suárez dies
(1981)

Spanish rider Antonio Suárez was born in Madrid in 1932 and died on 6 January 1981, aged just forty-eight.

Suárez is one of only three men to have won the general classification, the points competition, and the mountains prize at the Vuelta a España. Tony Rominger and Laurent Jalabert are the other two.

While Rominger and Jalabert won all three classifications in a single year (1993 and 1995 respectively), Suarez won the overall and the mountains prize in 1959 and then followed it with the points classification, two years later.

Suárez had a ten-year professional career that took him to no fewer than thirteen different teams. His standout year was 1959 when he won two stages at the Vuelta on his way to the overall and mountain titles. He also claimed the jersey of Spain's national champion that year, a title he successfully defended the following year.

Away from his homeland Suárez claimed a stage win and a podium placing at the 1961 Giro d'Italia.

7 January

The start of the modern era Bremen six-day races
(1965)

The inaugural six-day meet in Bremen was in 1910, one of the first such events to be held in Europe. Held in a banquet hall of the Schützenhof, with planks laid across a 95m-long track, 4,000 spectators saw Willy Arend and Eugen Stabe take the first title.

Then came a fifty-five-year hiatus before six-day racing returned to the German city.

In January 1965 the event returned, now housed in City Hall. Over the course of the six days more than 70,000 people made their way through the doors.

The overall title was claimed by Dutchman Ric Van Steenbergen, who was partnered by his son-in-law, Palle Lykke. Perhaps the greatest prize was taken by Willi Altig and Bernd Rohr, though. They took home a giant ham and twenty-five bottles of liquor following a win in a prime.

The event was hailed a huge success and has been an ever-present on the six-day racing scene since. Today the meeting has a reputation for being one of the liveliest on the circuit, with live music, discos, hog roasts and a 50m-long bar.

8 January

Jacques Anquetil is born
(1934)

Maître Jacques dominated cycling for over ten years. From the late 1950s through to the mid-sixties he was the patron of the peloton. Anquetil was the man to beat when the important races rolled round and big guns flexed their finely honed muscles. During that period he became the first man to win five Tours (1957, 1961, 1962, 1963, 1964), and the first to win all three Grand Tours, having also won the Giro (1960, 1964) and the Vuelta (1963).

He also claimed a number of one-day classics with wins in Liège–Bastogne–Liège, Ghent–Wevelgem and Bordeaux–Paris.

Anquetil was born in Mont-Saint-Aignan, near Rouen, where his parents owned strawberry fields. He entered his first race at the age of eighteen and won – the start of a pattern that soon would be oft repeated.

He came to national prominence at the 1953 GP des Nations and from there hardly looked back. His first tour win came in 1957, a tough year and one that saw more established riders either fail to start or abandon. It was Anquetil's first entry in the race and he took the yellow jersey on stage five. He lost it two days later but reclaimed it on stage ten, holding it to Paris.

His most dominant Tour performance came in 1961. That race opened with a split stage and while André Darrigade took the morning's skirmish, Anquetil claimed the afternoon time trial to steal the race lead from his countryman. That meant Anquetil ended day one in yellow. And that was exactly how he finished the final stage, twenty-one days and 4,232km later in Paris, with no one having been able to wrest it from him for even a single day. It was an all-conquering display but not one that pleased everyone. It prompted a damning article in l'Equipe from director of the Tour and founder of l'Equipe Jacques Goddet, who accused Anquetil's rivals of being 'satisfied with their mediocrity'.

Anquetil won races but never the affections of his public. He was victorious not because of daring escapades but because of carefully plotted tactics – take time against the clock and defend in the mountains. It was hugely effective. But it was also cold, calculated and methodical, slap-bang in the middle of arguably cycling's most romantic era.

9 January

Mat Hoffman, BMX Freestyle rider, is born
(1972)

Mat Hoffman is a pioneering BMX Freestyle rider, heralded as the greatest Vert-ramp rider in the sport's history and a man credited with inventing more than a hundred tricks. He is also regarded as the founder of 'Big Air', a BMX and skateboarding event.

Hoffman's big air adventures started in 1990. While he was performing on a television show a stuntman suggested that by building a bigger ramp he could double the height to which he could rise on his bike.

So, with the help of friends, Hoffman built a 21ft-high quarterpipe ramp. Using a motorcycle to tow him in, he was soon rising 20ft above the ramp, something no one else had ever done.

In 2001 he built an even bigger quarterpipe. This one was 24ft high and threw him 26ft above it – that's 50ft above the ground – an achievement that got Hoffman into *Guinness World Records*.

His exploits led to Big Air events at competitions like the X-Games. Hoffman had changed the game.

10 January

Bernard Thévenet, Tour de France winner, is born
(1948)

Bernard Thévenet is the man who brought the Eddy Merckx era of the Tour de France to an end.

By 1975 Merckx had won the Tour five times. As that year's race headed into the Alps he was again in the yellow jersey and, despite being punched by a fan (see 11 July), it seemed that a sixth was in the bag. But on the stage to Pra Loup, Merckx cracked and Thévenet took full advantage.

Thévenet powered past Merckx and Felice Gimondi, who had been leading the stage. At the finish Thévenet had nearly two minutes on Merckx. It was enough to give him yellow. The next day he won again, soloing over the Izoard and into Serre-Chevalier.

Thévenet had won his first Tour at his sixth attempt. It was a win of great panache ahead of the greatest cyclist the world had known. It was also the first time that the race finished on the Champs-Elysées in Paris. Thévenet became the first man to arrive on cycling's most prestigious finishing line in the yellow jersey.

Thévenet won the Tour again in 1977. He was made a Chevalier de la Légion d'honneur in 2001.

11 January

Cameron Meyer claims national title on his birthday
(2011)

Born in 1988, Cameron Meyer was celebrating his twenty-third birthday when he cemented his standing as one of Australia's premier riders against the clock, successfully defending his individual time trial title at Australia's national championships.

Meyer was already a force on the track. A junior world champion, who would later become a multiple world champion at elite level on the track, he turned professional on the road with the Garmin-Chipotle team in 2009. That year he helped his team take second in the team time trial at the Giro.

Seven months later he took his first ITT title at the Australian nationals, beating John Anderson by twenty-eight seconds over the 39km course. One year on, as he turned twenty-three, he defended that title, beating Jack Bobridge, so often his team-mate on the track, by just under thirteen seconds in Ballarat, Victoria. Meyer then crowned a fantastic January by winning a stage and the overall at the Tour Down Under, a race in and around Adelaide, South Australia, his biggest individual road race win to date.

12 January

Helen Wyman wins eighth national 'cross title
(2014)

Helen Wyman is Britain's most successful female cyclo-cross rider. At the time of writing she has won the British cyclo-cross championships nine times. With another legendary British female rider, Nicole Cooke, taking the inaugural title, Wyman took her first British champion's jersey home in 2006. She then won the next six titles before losing out in 2013 to Nikki Harris after crashing early in the race.

In 2014 Wyman returned to winning ways, claiming her eighth title and pushing Harris into second place by more than a minute. As well as claiming the British title nine times, Wyman has also won the European championships twice. She has also taken the Koppenberg Cross, one of the toughest races on the cyclo-cross circuit and one that includes the legendary Koppenberg climb. As far as the world title goes, Wyman's best result so far has been third place, in 2014. Her stated goal on the bike is to go two steps further up on that particular podium.

13 January

The Vélodrome d'Hiver hosts its first six-day race
(1913)

Affectionately known as the Vél' d'Hiv, Paris's Vélodrome d'Hiver hosted its first six-day race in 1913. The velodrome's origins lie in the Salles des Machines building near the Eiffel Tower where, in 1902, a 333m track was first installed and used for racing. Seven years later the building was listed for demolition. The track was moved and renamed the Vélodrome d'Hiver.

By 1913 six-day races, initially founded in Britain but then popularised in America, had begun to gain Europe's interest. The races, in which riders ride in pairs and try to cover as great a distance as possible in six days, attracted huge crowds. On 13 January 1913, the Vél d'Hiv hosted Paris's first six-day event.

Twenty thousand people crowded into the velodrome to watch the action. Unlike today, when in all but a few stadiums spectators sit around the outside of the track, in the Vél d'Hiv the crowds were located in the centre, pushing the riders and mechanics to the sides. The races attracted the rich and famous, who would enjoy fine dining and champagne as the action raged around them, while the masses would stand, drinking beer and roaring their heroes on.

That first race was won by Alf Goullet and Joseph Fogler, an Australian and an American respectively, who covered 4,467.58km, beating the French pair, Victor Dupré and Octave Lapize, into second place. The Vél d'Hiv continued to host six-day racing until 1958, when French stars Jacques Anquetil and André Darrigade won the final event.

For all the drama and excitement on its boards witnessed by thousands of spectators over the years, the Vélodrome d'Hiver had a far more sinister history. In 1942, while France was in the grip of Nazi occupation, 13,000 Jews were arrested in Paris in just two days. Many were imprisoned in the velodrome for five days, in appalling conditions, before being shipped

to internment camps. It is reported that fewer
than 400 of the 13,000 survived the war.

In 1959 fire broke out in the Vél d'Hiv,
after which the building was demolished.

14 January

Nicole Cooke retires
(2013)

On 14 January 2013, Nicole Cooke sat before cycling journalists in London and started to read out a statement. So began the retirement of one of Britain's greatest ever cyclists.

Cooke was born in 1983 into a family of cycling fanatics. Over the course of her eleven-year professional career she won virtually every race worth winning: the Olympic road race, Tour de France, Giro d'Italia, world championships, national championships, La Flèche Wallonne, Amstel Gold and the Tour of Flanders. As Cooke said in her retirement statement, she had amassed quite a collection of T-shirts over her racing career. She was the first rider of either gender to win the Olympic road race and the world championships in the same year.

Cooke's journey to the top of her sport was not a smooth one. While it was clear from the start that hers was a rare and precocious talent, the infrastructure to support her was missing. Not only was there no support, there were precious few events for her to enter. There is much truth in her words: 'It is somewhat of a handicap trying to demonstrate just how good you are on a bike when you are not allowed to ride.'

Cooke and her father set about trying to change that. They fought for more events and, if that failed, battled to get her into other races by examining the small print in race regulations. It was from just such an exercise that Cooke won her first national title. When she was sixteen, with no category for that age group, Cooke's dad discovered a ruling that allowed her to race in the group above, the Juniors. But with no Junior event either, this meant she could step up another category, to the Seniors. Thus did the sixteen-year-old race her first nationals against the senior, elite women of Britain. Cooke says that the winner's medal from that race remains one of her most prized.

Nicole Cooke blazed a trail for women's cycling in Britain and improved conditions immeasurably, and that is in no small part down to the tenacity shown by herself and her father. For all the T-shirts she has gathered, perhaps that is Cooke's greatest achievement.

15 January

Francesco Moser sets hour record for a veteran
(1994)

In 1994, Francesco Moser was forty-three years old. Ten years earlier he had travelled to Mexico City to break the hour record. He succeeded, twice bettering the previous mark over four days of riding.

His record of 51,151m stood for nine years but was beaten in 1993 by the Scotsman Graeme Obree. Shortly afterwards, Chris Boardman took the record. So, in January 1994, Moser returned to Mexico, intent on improving Boardman's record.

At 10.45 a.m., under clear skies and with barely a whiff of wind, Moser set off for sixty minutes of pain under the watchful gaze of fans who had travelled from Italy to support him.

Moser started well and after five kilometres was nine seconds ahead of Boardman's pace. However, he started to fade as the minutes ticked by. At the end of the hour Moser had ridden 51,840m, a significant improvement on his previous best but not enough to overhaul Boardman, falling short by 430m.

Moser's distance was at least the best achieved by a veteran. While not exactly what he had been hoping for, the Italian still entered the record books.

16 January

First edition of *L'Auto* is published
(1903)

Founded after the falling out of Pierre Giffard, editor of *Vélo*, and Albert de Dion (see 5 January), *L'Auto-Vélo* was first published on 16 October 1900, famously on yellow newsprint and with one Henri Desgrange as its editor. Desgrange had been working in the PR department of a car manufacturer owned by Adolphe Clément-Bayard. Dion, who had made his fortune in the motor car industry, turned to Clément-Bayard for help in setting up the paper and he nominated Desgrange as editor.

Vélo and *L'Auto-Vélo* went head-to-head in the battle for the French sports news-reading public. In 1903 Giffard won a legal battle to have the word 'Vélo' removed from his competitor's title, but his success was short-lived. On 16 January that same year the first edition of *L'Auto* hit the news-stands and just six days later its front page proudly announced the first Tour de France.

L'Auto would flourish on the back of its new race. *Vélo*, meanwhile, ceased publication a year later.

17 January

The first Flanders indoor cyclo-cross race is held
(2007)

What do Belgians do when it's too dark to race bikes around a muddy field? Bring the field indoors and switch on some lights, of course. Such is the popularity of cyclo-cross in Belgium that the small issue of daylight was never going to stop them racing.

And so was born the Flanders Indoor Cyclo-Cross race. First held in Mechelen, between Brussels and Antwerp, the inaugural race was won by Sven Nys, ahead of Niels Albert.

Featuring ramps and obstacles, mud and sand, the race took place on a circuit entirely within the 18,500sq m expanse of the Nekkerhal, in front of thousands of cheering fans. The race moved the following year, to the Ethias Arena in Hasselt.

In 2010, despite still taking place indoors, the event changed its name to the Cyclo-Cross Masters. Then, with the novelty of an indoor cyclo-cross race finally wearing thin, in 2013 the race moved outside under floodlights. That it is still run at night, under the glare of artificial light, at least means that the race retains something of its unique atmosphere.

18 January

Thor Hushovd is born
(1978)

Norwegian colossus Thor Hushovd was born in Grimstad in 1978. Nicknamed the God of Thunder, Hushovd enjoyed a fifteen-year career in the professional peloton until his retirement in 2014. A powerful rider who was too well built to challenge for podium places at Grand Tours but ideally proportioned for classics and long, rolling stages, Hushovd was no slouch in a sprint either.

As well as claiming the classics Ghent–Wevelgem and Omloop Het Nieuwsblad, and taking three national road race titles and three national individual time trial crowns, Hushovd won stages at all three Grand Tours, including ten at the Tour de France. He took the points jersey at the Tour twice (2005 and 2009) and wore the yellow jersey for nine days across three different years. He also won on the Champs-Elysées in 2006, a stage regarded as the unofficial world championships for sprinters.

In 2010 Hushovd got his hands on a rainbow jersey proper, winning the road race at the world championships in Geelong, Victoria, Australia, becoming the first Norwegian to win the title.

19 January

The inaugural Tour Down Under
(1999)

Before 1999, Australia did not have its own Tour. That changed thanks, at least in part, to Formula One.

Until 1995 the South Australian city of Adelaide was home to the Australian F1 Grand Prix. When Melbourne stole the race from Adelaide, the city was determined to find a replacement to bolster its international standing, hence the creation of the Tour Down Under. With heavy backing from the region's governing body, Adelaide lobbied the UCI and in 1999 they were rewarded with a slot in the racing calendar.

The inaugural race was a six-stage affair. All stages finished in a bunch sprint apart from stage three, won in a breakaway by Stuart O'Grady. His five-second win over his three fellow escapees was enough to ensure overall victory three days later, a feat he would repeat in 2001. O'Grady's two victories were first matched by André Greipel (2008 and 2010) and then beaten by Simon Gerrans (2006, 2012, and 2014).

Over the past few years the race has developed from what might be described as a sprint-fest into a more rounded race. Its standing in the sport has similarly grown so that today it is one of only four races outside Europe with UCI World Tour status.

20 January

Cyrille Guimard is born
(1947)

Cyrille Guimard was a French national champion on the track and forged a reputation as a decent sprinter. His best year at the Tour was in 1972, when he took four stage wins and wore yellow for eight days, taking it from Eddy Merckx twice before finally relinquishing it to the Belgian great.

After duelling with Merckx through the Pyrénées, over Mont Ventoux and across the Alps, winning at Aix-les-Bains and Mont Revard, Guimard abandoned the 1972 Tour just two days from Paris. Despite being second on GC and wearing the green jersey, Guimard's knees were shot – he had to be carried to his bike – and he couldn't continue. On the podium in Paris, however, Merckx handed the green jersey, relinquished by the Frenchman, back to Guimard.

It was as a team director that Guimard truly made his name, guiding three riders – Lucien Van Impe, Bernard Hinault and Laurent Fignon – to Tour victory. Hailed as a master of tactics, his methods were sometimes unorthodox. In 1976, for instance, on the stage to St-Lary-Soulon, he threatened to drive Van Impe off the road unless he attacked. Van Impe took the hint, won the stage, took yellow and held it to Paris.

21 January

Robbie McEwen wins his final TDU stage
(2007)

Australian sprint powerhouse Robbie McEwen sits second on the list of his national tour's stage winners. He has never won the race overall, but he crossed the finishing line of a stage in first place twelve times during his career, leaving him behind only Germany's André Greipel in the ranks of top stage winners at the Tour Down Under.

McEwen's first stage win at his national tour came in 2000, when he was riding for the Farm Frites team. It was the final stage of the race, a 96km circuit race around Adelaide, and McEwen took the win in a sprint ahead of Jaan Kirsipuu and Stuart O'Grady. Seven year later he took his final TDU stage in Adelaide. Over the course of his seventeen-year career McEwen won twelve tour stages and twelve Giro stages. He won the Tour's green jersey three times.

For a period in the mid-2000s the sight of McEwen crossing the line, arms spread as wide as his grin, was one of the most common in cycling.

22 January

Henri Pélissier is born
(1889)

One of the great French post-World War One riders, Henri Pélissier was the eldest of four brothers, three of whom (Henri himself, Francis and Charles) went on to ride professionally.

Pélissier was a champion with plenty of attitude and during his career he clashed repeatedly with Henri Desgrange over the conditions in which riders were expected to race. He was a semi-professional when he met his hero, Lucien Petit-Breton, in Paris in 1911. Invited to Italy for the Romany–Tuscany race, Pélissier didn't need to be asked twice.

That same year he went on to win the Tour of Lombardy, despite crashing with Costante Girardengo in the closing moments. Pélissier managed to remount and win in front of a baying Italian crowd, furious that their hero had been denied by this upcoming Frenchman.

In an eighteen-year career punctuated by war, Pélissier, who was advanced in his training methods, concentrating on speed, diet and equipment, rather than just pure endurance, won ten stages of the Tour de France as well as the overall title in 1923. He also claimed the Tour of Lombardy three times, Paris–Roubaix twice, Milan–Sanremo, Bordeaux–Paris, Paris-Tours and Paris–Brussels, to complete an impressive palmares.

23 January

Emile de Beukelaer, first President of UCI dies
(1922)

Emile de Beukelaer, son of François-Xavier de Beukelaer, the creator of Elixir d'Anvers, a herbal liqueur famous for its digestive benefits that has been produced in Antwerp for more than 150 years, was a racing cyclist through the 1880s who won the Belgian amateur national title twice.

With the family's liqueur business thriving and placing demands on him, de Beukelaer's cycling career was somewhat curtailed. Yet he kept himself involved with the sport, becoming chairman of the Ligue Vélocipédique Belge, as well as president of the Antwerp Bicycle Club and taking charge of the building of a new velodrome in Antwerp. He was also a member of various event organising committees.

In 1900 he was elected the first president of the Union Cycliste Internationale (see 14 April), a post he held for twenty-two years. In the winter of 1922, de Beukelaer's life was sadly cut short: he contracted flu and died on 23 January at the age of fifty-five.

24 January

Cycling Weekly is first published in Britain
(1891)

With the sport of cycling flourishing across Europe in the late 1800s, the Continent's printing presses were working furiously as entrepreneurs sought to jump on the gravy train and sate the appetite of the growing legions of cyclists taking to the road and the race tracks.

In Britain issue one of *Cycling* rolled off the press on 24 January 1891. Printed on pink paper and with a lively and enthusiastic style that set it apart from other publications of the time, in the opinion of former editor Arthur C. Armstrong, writing in 1946, nothing like it had been seen before.

Now published by Time Inc. UK under the title *Cycling Weekly*, the magazine has seen many changes over the course of the past 120 years or so. It has flirted with cars and mopeds and sometimes rather misguidedly resisted change in the sport, but still it continues and long may it do so. Cycling in Britain wouldn't be the same without a weekly copy of the magazine affectionately dubbed 'the Comic'.

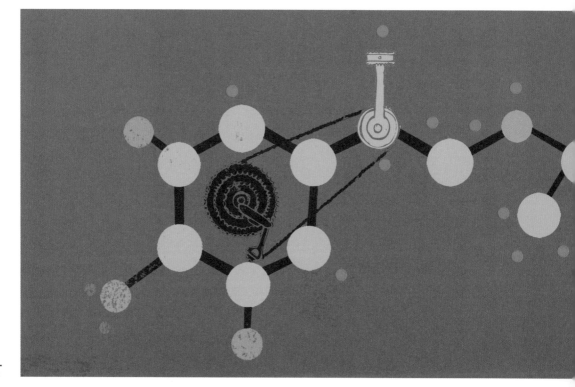

25 January

Alberto Contador's ban for clenbuterol starts
(2011)

The 2010 Tour de France was one of the closest in history and, at the end of the 3,642km race, the Spaniard Alberto Contador stood on the top of podium in Paris, having beaten Andy Schleck by just thirty-nine seconds.

His win was a controversial one. On stage fifteen, Schleck's chain dropped; Contador left him and gained time. Eyebrows were raised – it went against cycling's unwritten laws to take advantage of a rival's technical misfortune. The time Contador gained? Thirty-nine seconds.

The controversy was only just beginning.

After the race it was confirmed that Contador had tested positive for the banned substance clenbuterol, a decongestant used by asthma sufferers. Contador claimed it had entered his body through his eating contaminated meat. And so began a long and complicated legal process.

In January 2011, the Spanish Cycling Federation cleared Contador. The UCI and WADA appealed to the Court of Arbitration for Sport (CAS). Nearly twelve months later CAS overturned the decision and banned Contador. The ban was backdated to the time of that first hearing – 25 January 2011.

Meanwhile, Andy Schleck was confirmed as 2010's Tour de France champion, more than eighteen months after the race had finished.

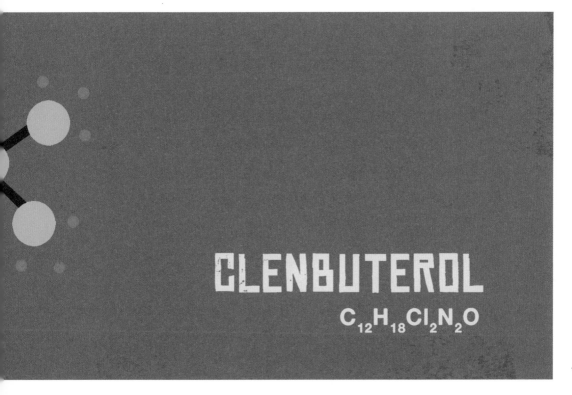

CLENBUTEROL

$C_{12}H_{18}Cl_2N_2O$

26 January

Ercole Baldini, Giro and World Champion in 1958, is born
(1933)

In the late 1950s, Italy thought it had found a worthy successor to Fausto Coppi. The campionissimo was nearing the end of his career and Ercole Baldini was the new champion elect.

Baldini was twenty-four when he hit the professional ranks, comparatively late to be turning pro, but he had already broken the hour record, taken national and world titles on the track and won gold in the 1956 Olympic road race. His pedigree was sound and his potential exciting.

And for a while Baldini didn't disappoint. In 1958 he won the Giro by over four minutes and then went on to claim the rainbow jersey in Reims. Look at the list of riders who have won a Grand Tour and a world championship in the same year and you'll see the list is a short one that is full of cycling royalty – Coppi, Merckx, Bobet, Hinault, Roche and LeMond.

Baldini never made it to the top table. He tended to put on weight easily and was criticised for appearing to enjoy the fruits of his early success a little too much. He never repeated his 1958 Giro victory and finally retired in 1964.

27 January

The 100th Berlin Six-day race starts
(2011)

The world's longest running six-day race celebrated its 100th edition in 2011 with the German pair Robert Bartko and Roger Kluge taking the win ahead of the Australian duo Leigh Howard and Cameron Meyer.

Berlin has been hosting six-day racing since 1909, making it one of the first on mainland Europe (see 21 March). It was first held in an exhibition hall at the Zoologischer Garten but over the years has moved to various locations in the city. Today it is hosted in a velodrome in Landsberger Allee, where it has been since 1999.

Klaus Bugdahl holds the record for the number of victories. One of the world's greatest six-day racers, with thirty-seven victories over a twenty-one-year career, he won nine times in Berlin between 1958 and 1970. Bugdahl also holds the record for the most appearances, having taken to the start line on twenty-six occasions.

28 January

Gustave Garrigou dies
(1963)

One of the pre-war greats, Gustave Garrigou turned professional in 1907 and rode for the Peugeot and Alcyon teams over the course of an eight-year career. He became France's first national champion in 1907, defending his title in 1908. He also won Paris–Brussels, the Tour of Lombardy and Milan–Sanremo.

Garrigou is best known for his performances in the Tour. He rode the race every year of his professional career, never finished outside the top five, claimed eight stage wins and recorded six podium placings, including the overall win in 1911.

That came after he took yellow on stage one to Dunkirk. He lost it the next day, but won it back on stage four and held it all the way to Paris, surviving the Tour's first ascent of the Galibier (see 10 July).

Garrigou's win owed something to good fortune. In the Pyrénées Paul Duboc was making serious inroads into Garrigou's lead when he fell victim to poisoning. As the main beneficiary of the poisoning, suspicion fell on Garrigou and he was advised to ride in disguise to protect himself from Duboc's followers. Later cleared, he died of pulmonary congestion in 1963.

29 January

First women's Cyclo-cross world championship is held
(2000)

While the first cyclo-cross world championships were held in 1950 (see 4 March), it wasn't until fifty years later that the UCI decided that women should also have a world title.

Germany's Hanka Kupfernagel won the inaugural title. In Sint – Michielsgestel, on a course made even harder by wet conditions, she powered away from the field at the start and stayed away for the entire 13km race. She won again in 2001, 2005 and 2008. This was her race. Between 2000 and

2010 only once did Kupfernagel fail to appear on the podium: that was in 2007 when she finished fifth, having led until the penultimate lap when she suffered a mechanical problem.

A multi-talented cyclist, as well as winning in cyclo-cross Kupfernagel has claimed world championship titles on the track and on the road. She completed her suite of titles across the disciplines in 2007 when she won the individual time trial at the worlds in her home country.

30 January

Tom Boonen dominates Tour of Qatar
(2006)

To say the Tour of Qatar is a happy hunting ground for Belgian classics specialist Tom Boonen is to understate his dominance of an event that first appeared on the calendar in 2002.

Boonen's first stage win in Qatar came in 2004. That was followed with two more in 2005, but it was in 2006 that he really took a stranglehold on the race. Over the course of the five stage 820.5km long race, Boonen won four stages and the overall.

The Belgian went one better in 2007, winning five stages, including stage one's team time trial. His team-mate Wilfried Cretskens won the overall, but Boonen returned to the top of the podium in 2008, 2009 and again in 2012. His haul of four wins is currently a record.

As of 2014 he also holds the record for most stage victories, with twenty-four to his name (two being team time trials). To put that in perspective, the next best is Mark Cavendish with eight.

31 January

Henri Desgrange is born
(1865)

It is tempting to ask what the cycling world today would look like had Henri Desgrange not entered the world in 1865.

Born in Paris, he became a successful cyclist, setting a number of records, including the first official hour record in 1893. In 1894 he published a training book, *La Tête et les Jambes* (the head and the legs), which took the form of a series of letters between a young cyclist and his trainer. He later worked in public relations for a car manufacturer but, by various quirks of fate, by the early 1900s Desgrange had become the editor of the sports paper *L'Auto* (see 5 and 16 January) and in need of an imaginative way of increasing circulation.

What followed changed the cycling world for ever. During a meeting with his staff, Desgrange asked for ideas. One journalist, Géo Lefèvre, suggested a long cycle race around the country and thus was born the Tour de France.

Desgrange was a man who liked to hedge his bets. Initially uncertain of the merits of the idea of the Tour, he stayed away from the start of the inaugural race's first stage, only appearing once it seemed certain the race would be a success. He was also a man who enjoyed both flowery prose and making his riders suffer. He demeaned the use of derailleur gears, refusing to permit their use in the Tour while he was in charge, and claimed that his ideal Tour would see just one rider finishing.

When Desgrange witnessed something spectacular, however, he let his readers know about it in no uncertain terms. Of the riders' first entry into the Alps in 1911, he wrote: 'Are these men not winged who today climbed to heights where even eagles don't go ... they seemed to dominate the world!'

Henri Desgrange ruled the Tour until 1936 when illness finally caught up with him. He died in 1940. Today a monument stands to the father of the Tour near the summit of his favourite mountain – the Col du Galibier.

1 February

La Course by Le Tour is announced by ASO
(2014)

With women's cycling enjoying a resurgence in popularity, in 2014 Amaury Sport Organisation (ASO), the organiser of the Tour de France, announced a new race: La Course by Le Tour.

A Women's Tour had been held until 2009. It was a prestigious race – after all, it was the women's version of cycling's most famous event – but it constantly struggled to get sponsorship. Over the years it was forced to change its name and reduce its length. By the time it folded it was just four stages long.

In 2013 a petition was circulating calling for a women's race to be run alongside the men's Tour, using the same roads and ridden a few hours before the men's race. There were more than 97,000 signatures.

In February 2014 ASO announced La Course by Le Tour. While not a full three-week race, it was instead a circuit race held on the Champs-Elysées a few hours before the traditional Tour finale.

It was a great success. Televised live around the world, the race was won by Marianne Vos, who outsprinted her rivals while wearing the rainbow jersey. In a press release ASO announced that La Course is destined to become an iconic event in the calendar. Time will tell, but having one of the best cyclists of all time win the inaugural event while wearing the rainbow jersey is as good a start as any.

2 February

Leon Meredith is born
(1882)

A three-time Olympian, between 1904 and 1913 Britain's Leonard Meredith claimed seven world champion titles.

Born in London, Meredith started riding in 1901. Success came quickly: by the end of the year he was a national champion. Fast-forward three years and he was on top of the world, winning the world championship stayers (motor-paced) race in London, easily beating all rivals in the eight-man field despite a heavy crash in the closing kilometres. He would go on to add a further six world titles to his name.

Meredith went to his first Olympic Games in 1908, where he won gold in the team pursuit, beating Germany in the three-lap final by more than ten seconds. He would return to Olympic competition in 1912, where he claimed a silver in the team time trial, and again in 1920, where he finished eighteenth in the road race.

Meredith was a versatile rider able to win races from five to one hundred miles in length. But that wasn't the end of his talent on wheels. He was also a keen roller-speed skater, a sport in which he claimed multiple national titles and broke a series of British records. He eventually went on to own a number of skating rinks.

Despite his obvious physical fitness, Meredith died young. He was just forty-seven when he died of heart failure, collapsing suddenly while in Switzerland.

3 February

Hennie Kuiper is born
(1949)

The 1975 world championships took place in Yvoir, Belgium. The country had high expectations for theirs was a formidable team: Merckx, De Vlaeminck, Van Impe and Maertens were among the thirteen-strong squad that started. The team was so powerful that Merckx called them to a breakfast meeting in the week prior to the race to discuss who would go for the win.

On race day the country turned out and tuned in to see which member of Belgian cycling royalty would seize the day. But one man had apparently not read the script: Hennie Kuiper.

Kuiper had turned professional just two years before and arrived in Yvoir as Dutch national champion. He escaped with just over two laps to go, quickly pulling out a lead. Behind, De Vlaeminck and Merckx were being marked by Kuiper's team-mates. Eventually the chase started in earnest but Kuiper managed to hold on to win by sixteen seconds in front of a disbelieving crowd. De Vlaeminck was left to sprint for second.

During a successful career Kuiper gained a reputation for riding tactically, summed up best by his famous quote: 'Racing is licking your opponent's plate clean before starting on your own.' Over the course of fifteen years he won four Monuments, and finished second at the Tour twice. He won three Tour stages, including two on l'Alpe d'Huez in successive years. His last major win came in 1985 when he claimed Milan–Sanremo.

4 February

Nairo Quintana is born
(1990)

Colombia's latest cycling superstar, Nairo Quintana, became only the second Colombian to win a Grand Tour when he won the 2014 Giro d'Italia, following Luis Herrera's 1987 win in the Vuelta. It was no surprise when Quintana stood in pink in Milan, showered in golden ticker-tape and holding the giant trophy awarded to the winner of the Giro, such had been his promise.

Born into a peasant family in the Boyacá Department of Colombia, Quintana honed his cycling legs over a distance of 16km to school. By 2010 he was in Europe racing at the Tour de l'Avenir. Quintana won two stages and the overall. He was on his way.

In 2012 he signed to the Spanish Movistar team and began to thrive. He won the Vuelta Ciclista a Murcia and then a stage at the Dauphiné that went over the Colombière and Joux-Plane climbs. Quintana, just twenty-two years old, had proved he could take on the very best in one of the world's biggest races and win.

In July 2013 he headed to the Tour. It was only his second three-week race (he'd finished thirty-sixth at the Vuelta in 2012). He was a sensation. He won a stage, finished second overall, won the King of the Mountains and the white jersey as best young rider. It was the best performance at the Tour by a Colombian, eclipsing Fabio Parra's third place in 1988.

Then came that Giro d'Italia win. It is surely only the start of what promises to be an exciting career.

5 February

First Dubai Tour
(2014)

The globalisation of road racing at the highest levels beyond Europe continued apace in 2014 with the inaugural edition of the Dubai Tour.

The four-day race attracted sixteen professional teams and 127 riders. In the bunch were some of the world's very best, with Fabian Cancellara, Marcel Kittel, Peter Sagan and Tony Martin all travelling to the Emirate for the race.

The race featured two flat stages, one time trial and one medium mountain stage. With the three road stages ending in a bunch sprint, all won by Germany's Marcel Kittel, it was the time trial that proved decisive with Taylor Phinney taking control of the race leader's blue jersey courtesy of a fourteen-second win against the clock. It was a lead he held until the end.

The Dubai Tour is the latest of a recent surge of early season stage races in Asia and the Middle East, taking its place alongside the Tours of Oman and Qatar in the UCI's February calendar. The initiative takes top-drawer cycle racing to fans outside its European heartland, as well as giving riders much needed warm-weather racing while Europe remains in the grip of winter.

6 February

Charles Bartlett is born
(1885)

The 1908 London Olympic Games were marred by terrible weather. With track cycling taking place on a 660-yard-long outdoor track at White City Stadium, not only were cyclists not protected from the harsh elements but the track was often flooded.

Britain's cyclists ruled the competition, winning five of the six golds claimed (there was a seventh race – the one-kilometre – won by France's Maurice Schilles but the result was declared void due to the time limit being exceeded).

Among Britain's gold-medal winners was Charles Bartlett. Born in south London, Bartlett was twenty-three years old when he lined up in the pouring rain at the start of the 100km Olympic final. He wasn't the favourite, in fact he wasn't even Britain's best hope – that was Leon Meredith the reigning world champion (see 2 February).

But as the race progressed others fell away, victims either to ill fortune or fatigue. Among them was Meredith, who had climbed off after an unsuccessful attempt to chase back following a crash.

As the finish drew near, Bartlett was in the leading group of four. At the start of the final lap, with the race slowing and tactics coming to the fore, he simply threw himself down the banking and went all out for victory. Roared on by thousands of spectators he held on to win by a wheel, claiming the biggest win of his career.

7 February

Learco Guerra dies
(1963)

A rider of great strength, terrific on the flat and against the clock but not so adept when the roads climbed skywards, Learco Guerra earned himself the nickname the Human Locomotive as he powered his way across Europe, picking up wins in some of the sport's biggest races.

He arrived on the scene at the tail-end of Alfredo Binda's peak years. Very different in personality and style, the pair competed on the road and off, vying for race wins and the affections of the Italian people.

Guerra was never able to match the incomparable Binda's results but Italy loved him nonetheless. Ruggedly good-looking and with a charismatic smile, his popularity was seized upon by the ruling Fascist party, which used his image to bolster their own.

And he still won more than most. In 1930 he went to the Tour as national champion in service of Binda. The *Campionissimo* would abandon on stage ten and Guerra set about making the most of his new-found freedom, picking up three stages, wearing yellow for seven days and finishing second in Paris. Three years later he would return, win another five stages and again finish second. That 1930 national championship win was the first of five consecutive titles for Guerra.

In 1931 he was one of the favourites for the Giro on a course light on mountains, barring a slog up to Sestrière on the penultimate day. Guerra won the opening stage becoming the first rider to wear the pink jersey in the process (the jersey was introduced that year) but the race ended in disaster for him. A crash on stage nine, while he was leading the race, caused by a fan running alongside him, forced him to abandon. Italy was distraught.

But Guerra would return. He won stages in both the 1932 and 1933 Giri and in 1934, utterly dominated the race, claiming ten stage wins and the overall. He had at last realised his destiny.

A world champion in 1931, winner of Milan–Sanremo and the Tour of Lombardy, Guerra won all there was to win in Italy. His record of thirty-one stage wins at the Giro places him third on the all-time list of winners.

The outbreak of war in 1939 effectively ended Guerra's career. He died in 1963, having suffered from Parkinson's disease. 'He was my teacher,' said the legendary Gino Bartali.

8 February

Six Days of Milan starts
(1999)

First held in 1927 in the Sport di Piazza VI Febbraio, the inaugural Six Days of Milan was won by Italian cycling royalty, with Costante Girardengo and Alfredo Binda coming together to claim the first title. Girardengo would repeat his win in 1928, partnered with Pietro Linari, winner of the 1924 edition of Milan–Sanremo.

Despite its auspicious beginnings, the event then disappeared from the calendar, returning only in 1961. Now came its heyday. Until 1984 the race was held every year except for 1974 and 1975, with cycling legends Peter Post, Gianni Motta, Eddy Merckx, Felice Gimondi, Patrick Sercu and Francesco Moser among the names to have tasted success on the boards of Milan.

When heavy snow in 1985 caused damage to the roofs of both the Vigorelli Vélodrome and the Palasport di San Siro, the event folded. It returned in 1996 when Italian rider Silvio Martinello started his assault on the race. Martinello, who also won Olympic gold in the points race in 1996, claimed four Milan six-day titles in a row. Three came with Marco Villa, with whom he also won two Madison world championships, and one with Belgian Etienne De Wilde.

Martinello's run ended in 1999 when the event again disappeared. It came back for one year only in 2008, when former world champion and Olympic gold medallist Paolo Bettini took his last win as a professional.

9 February

Herald Sun Tour hit by bush fires
(2014)

With Australia wilting under insane summer temperatures, and with fierce, hot winds blasting the country, on 9 February 2014 the peloton prepared to ride the final stage of the sixty-first Jayco Herald Sun Tour. First held in 1952 as the Sun Tour, the event is Australia's oldest stage race. Keith Rowley won the inaugural edition with half a million people estimated to have watched the sheep farmer ride to glory.

By 2014 the race had become a UCI-rated event. The final stage was to include three ascents of Arthurs Seat, a 300m high hill that overlooks Port Phillip Bay on the Mornington Peninsula, with the finish at the end of the third climb: an iconic finish to a now iconic race.

But Australia was experiencing one of its most devastating summers. Echoing the name of the race, the sun beat down mercilessly on the whole country for weeks on end. By February dozens of bush fires raged around Victoria, homes had been lost, lives were at risk. Emergency crews were stretched. Bike racing was firmly put into perspective.

With fire crews deployed to other areas around Victoria and with the ever-present risk of more fires starting, just minutes before the scheduled start the stage was pulled. Simon Clarke, the leader going into the final day, was awarded the win against the terrible backdrop of a state under a fire-fuelled siege.

10 February

Gunn-Rita Dahle Flesjå is born
(1973)

In August 2004, Norway's Gunn-Rita Dahle Flesjå stormed to victory in the Olympic Mountain Bike race. She led from the start, even surviving a fall and a mechanical problem, to complete the race nearly a minute ahead of second place. She was only the second Norwegian to win cycling gold after Knut Knudesen's individual pursuit win in 1972.

Dahle Flesjå had started mountain biking in 1995 at the age of twenty-two. If written as a work of fiction her rise through the ranks of the sport would be dismissed as unbelievable. But this is fact. Within two months she was national champion. Three months later she was crowned Nordic champion. Then, just six months after starting out, she signed as a professional for the American Eagle Team.

Since then Dahle Flesjå hasn't stopped. At the time of writing she has four cross-country world championship titles, four cross-country world cup titles, five mountain bike marathon world championships, twenty-seven world cup race wins and six European and eight national titles to add to that Olympic gold.

Her 2004 season was particularly noteworthy. She claimed six of seven world cup races leading to the overall title, won Olympic gold, the world championships in both cross-country and marathon, the European title and the national title. She was unbeatable.

Still riding, Dahle Flesjå will go down in history as one of the finest mountain-bike riders ever to have turned a pedal.

11 February

The Boston Cycling Club is formed
(1878)

Holding a special place in the history of cycling in the USA, the Boston Cycling Club was the first of its kind to be formed in America. The state of Massachusetts grasped the joys of riding on two wheels before most other states and the Boston Cycling Club was at the forefront of the sport's development. The first mass 100-mile ride, the first bike race, the first tricycle race, the first 100-mile race, the first hill climb – they all came courtesy of the Boston Cycling Club.

It became a club of national importance. In 1880 the League of American Wheelmen (LAW) was formed. Its president was one Charles E. Pratt, who also happened to be the editor of the Boston published *Bicycling World* magazine and the president of the Boston Cycling Club.

By 1894 Massachusetts was described as the 'banner cycling State of the Union', with nearly a quarter of the LAW's membership hailing from the state. That rapid growth was in no small part due to the work of the Boston Cycling Club.

12 February

Melinda McLeod is born
(1993)

With eyes currently set on making her Olympic entrance in Rio in 2016, Australia's BMX speed machine Melinda McLeod is a world champion at both girl and junior level. Attracted to BMX at the age of four after first seeing a track from the back seat of her father's car, McLeod has developed into one of Australia's best BMX racers.

And the competition Down Under is fierce. At the end of the 2014 season Australia had three of the UCI's top fifteen ranked women, including the number one rider, Caroline Buchanan, with McLeod, three years younger than Buchanan, fourteenth.

McLeod took her first world title in 2007. Then, in 2011, she went to the world championships in Copenhagen. She returned with two gold medals in her bag, claiming both the junior women time trial and the junior women's race titles. In 2012 and 2013 she won back-to-back national titles, her first at elite level.

13 February

Freddy Maertens is born

(1952)

Belgian-born Freddy Maertens enjoyed a six-year peak period between 1975 and 1981 when he claimed all of his important victories. In those six years Maertens won thirty-four Grand Tour stages. He took home three green jerseys at the Tour, added a couple of world championships and won the Vuelta.

In 1976 Maertens won fifty-seven races, a record he shares with Eddy Merckx. That included eight stages at the Tour, another record he shares with Merckx.

Maertens held that terrific form into 1977. In early April he was in the thick of things at the Tour of Flanders. At the head of the race with Roger De Vlaeminck, Maertens made a bike change on the Koppenberg. Officials deemed the change illegal and Maertens was disqualified. When told of the decision he nonetheless kept riding.

Wearing the rainbow jersey of world champion, Maertens rode at the front for the rest of the race. For two hours he towed his rival, leaving De Vlaeminck to come around and take the win on the line. Every winner of the Tour of Flanders has their name inscribed on a cobblestone, which is placed in the race museum in Oudenaarde. For 1977 there are two names: one for De Vlaeminck and one for Maertens, under which is written: 'Morele Winnaar'. Moral Winner.

Maertens then headed to the Vuelta, winning his only Grand Tour. His overall margin of just under three minutes doesn't do justice to his dominance of that race. Maertens won thirteen of the twenty stages and held the race lead from start to finish. That haul of stage wins remains a record in a single Grand Tour.

After Flanders and the Vuelta came the Giro. There he won seven of the first eleven stages before having to retire with a broken wrist. He returned to winning ways the following month at the Tour of Switzerland.

He ended 1977 with fifty-six wins. Without that month off the bike he would almost certainly have smashed his 1976 tally.

His career was one of ups and downs. His final win of note came in 1981 when he claimed his second world title. One of the finest one-day riders never to have won a Monument, he carried on riding until 1987, collecting only two minor wins in his final six seasons.

14 February

Marco Pantani dies

(2004)

Described after his death by Lance Armstrong as 'more of an artist than an athlete', Marco Pantani was a gifted climber who scaled cycling's greatest heights for an all too brief period.

Talented yet troubled, Pantani died in a hotel in an out-of-season Rimini on Valentine's Day. The coroner would later record a verdict of 'acute intoxication from cocaine', although in 2014 the cyclist's family would be successful in requesting the inquiry be reopened. At the time of writing investigations continue.

Whatever may yet be revealed, Pantani's tale is one of triumph followed by tragedy. Armstrong's description of him as an artist is apt. To watch the Italian scale a mountain was to observe a master craftsman at work. With the bike as his chisel and his legs as his hammer, Pantani sculpted legendary tales from the mountains of the Tour and Giro. For it was in those races that Pantani truly soared. He couldn't turn his attention to the one-day classics; the worlds weren't for him; ditto short stage races. Pantani was a pure climber and he needed the high mountains to do his best work. Short, punchy climbs were no good: Pantani needed kilometre after kilometre of relentless uphill slog because it was then that he could dance away while others floundered.

Yet for one so gifted his palmares is shockingly brief. One Giro. One Tour. Both in 1998. That's it. Finito. He was susceptible to misfortune and suffered a number of horrible crashes that lost him many a season. Later, allegations of doping would come. In pink and two days from Milan, he would be thrown off the Giro in 1999 for failing a 'health check' as his haematocrit level breached 50 per cent (raised haematocrit being an indication of EPO use).

In an era when racing was increasingly becoming controlled and numbers-driven, Pantani rode with feeling. He didn't wear a heart monitor or measure wattage. If he felt good and if the time felt right, he simply went. His wins always came with panache. Whether it be his back-to-back stage wins in the Dolomites in the 1994 Giro, his climb of l'Alpe d'Huez in 1997, or the claiming of his Giro on Plan di Montecampione in 1998, Pantani always crafted a story worth telling.

15 February

Antonin Magne is born
(1904)

When Frenchman Antonin Magne won his first Tour in 1931 he said that if he had to suffer the psychological pain he'd just been through again, he wouldn't start for all the money in the world.

To think those words came as he 'celebrated' victory in Paris. Leading from the race's ninth stage for more than two weeks he had faced wave after wave of attacks, relying on team-mates to pull him through. It had all taken its toll, his win exacting a heavy price.

Magne didn't start the following year but luckily for France he did return and won the race again in 1934. This time he owed his win to René Vietto (see 17 February).

With two Tour wins in his pockets he travelled to Berne in 1936 for the world championships. On a hilly course, in wind and in rain, Magne spent the day at the head of the race, ready to respond when the serious attacks came. Those who had the strength to stay with him at the front gradually fell away until Magne was left with only Gundhal Hansen of Denmark for company.

As the race neared its conclusion Hansen was fading. Magne launched his attack. Hansen punctured. He was so exhausted he didn't bother to return. Magne won by over nine minutes to add a rainbow jersey to the two yellows he had at home.

On his retirement Magne became a highly respected *director sportif*, with Louison Bobet and Raymond Poulidor among the riders he managed.

16 February

Chris Hopkinson retains Sebring 24-hour title
(2014)

In a feat that almost makes today's Tour de France riders look a little soft, in 2014 Britain's Chris 'Hoppo' Hopkinson retained his Ultra Marathon Cycling Association Sebring 24-hour title.

One of the world's premier endurance riders, in twenty-four hours Hopkinson rode a total of 468.1 miles in Florida. He won by twenty-seven miles, thirty-six further than the mark he had reached when winning the title the previous year.

Hopkinson only began cycling in 1998 at the age of thirty-one when he started to ride to work. To say he caught the cycling bug is a slight understatement. Today he has a string of endurance records and titles to his name.

In 2005 he became the first Briton to complete the Race Across America (RAAM) solo, completing the 3,052-mile route in just under twelve days. He returned to the RAAM in 2013, going a couple of hours faster than his 2005 time. In 2014 he did even better, knocking a day off his previous best.

But Hopkinson was far from done. He grabbed a couple more domestic records, setting best times for London–Cardiff and then Cardiff–Edinburgh, won a 1,000-miles time trial by more than seven hours in Texas, and then took the twenty-four-hour world championship for his age group. At the time of writing Hopkinson is assisting Steve Abraham's attempt to break Tommy Godwin's Year Record (see 31 December).

17 February

René 'Le Roi' Vietto is born
(1914)

Born just outside Cannes in 1914, René Vietto entered cycling legend in 1934 when his sacrifices in the Pyrénées saved the Tour for his team leader, Antonin Magne.

Vietto was a climber of rare talent and when the 1934 Tour hit the Alps he put his gifts to stunning use. He won stage seven, over the Galibier and into Grenoble, by over three minutes. Two days later he won again. This time he tamed the Vars and the Allos on his way into Digne. Then he won the stage into his home town, in front of adoring fans who had crowded on to the Boulevard de la Croisette to watch their favourite son triumph. 'He presented himself as a conqueror as the Croisette was invaded by the crowd,' wrote Louis Nucera in his biography of Vietto.

If King René had announced his arrival, he is perhaps best remembered for what happened later in that same Tour when he saved Magne's race.

Magne crashed on the Puymorens and buckled his wheel. His biggest rival for the race win, Giuseppe Martano, sped off. Vietto immediately offered his leader a wheel. Magne accepted and continued but the wheel didn't fit properly and he ended up grabbing another team-mate's bike further down the mountain. That would have done little to improve Vietto's mood: he was still waiting for his team to arrive with a replacement wheel. A photograph from the time shows him sitting forlornly on a wall, head in hands, waiting in anguish for his team car.

The next day Magne's bike broke again as he climbed the Portet d'Aspet. This time Vietto was up the road, over the climb and on the descent. Vietto got wind of his leader's problem and turned around, riding back up the climb to appear like a mirage in front of Magne. He handed over his bike. Magne sprinted off on a mission to save his Tour. Magne won in Paris. Vietto, who had bailed his leader out twice, finished fifth. He was hailed as the moral victor, his place in cycling history assured.

Le Roi René never would win the Tour – injuries, disputes and war saw to that – but he was once described by cycling writer Christophe Penot as the finest climber the sport ever saw. 'Superior to Gaul, to Bahamontes ...' he wrote. 'Only ... this peerless rider danced just one summer.'

18 February

Henry George is born
(1891)

Returning after an eight-year absence caused by the outbreak of the First World War, the 1920 Olympic Games were held in Antwerp, Belgium. Cycling was again part of the programme. In 1912 the only cycling medals on offer were for time trials, the only time in history that no track events were included. But now track races were back.

Born in Charleroi, Belgium's Henry George was one of the riders competing for the host nation. Surprisingly for a country where cycling was an integral part of its culture, Belgium had never won a cycling gold medal.

George was riding the 50km race. Reports of the time state that the cycling races were sparsely attended, but the people of Antwerp who did venture out to the velodrome to watch their countryman ride were rewarded with a little piece of history. George won by 15cm from Britain's Cyril Alden to record Belgium's first cycling gold medal.

It would be another forty-four years before another would come at the track, Patrick Sercu winning the one-kilometre time trial in 1964 (although Belgium did win the team time trial on the road in 1948).

George never won another important race but his place in Belgium's cycling history was assured.

19 February

Valverde wins opening stage of Vuelta a Andalucía
(2014)

A one-week stage race, the Vuelta a Andalucía was first held in 1925. Won by Ricardo Montero Hernández, Spain's national champion at the time, the race then promptly disappeared. It would be thirty years before it returned.

The race has become one of the favourite hunting grounds of Alejandro Valverde. The Spanish rider took his second straight win there in 2013 and returned for more twelve months later. Valverde smashed the opposition in the opening stage, blasting around the seven-kilometre time-trial course a full seven seconds faster than his nearest rival, even passing his motorcycle outrider in the process.

He went on to claim the next two stages, the hilly parcours suiting him perfectly and confirming his status as the strongest in the race. Two days later he was crowned overall winner.

Valverde's tally of three wins is a record in a race that has been dominated by the Spanish, the country claiming more than half of the sixty-one races held to date.

20 February

Sarah Hammer wins fifth Individual Pursuit title
(2013)

American cyclist Sarah Hammer is a multiple world champion on the track, her fifth individual pursuit world title won in 2013 leaves her just one rainbow jersey shy of the record shared by Rebecca Twigg (USA) and Tamara Garkushina (Russia).

Hammer's career nearly didn't happen. After impressing as a junior and becoming an elite rider at just seventeen, she left the sport before her twentieth birthday. She didn't intend to return and instead of cycling went to work in a bagel shop.

Fortunately for US cycling her absence proved temporary for, after watching the Athens 2004 Olympic Games, Hammer took to the bike again. 'I needed to step away from it [racing] to know how much I really loved it,' she told *Bicycling* in 2012.

At the time of writing Hammer is a seven-time world champion, with two omnium titles added in 2013 and 2014 to her five individual pursuit wins. Away from the worlds she has amassed twenty national championships, holds the world record for the pursuit and has two silver medals from the London 2012 Olympic Games.

21 February

O'Grady wins the Classic Haribo
(1999)

A world champion on the track and national champion on the road, Australia's Stuart O'Grady had an eighteen-year professional career running from 1995 until 2013. During that time he won Paris–Roubaix and two stages at the Tour, where he shares the record for most appearances with seventeen starts, finishing fifteen of them. He also wore the yellow jersey for a total of nine days.

In 1999 he took his first win in France by winning the Classic Haribo. The Aussie was active all day, attacking several times, at one point building a solitary lead of forty-five seconds. He eased off, waited to be caught, and then won the sprint to the line.

The Classic Haribo was a short-lived one-day race held in southern France. Starting outside the Musée du Bonbon (the Sweet Museum) in Uzès and finishing in Marseilles, the race was part of the season-long Coupe du France competition. Sponsored by the confectionery company, attacking riding was encouraged with the most aggressive rider rewarded with his weight in Haribo sweets.

Often ridden in the face of the fierce mistral, the race was held between 1994 and 2006. O'Grady's win was the only time a rider from outside Europe won. Jaan Kirsipuu was the only rider to have won the race more than once, the Estonian rider claiming three victories in four years.

22 February

Romain Maes dies
(1983)

Small but strong, Romain Maes rode professionally from 1933 until the outbreak of the Second World War effectively ended his career.

Maes stunned the cycling world when he won the Tour in 1935. And it wasn't just any old win: he did something that only four men had done before (Garin, 1903, Thys, 1914, Bottecchia, 1924 and Frantz, 1928), and no one has done since: he led the race from the first stage to the last.

Maes had done little to show he was a Tour contender. He'd ridden the race just once before, abandoning on stage ten. His best result was one Paris–Nice stage win. But on the Tour's opening stage he escaped the peloton and rode into Lille alone, fifty-three seconds ahead of the rest.

Described by Henri Desgrange as a 'ball of muscle', Maes set to defending his lead. A sprinter rather than a climber, most expected him to falter in the mountains. Not so. He emerged from the Alps with three minutes' advantage. Then he won a second stage in Cannes and retained a two-minute gap through the Pyrénées. In the final week he got even stronger, increasing his lead and winning the final stage in Paris. Come the end, his overall margin was nearly eighteen minutes.

Maes never finished the Tour again. In 1936 he crossed the line of Paris–Roubaix first but was mistakenly awarded second place, the commissaires erroneously judging Georges Speicher to have won the sprint.

Maes died in 1983 aged seventy.

23 February

Erik de Vlaeminck wins cyclo-cross world championship
(1969)

Born in Eeklo, Belgium, Erik de Vlaeminck is probably the greatest cyclo-cross rider the world has seen.

A world champion by the time he was twenty, Erik ended his career with seven world titles to his name, six of them won consecutively. He would have made it eight in a row but for a damaged bike forcing him down to fifth in 1967. His brother Roger also took the world title in 1975 so that between 1966 and 1975 there were only two editions of the cyclo-cross worlds that didn't end with a de Vlaeminck brother top of the podium.

This 1969 win was Erik's third and came in Magstadt, Germany. He finished over a minute and a half ahead of Germany's home favourite and three-time world champion Rolf Wolfshohl.

De Vlaeminck also claimed four national titles. This was the start of Belgium's domination of cyclo-cross, an era when the country was beginning to grow into the force it has since become. At the time of writing, in the fifty years since de Vlaeminck won the country's first world title in 1966, Belgium has claimed a total of twenty-seven championships. The next best is France with ten.

Away from dominating cyclo-cross, de Vlaeminck also competed on the road. He collected a stage win at the Tour and a handful of top-five placings in one-day classics. On retiring he went on to become a coach for the national team.

24 February

Last edition of Mont Chauve
(1975)

One of the most feared climbs in cycling, Mont Ventoux rises high above the Provençal landscape. Three roads lead to its summit, but it is the route from Bédoin, a town at the south-western base of the mountain, that has become the most famous.

Steep and long, the road cuts through woods before emerging into a landscape devoid of vegetation. White rocks mercilessly reflect the heat of the sun all the way to the top. Thus cruelly exposed, fierce winds blast any soul brave enough to venture this far up the Ventoux. It is here that France's strongest winds have been measured and, as everyone involved with cycling knows, it is here that the Englishman Tom Simpson lost his life (see 13 July).

Cyclists have been tackling Ventoux since the early 1900s – perhaps most notably Vélocio (see 29 April) in 1903 – but it wasn't until 1922 that the first true bicycle race took place on the mountain.

Called Mont Chauve (after Ventoux's nickname – the bald mountain – due to its appearance from afar), it was a race against the clock to the summit. The first winner was Jean Alavoine, a national champion of France. Third was a nineteen-year-old, Alfredo Binda. The Italian would go on to win the race the following year.

Held only sporadically, the last of the race's eleven editions took place on 24 February 1975. By now it had become a two-stage format, with a mass-start race followed by a time trial. Raymond Delisle won both, adding the race to a palmares that includes a national championship title and stage wins at the Tour and Vuelta.

25 February

Antoine Gutierrez wins final GP Valencia
(1979)

First held in 1969, the final edition of the GP Valencia was won in 1979 by Antoine Gutierrez, a French rider who had a short career in the professional ranks. Two years later the race returned, now renamed the Trofeo Luis Puig, after the man who saved the Vuelta.

While not a top athlete himself, Puig, a Spaniard, devoted his working life to sport. He was the president of numerous sporting federations in Valencia and the president of the Spanish cycling federation. He also organised a number of bike races and is credited with saving the Vuelta when he stepped in to secure backing for the race and lead a technical committee hastily assembled to oversee the race after the previous organisers withdrew two months before the scheduled start. He was later elected to the presidency of the UCI.

The Trofeo Luis Puig ran from 1981 until 2005. Bernard Hinault, Sean Kelly, Mario Cipollini and Erik Zabel are among its winners. Puig himself died suddenly of a stroke in 1990, aged seventy, while still in office at the UCI.

26 February

Team Sky is announced
(2009)

When it was announced that BSkyB would be sponsoring a new cycling team, with the stated aim of putting a British cyclist on the top step of the Tour's podium within five years, more than a few eyebrows within the sport were raised. Britain hadn't placed anyone on any step of the final podium in the seventy-two years since the country had first sent a rider across the Channel to take on the Tour. And Sky thought they could do it in five?

The team's entrance in 2010 sent shock waves through the sport. Their forensic-like attention to detail was impressive, most vividly illustrated by their new team bus, which seemingly gained more column inches in the UK than the majority of Britain's cyclists had ever attracted.

Initially things went well. A stage win at the Tour Down Under was followed by a time-trial win for Bradley Wiggins at the Giro. But at the Tour the wheels came off. The team recorded top three finishes in just three stages. Only one rider finished in the top twenty overall. 'We are a young team, we have learned invaluable lessons and will be back and start all over again,' team boss Dave Brailsford said afterwards.

How right he was. Two years later Wiggins was in yellow in Paris. Twelve months on Chris Froome followed. From first race to two Tour champions in four seasons. The impossible deadline smashed.

27 February

André Leducq is born
(1904)

Winner of two Tours, Paris–Roubaix, Paris–Tours and an amateur world championship, André Leducq was one of the peloton's best riders through the late 1920s and into the 1930s.

Known for his looks, charm and good humour, Leducq was popular with the opposite sex (his nickname was *le joyeux Dédé*, but at least one writer dubbed him *le beau Dédé*). He was one of cycling's first sex symbols and women flocked to the roads of France to see him race.

Born in Paris, Leducq was first given a bike at the age of five. It put him on the road to greatness. Fifteen years later he stood in his home city as world champion.

He turned professional in 1927 and promptly placed fourth at the Tour, picking up three stage wins on the way. Many more would come – he ended his career with twenty-five stage wins, a record that stood until Eddy Merckx came along.

A good all-rounder who could mix it in a sprint or in the mountains, in 1928 Leducq won Paris–Roubaix. He claimed his first Tour in 1930, after duelling with Italian Learco Guerra for three weeks. It was the first Tour to be competed between national teams and Leducq benefited from rare harmony within the French team. France was smitten with her new champion. Leducq repeated his Tour win in 1932.

His final victory came at the 1938 Tour, where he won the last stage, finishing arm-in-arm with Antonin Magne, who was also riding his final Tour.

28 February

Djamolidine Abdoujaparov is born
(1964)

Nicknamed the Tashkent Terror, Djamolidine Abdoujaparov won three green jerseys at the Tour, as well as the points competitions at the Giro and the Vuelta. A sprinter who duked it out with the toughest in the peloton, to put it kindly his style was unconventional. More than once riders complained he was a danger; that he was an accident waiting to happen.

And an accident was exactly what did happen.

Going into the final stage of the 1991 Tour, Abdoujaparov was leading the points classification. He couldn't be caught. He only had to finish the race to secure his first green jersey.

But the final stage of the Tour, when the world watches the riders race on the Champs-Elysées, is one of the biggest days in cycling. And Abdoujaparov wanted the win. As the stage entered its closing moments, with the excitement at fever pitch, the Tashkent Terror was ready to go into battle.

The sprint wound up. Abdoujaparov, head down, legs pumping, was close to the barrier. Too close as it turned out. Fully focused on going for the win, he clipped a railing and was propelled over the handlebars. It was a spectacular high-speed crash that brought down at least two others. Abdoujaparov broke a collarbone and was badly concussed. More than fifteen minutes later he was helped across the finish line. Then, instead of standing on the podium in green, he was put straight in an ambulance and whisked off to hospital.

MARCH

1 March

Reg Harris is born
(1920)

In almost complete darkness on the evening of 11 August 1948, Reg Harris and his racing partner Alan Bannister lined up at the Herne Hill Velodrome, south London, for the 2,000m Tandem Olympic final. Racing against Italy, the final stood at one race apiece. This one would decide who took gold.

One week earlier it had looked as if Harris wouldn't be at Herne Hill at all. Unimpressed by the training offered to the Olympic team, he had returned home to train by himself. The National Cycle Union ordered him back and then cancelled his Olympic nomination when he refused to do so. It took a hastily arranged hearing to get him reinstated.

The tandem final was later described in the Games' official report as the most exciting race of the cycling programme. Too bad, then, that no one could see it taking place: it was so dark when the pairs crossed the line at the same time that no one could be sure of the result. Eventually the win was awarded to Italy. Even so, while certainly not what Harris had aimed for, it wasn't a bad result considering that less than six months earlier he had been in hospital with a broken back.

After the Olympics Harris turned pro and went about becoming one of the world's greatest sprinters. He added four professional world championships to the amateur title he'd won in 1947, a day described in the *Golden Book of Cycling* (created in 1932 by the British magazine *Cycling* to celebrate the glories of the sport) as 'British cycling's greatest day in a generation'.

Reg Harris died in 1992. A statue of him now stands in Manchester's velodrome.

2 March

Peter Van Petegem wins Omloop Het Volk
(2002)

One-day specialist Peter Van Petegem won a number of spring classics during the course of his sixteen-year career. While two wins at the Tour of Flanders (1999, 2003) and one at Paris–Roubaix (2003) – Van Petegem is one of only ten riders to have completed the Flanders/Roubaix double in the same year – are by far the biggest of his career, it was at the Belgian semi-classic Omloop Het Volk that he recorded most wins.

Currently called Omloop Het Nieuwsblad, the race has undergone four name changes in the course of its seventy-year history.

From 1961 until 2008 it was known as Omloop Het Volk and it was during this period that Van Petegem secured his wins.

Like most classics with a long history, the race's route has evolved over the years but its essence has always remained the same: cobblestones and climbs.

The 2002 win was Van Petegem's third. Bridging across to the lone leader with 12km to go and then winning the two-man sprint at the finish, victory brought him level with Ernie Sterckx and Jos Bruyere as the riders with most race wins.

3 March

Maurice Garin is born
(1871)

His name now enshrined in cycling history as the first winner of the Tour, Maurice Garin was born in Arvier in north-west Italy in 1871. His was a large family. He had four sisters and four brothers and life in Italy was tough. So tough, in fact, that his parents decided to move to France when Maurice was fourteen. Whether they went together or separately is unclear – some accounts even claim the young Maurice was sent by his family to work for a Frenchman in exchange for a wheel of cheese.

However he ended up getting there, by the 1890s Garin was sweeping chimneys in northern France (he would bear the nickname the Chimney Sweep throughout his cycling career). In 1893 he recorded his first race win at Dinan and turned professional the following year.

While Garin's list of wins is not particularly lengthy, what it lacks in quantity it makes up for in quality. In 1896 he came third in the very first Paris–Roubaix, before going on to claim the next two editions. In 1901 he won the second edition of Paris–Brest–Paris. One year later he finally claimed Bordeaux–Paris, having finished second on two previous occasions.

By the time of the first Tour, Garin was firmly in place as one of the world's best long-distance racers and so was among the favourites. He more than lived up to the billing. He won the first stage – 467km from Paris to Lyon – taking the overall lead and keeping it until he rode back into Paris eighteen days later with more than 2,400km under his wheels. In total he won three stages and the race by over two hours.

Roundly celebrated as the Tour's first ever winner, Garin's relationship with the race soured in 1904 when he was disqualified having provisionally been awarded the win (see 2 December). Garin never rode the race again after that. He died in 1957 at the age of eighty-five. Even after his death he continued to make news. In 2004 documents were found that revealed his French naturalisation had come later than previously thought. It was a revelation that would affect cycling history (see 28 March for more).

4 March

Jean Robic wins the first cyclo-cross world championship
(1950)

While the first cyclo-cross national championships can be traced to 1902, when France held its first national competition, it wasn't until 1950 that the inaugural world championships were held.

Before 1950 the Critérium International de Cyclo-cross had acted as the unofficial world championships. That race had first been held in 1924 but as the popularity of the sport grew, the UCI finally decided to sanction an official championships.

Held in the Bois de Vincennes, a public park on the eastern fringes of Paris that was created by Napoleon III, the race turned into a battle between two French cycling champions. Jean Robic had won the Tour and the Critérium International de Cyclocross in 1947; Roger Rondeaux was three-time cross national champion and two-time Critérium International winner. Here, the two friends went head-to-head.

Rondeaux crashed on the third lap and lost time. He fought to claw his way back to Robic. That was impressive in itself, but it was the 1947 Tour champion who prevailed in the sprint to become the first cyclo-cross world champion. 'I reached my goal, it is a great joy for me,' Robic said afterwards.

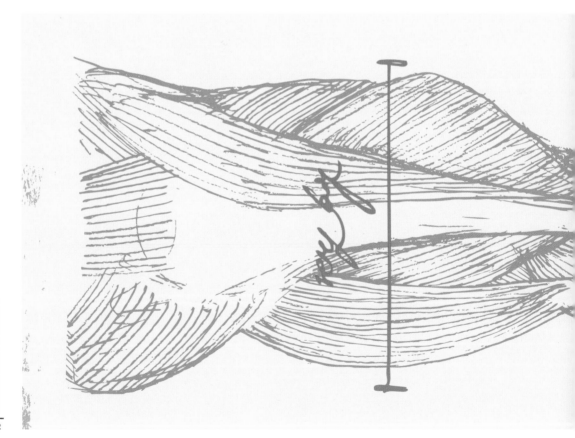

5 March

Robert Förstemann is born
(1986)

Robert Förstemann is a German track cyclist and a national champion in the one-kilometre time trial, sprint and team sprint disciplines. He is a world and European champion with World Cup wins to his name and an Olympic bronze medal.

An impressive track rider, then, but there are many impressive track riders out there. So what exactly sets Robert Förstemann apart from the rest? It is not so much his race wins but, rather, his physiology. More specifically, his legs. Put bluntly, the man has simply enormous thighs.

Förstemann's thigh size came to international attention during the 2012 Olympic Games in London when Kiwi cyclist Greg Henderson tweeted a photograph of Förstemann and fellow German cyclist André Greipel in their pants, having what was described by the *NY Daily News* as a 'quad-off'. Having been variously reported at a barely believable 28–34 inches in diameter, Greipel was never really in the running. Förstemann is the thigh king. Pure and simple.

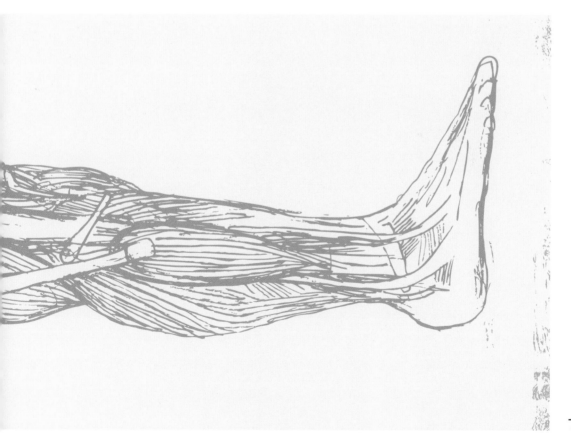

6 March

Gerrie Knetemann is born
(1951)

A world champion, winner of multiple Tour stages and one-day classics victor on the road, and a European, national and six-day champion on the track, Gerrie Knetemann had a fifteen-year career during which he amassed more than 125 wins.

Knetemann was born in Amsterdam and turned pro in 1974. He won his first classic, Amstel Gold, in his debut season. The following year he collected his first stage win at the Tour, escaping the bunch with Italy's Giovanni Cavalcanti with 80km to go and winning the two-man sprint in Albi.

His best year came in 1978. He won three stages and the overall at Paris–Nice and followed that with two stage wins (including the final sprint on the Champs-Elysées) and two days in yellow at the Tour, before heading to the world championships.

The 1978 worlds were held at the Nürburgring. With less than 10km to go Knetemann found himself at the front of the race with just Francesco Moser for company. The Italian was defending the title he'd won in Venezuela the previous year and most expected him to repeat that win. Moser launched his sprint with around 150m to go, but Knetemann fought back, nicking the rainbow jersey by less than a tyre's width.

Gerrie Knetemann retired in 1989 and died suddenly fifteen years later, suffering a heart attack while out mountain-biking with friends.

7 March

Jörg Jaksche wins first stage of Paris–Nice
(2004)

The best year of Jörg Jaksche's twelve-year professional career came in 2004 when riding for the CSC team. Previously wins had been hard to come by for the German, who plied his trade principally as a domestique for the brighter lights in the peloton. But in February 2004 he won the Tour of the Mediterranean in February and then headed to Paris–Nice.

There Jaksche won the opening 13km time trial over Davide Rebellin. The next day's stage looked to be a straightforward sprintfest, but a strong wind was blowing and Jaksche's CSC team were ready. They drove hard at the front of the bunch, shelling many of the favourites out the back. At the end of the day Jaksche still had yellow.

And so it was for the rest of the race. While stage wins went elsewhere, including three to T-Mobile's Alexandre Vinokourov, Jaksche kept his grip on yellow. He finished the race with a fifteen-second advantage over Rebellin. It would prove to be the best result of the German's career and only the tenth time a rider had led the race from start to finish, with Jaksche joining such luminaries as Merckx, Maertens and Kelly.

Three years later Jaksche was out of cycling. Caught up in Spain's Operación Puerto doping case he confessed to using performance-enhancing drugs and spoke of systemic doping programmes. He never rode professionally again.

8 March

Roger De Vlaeminck wins Milan–Turin
(1972)

In March 1972 Roger De Vlaeminck was still at the beginning of what would be a startling career (see 24 August). He'd already won Liège–Bastogne–Liège but now the classics legend was about to enter his prime.

After De Vlaeminck opened his 1972 account with a stage win at the Tour of Sardinia, he headed to Milan–Turin, the oldest of the Italian classics. First held in 1876, the race has been held only sporadically (after that inaugural race there was an 18-year gap before the second edition was held and there have been many more breaks since), but over time it grew in prestige with winners including Girardengo, Magni and Kübler.

The race route includes the Superga – the hill with a basilica on its summit overlooking Turin where the Torino football team was wiped out in a plane crash in 1949.

And it was on the Superga that De Vlaeminck began to make his move in 1972. Accelerating away, at first only the Swede Gosta Pettersson went with him. Ultimately the Belgian was brought back but held on to take the win in a sprint. It was the start of a terrific spring for him. Five days later he would start his run on Tirreno–Adriatico (see 16 March) before then claiming his first Paris–Roubaix (see 17 April).

Milan–Turin returned to the modern cycling calendar in 2012 after a five-year break, with the finish now on top of the Superga.

9 March

Paris–Nice arrives in Nice and ends five days later in Rome
(1959)

For reasons best known to themselves, in 1959 the organisers of Paris–Nice decided that once the race hit Nice it should keep going. So for one year only (as it turned out) Paris–Nice became Paris–Nice–Rome.

The change added around 800km to the race distance and increased the length of the race to eleven days. It was split into two sectors: Paris–Nice and Nice–Rome (though actually starting in Menton), with three different classifications. Separate winners would be declared for each of the two sectors of the race and, the rider with the best combined time awarded the overall win.

Ninety-six riders started, of whom forty-six finished. Only those who made it to Nice were allowed to start the second phase to Rome. The race was won by France's Jean Graczyk. Riding on Jacques Anquetil's Helyett-Hutchinson team, Graczyk led the race into Nice. While Gérard Saint won the Nice–Rome phase, Graczyk had the best overall time in Rome and so was awarded the overall win.

The experiment wasn't a success. Criticised as being too long and needlessly complicated, the Nice–Rome phase was dropped and never repeated. (See 10, 12 and 14 March for more on Paris–Nice.)

10 March

Introduction of points jersey to Paris–Nice
(1954)

Paris–Nice first introduced a points competition back in 1938 but the winner, Jules Lowie, didn't get to wear a special jersey. Not that he would have been too bothered – he won the overall race as well so got to wear the (then) blue and orange jersey of the race leader. There wouldn't be another points competition at Paris–Nice for sixteen years.

When the classification was reintroduced in 1954 it came with its own jersey. In 1953 the Tour had introduced a green jersey to identify the leader of the newly introduced points classification and now Paris–Nice followed their lead and, like the Tour, the jersey was green. Raymond Impanis became its first winner on his way to the overall win.

Over the years the classification has fallen in and out of fashion, held some years but not in others. Rik Van Looy and Sean Kelly have won the classification four times each, Freddy Maertens three times. Other winners of Paris–Nice's green jersey include Eddy Merckx, Laurent Jalabert and Bradley Wiggins.

11 March

First Tirenno–Adriatico starts
(1966)

A one-week stage race from the west coast of Italy to the east, if you want to measure the importance in today's calendar of Tirenno–Adriatico just look at the names of the riders who pitch up at the start and who make it on to the podium.

Despite coming early in the season, this is a race that the biggest stars in road racing take seriously. Over the past few years Nibali, Froome, Contador and Quintana, all recent Grand Tour winners, have stood on the final podium.

First held in 1966 – a race won by Dino Zandegù, a multiple Giro stage winner and winner of the Tour of Flanders in 1967 – it is the race's route that attracts the world's best.

Known as the Race of the Two Seas, it starts on the coast of the Tyrrhenian Sea, travels inland, over the spine of Italy and finishes on the Adriatic coast at San Benedetto del Tronto. Featuring time trials, climbing, sprint finishes and at least one long, rolling day, the race has a little something for everyone.

Held in early March, as well as being a desirable race to have on the palmares it is ideal preparation for the new season. And if that's not enough incentive the winner also receives a huge, Neptunesque trident trophy.

12 March

Sean Kelly wins a record seventh Paris–Nice

(1988)

Sean Kelly first rode Paris–Nice in 1977 as a domestique on the Flandria team riding for Freddy Maertens. Maertens dominated the race, claiming five stages and taking the overall win, while Kelly spent his week grabbing bottles and riding in the wind. He finished in fortieth place, more than half an hour down.

Kelly won his first Paris–Nice five years later. It was the start of a remarkable run and by the end of the 1980s the Irishman had been firmly crowned as the King of the Race to the Sun.

For seven years Kelly reigned over Paris–Nice, winning every edition from 1982 until 1988, collecting fourteen stages along the way. Over the years he had been so dominant that in 1988, on his way to his final win, he was handed the leader's jersey after the stage to Mont Faron, only for the organisers later to realize that Sean Yates was the true leader of the race. Force of habit, you could say.

Kelly grabbed the lead for real the following day: 12 March was the penultimate day of the 1988 race and overnight he had sixteen seconds on second-placed Ronan Pensec. The final day brought two stages. King Kelly maintained the margin on the 100km road stage, then won the final time trial up the Col d'Eze to take his seventh and final win.

13 March

Louison Bobet dies
(1983)

In 1953 Louison Bobet was riding his sixth Tour. His record so far had been a little inconsistent. He'd finished fourth in 1948 and secured a podium place and the mountains classification in 1950, but he'd also abandoned twice and only managed twentieth in 1951. However, going into the 1953 race Bobet was still one of the fancied riders, even if he had to deal with squabbling within the French team.

'It's on the Izoard where the Tour will be played out. It's there that it will be won,' Bobet said. True to his word, it was on that climb that Bobet went to work. He grabbed the yellow jersey after an imperious ride over the Alpine giant and into Briançon, during which the rest of the race was left trailing in his wake. Coppi had stood on the Izoard that day and watched, camera at the ready, as Bobet laid the foundations for his first Tour win. Today a monument to them both stands on the Izoard's slopes.

A marvellous climber and great against the clock, Bobet would be the first rider to record three Tour wins in a row (1953–1955). The early to mid-1950s were his greatest years, adding to those three Tours, wins in Milan–Sanremo, the Tour of Lombardy and Paris–Roubaix. In 1955 he took a Tour of Flanders win that Pierre Chany described as being such a surprise that spectators dropped their cartons of chips in shock.

He also claimed a world championship win in 1954, having to chase back after a wheel change on the penultimate lap to prevail by twenty-two seconds, ahead of the likes of Coppi, Gaul and a youthful Anquetil. It was the first time in eighteen years that a Frenchman had become world champion. 'Maman, je suis champion du Monde!' he exclaimed afterwards. It needed no translation.

Bobet rode his last Tour in 1959. The Alps, over which he had soared for so many years, finally got the better of him and he climbed off his bike on top of the Col d'Iseran.

He died in 1983 aged fifty-eight.

14 March

First Paris–Nice gets underway
(1933)

It was a 4 a.m. start for the riders of the first Paris–Nice. After assembling at the Café Rozes on the Place d'Italie for the roll-out, by 5 a.m. they were racing towards Dijon, over 300km away.

The race was the idea of Albert Lejeune. Lejeune owned two papers: *Le Petit Journal* and *Le Petit Niçoise*, the former based in Paris, the latter in Nice. Lejeune wanted to link the two papers in some way and a bike race between the cities seemed to be just the ticket.

Originally dubbed 'Le Six Jours de la Route' – the six days of the road – the idea was to build on both the success of winter six-day racing and the huge popularity of the Tour. Heavily promoted by his two newspapers, the inaugural race was won by Alfons Scheppers, who took the first stage and held the lead until the end.

Today known as the Race to the Sun, Paris–Nice is one of the most prestigious week-long stage races. Many of cycling's greats have claimed the *course au soleil*, among them Bobet, Anquetil, Merckx and Indurain. Sean Kelly holds the record for most wins (see 12 March).

Having passed through a number of owners since its start, the race is now run by ASO, organisers of the Tour. In 2015 it celebrated its seventy-third edition.

15 March

Jean-Pierre Monseré is killed during a race
(1971)

On this day in March 1971 'Jempi' Monseré was riding a kermesse race in and around Retie, a small town in north-east Belgium. He was one of the brightest lights in the peloton, a young man who had already won more than most riders dared dream, and one who had the potential to become a true great.

Monseré was twenty-two years old and preparing an assault on the spring classics. He was already in the record books as a winner of a Monument, having been awarded the 1969 Tour of Lombardy win after Gerben Karstens failed a doping test. Jempi had only been a pro a matter of weeks.

Less than one year later he became world champion when he out-thought Felice Gimondi to claim the rainbow jersey in Leicester, England. Only Karel Kaers had won the world championships younger (see 18 August). The scene was set for a terrific professional career.

Jempi would die wearing that rainbow jersey. Riding in a bunch at the head of the kermesse, on the road between Gierle and Lille, Jempi collided with a car. He was killed instantly. A young life and a young career brought to a sickening end. A monument now stands where Monseré fell.

And as if that wasn't sad enough, fate wasn't yet finished with Monseré's family. Five years after his death, Monseré's young son, Giovanni, was also hit by a car while riding his bike. Tragically he was also killed.

16 March

Roger De Vlaeminck wins record Tirenno–Adriatico
(1977)

The record for the most wins in the Tirenno–Adriatico is held by Roger De Vlaeminck. While better known for his haul of classics wins, De Vlaeminck also found the Race of the Two Seas to his liking.

The Belgian's record haul of six wins came in successive years, from 1972 to 1977, a tally that no one else has come close to matching. The 1977 edition started in Ferentino with a 182km slog to Santa Serena, a stage that was won by Italian Alfio Vandi. That would prove to be about as good as it got for the host nation as De Vlaeminck won the next two stages, laying the foundations of his overall win. Compatriot Rik Van Linden took stage four while the final 18km TT was claimed by Knut Knudsen of Norway. De Vlaeminck won by five seconds ahead of Francesco Moser.

While he would never again claim the overall win, the Belgian would win stages in 1979 and 1980. He would finish his Tirenno–Adriatico career with fifteen stage wins to his name. Another record.

17 March

Albertus Geldermans is born
(1935)

Geldermans' professional career may have been brief but the Tour was pretty much a perennial entry on his calendar.

The Dutchman turned pro in 1959 with the Saint-Raphael-Geminiani team. While he missed that year's Tour from that point on he started every edition until he left the professional ranks in 1966, though he only made it to Paris four times.

His best year at the Tour came in 1962. On stage six he was part of a fifteen-man breakaway that contested the sprint into Brest. He didn't win the stage but out of the bunch he was the best placed rider on the general classification so when the previous leader, Rudi Altig, rolled in over five minutes later, the yellow jersey passed to Geldermans. Geldermans held the jersey for two days to become, at the time, just the fourth Dutch rider to lead the race. He would finish fifth in Paris.

His biggest career win came in 1960, when he won Liège–Bastogne–Liège, recording the Netherlands' first win in the oldest of all the classics. After retiring from racing in 1966, Geldermans turned to management and was at the head of the Dutch team two years later when Jan Janssen recorded another first by becoming the first Dutch winner of the Tour.

18 March

Costante Girardengo is born
(1893)

Born in Novi Ligure, Italian Costante Girardengo was the original *Campionissimo* – the Champion of Champions. The name was later also given to Alfredo Binda and then Fausto Coppi, but it first belonged to Gira when, in 1919, the editor of *La Gazzetta dello Sport*, Emilio Colombo, bestowed it on him during the Giro.

That 1919 Giro was dominated by Girardengo. He won seven of the race's ten stages, took the race lead after the opening stage and never lost it. It was the first time anyone had led the race from start to finish and only Binda, Eddy Merckx and Gianni Bugno have matched it since. In Milan his winning margin was nearly fifty-two minutes.

He first rode the Giro at the age of twenty, in 1913, winning a stage and finishing sixth overall. If his performance showed signs of great promise it would take him a few years to realise it. The following year he abandoned. Then came the war.

Wins in Milan–Turin and Milan–Sanremo would come during the war years but the start of the Girardengo era really came in 1919 with his Giro win.

What followed was quite startling. Between 1919 and 1928 Gira would claim five more Milan–Sanremo titles, three Lombardy crowns and another three Milan–Turin triumphs. In 1921 he started the Giro full of intent, claiming the first four stages to lead overall before a crash on stage five left him with a frantic pursuit of rival Gaetano Belloni. Ultimately he could give no more. He stopped and drew a cross in the road. Until the crash he had looked the strongest but Gira's Giro was over for another year.

Two years later he made amends for that disappointment by recording his second Giro win. He won eight of that race's ten stages but his margin of victory was significantly tighter than his 1919 vintage – just thirty-seven seconds separated him from second-placed Giovanni Brunero.

Girardengo still holds the record for Italy's national championship. From 1913 until 1925 he won every edition that was held, bringing him nine titles. In 1927 he finished runner-up to Binda in the inaugural world championships. His time at the top was coming to an end. The old *Campionissimo* was about to give way to the new.

19 March

Coppi wins his first Milan–Sanremo
(1946)

Otherwise known as *la Primavera*, Milan–Sanremo is the first Monument on the cycling calendar. At 293km, it is also the longest, taking the riders south to Sanremo via the Passo del Turchino and the famous Cipressa and Poggio climbs.

Fausto Coppi had trained all winter with the race in mind. He'd already won the Giro, now he wanted his first classic. With just 50km of the race gone Coppi found himself chasing a breakaway. The move went against all cycling logic. It was far too early to be expending unnecessary energy – let others bring the escape back, then attack nearer the finish. But on this day Coppi ignored his head. He rode with his heart.

By the time he exited the tunnel at the summit of the Turchino he was alone at the front of the race. He was only halfway but on he rode. Alone. One minute became two became five. Legend has it that in a café crowded with people listening to the race on the radio, a shout went up as Coppi arrived. Such was his advantage that he pulled over, downed an espresso, paid and went calmly on his way.

Coppi's final margin of fourteen minutes remains the largest in the post-war era. The radio commentator announcing his arrival had to call for music to be played while he waited for the rest of the riders. Coppi hadn't just won his first Monument, he had sent shock waves through the sport.

20 March

First edition of Critérium International held
(1932)

Initially called the Critérium National de la Route and organised by the newspaper *Paris-Soir*, the first edition of the Critérium International took place in 1932. Initially a single-day race, open only to the French, it was won by Léon Le Calvez, his first and only win of note.

Since that first edition the race has seen a number of changes. Now a three-stage race, in the late 1970s its entry criterion was changed to allow non-French riders racing on French teams to enter. With non-French teams added in the 1980s the race changed its name to the Critérium International.

Currently held on the island of Corsica, comprising a flat stage, mountain stage and time trial, it boasts Bobet, Anquetil, Hinault, Kelly, Fignon and Indurain among its former winners. Raymond Poulidor and Jens Voigt share the record for most wins, with five apiece.

Perhaps the race's most famous participant, however, is of the four-legged variety. In 1997 the peloton was joined by a horse that, attracted by the colourful blur of Lycra speeding by its field, jumped a fence and took its place in the bunch. Chaos ensued until, having led the peloton for a while, it finally ran off course, ending a very brief but well-documented equine cycle-race career.

21 March

Mainland Europe's first full six-day race finishes
(1909)

Born in Britain and growing to maturity in the USA, six-day racing finally hit continental Europe in the 1900s.

The first documented race was held outdoors in Toulouse, France, in 1906. It was won by Emile and Léon Georget but the race suffered from interruptions. It was suspended after two days of racing and only restarted after nearly a full day's break.

The first full six-day race on mainland Europe took place three years later, in 1909, when Berlin hosted its inaugural meet. Now the world's longest-running six-day race (see 27 January), the first Berlin

Six was won by the Americans Floyd McFarland and Jimmy Moran, who covered 2,425 miles in the six days they spent circling the Berlin track. Just one lap separated them from second-placed pair Marcel Berthet and John Stol.

It was a huge success and soon six-day races were springing up all over Germany. Within a few years Bremen, Dresden, Frankfurt, Hanover and Hamburg had all held their own events as the unique spectacle of six-day racing started its march across Europe.

22 March

Marcel Buysse wins the second Tour of Flanders
(1914)

Brother of Lucien, who would go on to win the 1926 Tour (see 11 September), Marcel Buysse claimed the most significant race of his career in 1914 when he won the second edition of the Tour of Flanders.

At the time the race, starting and finishing in Ghent, had yet to win its place as one of the most prestigious in the cycling year. Buysse's win, which came when he outfought seven other riders after ten hours of racing, attracted only two brief paragraphs in Le Petit Journal, one of the most pro-cycling

publications of the time. Only nineteen riders finished. Safe to say, then, that Flanders was not yet attracting the feverish attention of some other races of the same era.

Buysse had already finished on the podium of the Tour, completing the 1913 edition in third place and claiming six stage wins. He would later add a second place at Bordeaux–Paris and a podium spot at the Giro, but he would never again taste victory in a race that would go on to become as important as the Tour of Flanders.

23 March

Van Lerberghe springs a surprise in Ghent
(1919)

In 1914 Henri Van Lerberghe finished second in the Tour of Flanders. Then he headed off to war to fight far more serious battles in the fields of Flanders than he had on its roads, battles that put bike racing firmly into perspective.

Peace finally came in November 1918. Four months later the Tour of Flanders returned with forty-seven riders turning up to the start in Ghent. Among them was Van Lerberghe.

Van Lerberghe was a Tour de France stage winner but also a man with a curious personality. He arrived at the start with an old bike clearly not up to the job of taking on the Flanders course. Jules Masselis, a rider who had claimed a couple of top-three Monument finishes himself, couldn't believe his eyes. He told Van Lerberghe that he couldn't ride the race on 'that piece of junk', and handed him a racing bike.

The other starters laughed. Van Lerberghe told them to button it. He said he'd ride them all off his wheel. Still they laughed. Van Lerberghe, they considered, was not to be taken seriously.

Their mistake. Van Lerberghe found himself in a group of four on the climb of Kwaremont. He attacked and quickly opened a gap. He wouldn't be seen again. By the time the chasers realised he had a significant lead it was too late.

On the road to the finish Van Lerberghe came to a level crossing with a stationary goods train blocking the way. A mere inconvenience. Van Lerberghe shouldered his bike, clambered over an open carriage, and continued on his way. The story goes that near the finish, and with an advantage of such scale that victory was all but assured, Van Lerberghe decided to start his celebrations early. He stopped at a bar and ordered a beer. And then another. And another. His trainer had to drag him out. At the finish, and now a little worse for wear, he told the crowd they might as well go home because he had half a day's lead.

Van Lerberghe's winning margin turned out to be fourteen minutes, a mark that remains the biggest in the race's history.

24 March

Johan Museeuw wins final Dwars door België
(1999)

First held in 1946, the last edition of the Dwars door België took place in 1999, after which the race became known as the Dwars door Vlaanderen.

The first of a series of Flemish one-day races that culminates in the Tour of Flanders, the race takes in many of the same roads and hills of its more famous older sibling. This 1999 edition was won by Belgium's Johan Museeuw, who broke away with Michel Van Haecke in the closing kilometres and then easily won the final sprint. It was his second win at the race after he claimed the 1993 edition. No rider has won the race more, with Museeuw joined on two wins by eleven other riders.

Museeuw, nicknamed the Lion of Flanders, was a superb classics rider who, over the course of his seventeen-year professional career, collected three wins in both the Tour of Flanders and Paris–Roubaix. He also won Paris–Tours and claimed a rainbow jersey, winning the 1996 world championships.

25 March

Wim Van Est is born
(1923)

Dutchman Wim Van Est won the Tour of Flanders and Bordeaux–Paris but is best remembered for an incident on the Col d'Aubisque during the 1951 Tour.

On stage 12 Van Est won into Dax and took yellow. He was the first Dutchman to slip the golden fleece over his head. A stage win and the yellow jersey: his Tour was going well.

The next day took the Tour's peloton into the Pyrénées and over the Aubisque.

The descent of the eastern side of the Aubisque is narrow and technical. Van Est didn't handle it well. After a few near misses he hit a low wall and was catapulted from his bike and into a ravine 70m below. Incredibly, he survived. There was just one problem. How to get him out?

A safety rope was fashioned from spare tubulars, which rescuers used to lower themselves down to Van Est and help him to safety. He abandoned there and then. The incident inspired one of the Netherlands' most famous advertisements. Pontiac Watches, who supplied the Dutch team, ran an ad in the press featuring Van Est sitting on a mountainside wearing cycling gear and a pained expression. The slogan ran: 'Seventy metres I fell. My heart stood still. But my Pontiac never stopped! Indeed, a Pontiac can take a beating'.

A plaque now marks the spot where Van Est fell.

26 March

Simpson takes his first major win
(1961)

Born in County Durham, Britain's Tom Simpson headed to France in 1959 determined to forge a career in professional road racing. He was already a national champion and Olympic bronze medallist on the track, but the road was where he saw his future and that meant only one thing: he had to move to continental Europe.

After riding on a semi-pro basis for a couple of months, immediately picking up wins, he was soon given full professional terms by the Saint-Raphael-Geminiani team. He was a fully-fledged professional rider racing against the world's greatest cyclists. Now he turned his attention to beating them.

His first major win came in 1961. Simpson had led some of the biggest races in the world before – most notably Milan–Sanremo and Paris–Roubaix – but had failed to hold on to the end. The 1961 Tour of Flanders would prove to be different.

Towards the finish Simpson found himself at the front of the race with the Italian Nino Defilippis. Defilippis was a vastly more experienced rider, with a Tour of Lombardy win and stage wins at the Tour, Giro and Vuelta to his name. As they approached the line, in a bid to outwit his rival Simpson decided to try something a bit different.

He started his sprint early, with around a kilometre to go, and then deliberately slowed. Defilippis, sensing Simpson had erred in sprinting so early and had tired, launched his bid for the line earlier than he might otherwise have done. But Simpson was faking. He kicked again, moved alongside the Italian and sprinted past him on the line.

A protest was filed by the Italians – there had been high winds and the finishing banner had been taken down, leading the Italian contingent to claim the position of the finish line was unclear. But the result stood. Simpson had his first Monument.

He would add two more: Milan–Sanremo in 1964 and the Tour of Lombardy in 1965, five weeks after he had claimed his one and only rainbow jersey. He died on the slopes of Ventoux during the 1967 Tour (see 13 July).

27 March

Pacing is banned in Paris–Roubaix
(1910)

From its first edition in 1896 (see 19 April), Paris–Roubaix was a paced race. Riders would follow pace-setting outriders – some on bikes, some on motorbikes, some even in cars.

Pacing was common practice. Paris–Roubaix was originally considered a training race for the then much more prestigious, and also paced, Bordeaux–Paris. In the 1900s, however, the race began to alter its rules, restricting the amount of pacing allowed. Some riders welcomed the change: they didn't like the extra traffic it brought. Octave Lapize, the first three-time winner of Roubaix, was one: 'With all these coaches the risk of crashes is increased,' he said. 'I put myself in the wake of others, taking care to open my eyes wide.'

By 1909, Lapize's first win, pacing was restricted to the opening section of the race only. From Beauvais onwards, around a third of the way into the race, the riders were on their own. One year later and pacing was banned completely. Cars could follow the race but no pace-setting was allowed at any time, with severe consequences promised for those who ignored the rule.

Lapize won the race by two lengths, taking the second of his eventual three wins. Pacing never returned to Paris–Roubaix as it went on to secure its place as one of cycling's most distinguished races.

28 March

Rossi becomes first Italian winner of Roubaix. Or does he?
(1937)

When Jules Rossi crossed the finish line of the thirty-eighth edition of Paris–Roubaix in first place, ahead of Belgium's Albert Hendrickx, it seemed that history had been made. The record books showed that no rider from Italy had won the race before. While Rossi had moved to France from Italy, the country of his birth, at a young age, he remained Italian, having not sought French naturalisation. 'Certainly, Rossi has, over Girardengo, Belloni, Linardi and Binda, the advantage of being raised under our sky,' said France's *Le Petit Journal*, 'but that doesn't stop his success having an impact on the other side of the Alps.'

Rossi had achieved something that had escaped even those legendary Italians. Indeed, something that had escaped any Italian before him. Or had he?

In 1897 Maurice Garin, the man who would go on to win the first Tour, won Paris–Roubaix. In 1898 he won it again. Like Rossi, Garin had been born in Italy but had moved to France (see 3 March). Unlike Rossi he had taken French naturalisation. It was assumed this had taken place in 1892, when Garin turned twenty-one. That meant that all of his wins as a professional were awarded to France. However, in 2004 the author Franco Cuaz was researching Garin's life and unearthed documents that stated Garin's naturalization didn't occur until 1901, nine years later than previously thought. The startling discovery meant that Garin was still Italian when he won Roubaix, changing cycling history in one fell swoop.

29 March

Cadel Evans wins Settimana Internazionale Coppi e Bartali
(2008)

First held in 1984 as the Settimana Ciclistica Internazionale, or International Cycling Week, over its thirty-one-year history this five-day stage race has changed both its name and its location.

Moreno Argentin won the inaugural edition in Sicily. There the race stayed for a decade before moving briefly to Sardinia, then settling in Emilia. In 1999 it became the Memorial Cecchi Gori before changing its name in 2001 to the Settimana Internazionale Coppi e Bartali, in celebration of two of Italy's greatest riders.

Only two riders from outside Europe have ever won the race and both are Australian.

Phil Anderson won in 1991 and then, seventeen years later, Cadel Evans claimed this 2008 edition, winning one stage along the way.

It was the start of the peak years of Evans' road career. He'd already claimed a Tour of Romandie and a second place at the Tour, but over the next five years he would become the first Australian to win both the Tour and a world championships (see 15 May for more). As well as winning the Flèche Wallonne classic, Tirreno–Adriatico and another Romandie title, he also added podium spots at the Giro and the Vuelta.

30 March

Pollentier gambles and wins a Classic

(1980)

When the 1980 edition of the Tour of Flanders entered its final kilometre only three men were left in contention: Italy's Francesco Moser, the Netherlands' Jan Raas and Belgium's Michel Pollentier.

Moser was a former world champion and a two-time winner of Paris–Roubaix. He also had a couple of Lombardy titles to his name. Raas was the current world champion. He had also won Paris–Tours, and the Amstel Gold race three times. He'd won Milan–Sanremo and the Tour of Flanders. Both men were among the strongest one-day riders of their era. They knew what it took to win a classic.

Pollentier was no mug either – he'd come second in Flanders and taken top fives in other one-day classics, but he was more of a stage-race rider. He'd won the Giro and the Tour of Switzerland but up against Moser and Raas in the closing moments of Flanders? Not a hope. Right?

Wrong.

Moser had been aggressive all day, forcing the pace, wearing down the opposition. But he hadn't managed to shake off Raas or Pollentier. With 500m to go, knowing he couldn't win a sprint, Pollentier gambled and launched an early bid for glory. Moser and Raas hesitated. Their indecision proved fatal. Pollentier, prepared to lose in order to win, had rolled the dice and triumphed. *La Stampa*'s headline the next day summed things up nicely: 'Moser dominates, Pollentier wins'.

31 March

Oude Kwaremont is introduced into Flanders route
(1974)

First used in 1974 when it replaced the Kwaremont climb that had been a feature of the race since 1919, until recently the Oude Kwaremont had been in the shadow of the Muur van Geraardsbergen – the most famous of the climbs that punctuate the Tour of Flanders. But no more. Today the Oude Kwaremont is arguably the race's most significant ascent.

The Muur was dropped from the race's route in 2012, prompting howls of disbelief. The climb had come to define the race: steep and cobbled, with tight corners and grassy banks offering the perfect viewing platform for the thousands that crowded its slopes to watch the Flanders peloton explode. Positioned beautifully about 15km from the finish in Meerbeke, it was here that anyone wanting to add Flanders to their palmares made their move. There was even a little chapel at the top for the photographers to use as a backdrop when the attacks came.

So when the organisers opted to move the race's finish to Oudenaarde there was only one question: what would happen to the Muur? Answer: it was dumped.

It wasn't the first time that a race had taken a brave decision to let its route evolve for the greater good and it certainly won't be the last. But it meant that something was needed to replace the rather large Muur-shaped hole that the decision left.

It was filled by the Oude Kwaremont which, after decades of featuring in the race, suddenly found itself propelled up the pecking order of importance. It's not as steep as the Muur, but at 2.2km, 1,500m of which is cobbled, it is longer. More crucial, though, is the fact that it is climbed three times. The first ascent comes early on but then, in the final 55km, the peloton face it twice more, both times followed by the Paterberg. The Oude Kwaremont/Paterberg combo is now the most important part of the race – a vital one-two punch that can land knockout blows as riders with heavy legs and empty lungs fight to realise their monumental dream.

1 April

Heiri Suter wins Flanders/Roubaix double
(1923)

On 18 March 1923, Switzerland's Heinrich 'Heiri' Suter won a three-man sprint to become the first non-Belgian to win the Tour of Flanders, a feat that wouldn't be repeated until Italian Fiorenzo Magni won the race some twenty-six years later.

Two weeks on from that Flanders first and Suter was making history again. Suter, born in Gränichen, in the Aargau canton of Switzerland, had turned professional in 1918. By the start of the 1923 season he had already claimed three national championship titles (he would go on to take another two before he retired, bringing his total to five, a record haul which he shares with Ferdi Kübler).

The start line of the 1923 Paris–Roubaix race was a crowded one, to say the least. Joining the professionals were semi-pro *indépendant* and amateur riders, bringing the total number of starters for the 270km race to 389. At 6.30 a.m. they were on their way.

Henri Pélissier, winner of the race in 1919 and 1921, was at the forefront of the action, along with his brother Francis and Belgians Charles Deruyter and René Vermandel. Together they forced the pace as the race hit the cobblestones, causing the bunch to splinter as those with less firepower in their legs than the Pélissier brothers fell away.

Suter had held his Flanders form. More importantly, he had ridden an intelligent race. Despite the best efforts of the French and Belgians, which at one point had seen him dropped, he was back with the leaders for the race's finale as he and twenty-two others wound up for the final sprint.

After nearly nine hours of riding Suter outgunned everyone to win by two lengths. He became the first Swiss to win Paris–Roubaix and the first of any nationality to win the now fabled Flanders/Roubaix double, something that only nine other riders have achieved since.

2 April

Van Steenbergen wins Flanders
(1944)

In April 1944 Rik Van Steenbergen was nineteen years old. Born in Arendonk, Belgium, he had turned professional just the year before and promptly won Belgium's national championship. Now he was riding his first Tour of Flanders.

No one expected much from Van Steenbergen. This was a race for the experienced riders in the peloton. Among the favourites was Alberic 'Briek' Schotte, a former winner and a man whose career would see him for ever associated with the race (see 7 September).

But, belying his youth, approaching the finish of the 225km race in Ghent, Van Steenbergen was still at the front of the race with eight others.

On the approach to the Kuipke velodrome Georges Claes collided with Frans Sterckx.

Both fell heavily. Others were forced out wide in order to avoid the chaos. While Sterckx quickly remounted and rejoined the leaders, the crash ended Claes's chances and he trailed in over one minute down. It was Van Steenbergen who had the freshest legs in the sprint and he who claimed the win by one length over Schotte. He became the youngest winner of the race, a record he still holds.

Van Steenbergen would add another Flanders title in 1946. He also claimed Paris–Roubaix in 1948 and 1952 and Milan–Sanremo in 1954 and three world championships. (See 13 April for more on his 1952 Roubaix win.)

3 April

71 start, four finish Milan–Sanremo
(1910)

Heavy rain and biting wind greeted the seventy-one starters in Milan for the fourth edition of Milan–Sanremo. Worse was forecast. A snowstorm was predicted to hit the Turchino Pass, the race's highest point. Riders wondered if the race might be postponed, or rerouted, but this was 1910 and race organisers liked their cyclists to suffer. The race went ahead as planned.

Sure enough, as the race approached the Turchino the rain turned to snow. Riders were forced to dismount. Soon more than 20cm of the white stuff lay at the roadside. Frozen to the bone, battered by the wind, caked in mud and drenched to the skin, riders abandoned in droves.

Among the starters was Eugène Christophe.

He wasn't about to abandon, but he was in trouble. Blighted by stomach cramps and numbed and exhausted after the Turchino, he badly needed shelter. Christophe was helped to an inn by a passer-by, where he was given blankets, rum and dry clothes.

Deaf to the protests of the innkeeper, and having seen a handful of riders pass, Christophe went back into the storm, caught those who had passed him and rode into Sanremo alone. He had been on the road for nearly twelve and a half hours.

Just seven riders finished from the field that started. Three were later disqualified, leaving just four classified finishers. Christophe took a famous win – and spent the next month in hospital recovering.

4 April

Tour of Flanders starts in Ghent for final time
(1976)

Since its inception in 1913 the Tour of Flanders had always started amid Ghent's cobbled streets. But the race was growing in scale and, with the need for a new start point to be found, race organisers announced that in 1977 the race would move to Sint-Niklaas, 40km north-east of Ghent.

Among the riders waved off from Ghent for the last time in 1976 was Walter Planckaert. Six hours, ten minutes later, after 261km of racing, Planckaert won the three-man sprint ahead of Francesco Moser and Marc Demeyer, recording the best win of his sixteen-year career.

Planckaert's win was not met with universal approval. He was accused of enjoying a free ride, of not contributing to the escape. Roger De Vlaeminck called it a scandal that a 'wheel-sucker' had won.

While the 1976 race brought the curtain down on one aspect of the race it opened another. For the first time the Koppenberg was included. Cobbled and insanely steep, with gradients over 22 per cent in places, only five riders managed to cycle up the entire climb (perhaps not coincidentally, the same riders filled the top five positions in the final standings). Even Eddy Merckx had been reduced to walking.

The peloton wasn't happy about its inclusion but the Koppenberg was to stay, that is until the events of 1987 (see 5 April).

5 April

Jesper Skibby gets run over on the Koppenberg
(1987)

Jesper Skibby was a second-year pro when he started the 1987 Tour of Flanders. He set off with the enthusiasm of youth and built a sizeable lead. By the time he reached the Koppenberg that lead was coming down fast. Everything was pointing to him being caught but, hey, you never know, right? When the bunch hit the narrow and steep Koppenberg chaos would ensue. By then Skibby would be over the top and away. Maybe he could grow his lead again. Maybe there was still a chance.

Chaos certainly did ensue. Unfortunately for Skibby he was at the heart of it. As the Dane wobbled his way up the Koppenberg the driver of the official car following him was in a dilemma. Ahead of him was a rider at a virtual standstill, behind him a fast-gaining peloton. Not a good situation. He panicked and went to overtake.

Suddenly Skibby lost all momentum and weaved across the road. The car hit Skibby's back wheel and the Dane fell. Knocked from your bike by a car while fighting to hold a lead – it couldn't get any worse than that, could it? Turns out that, yes, it could. Especially if the driver then ran right over your bike before disappearing up the road.

Claude Criquielion finally won the race as Skibby tried to come to terms with what had just happened. The car that had knocked him off and then wrecked his bike continued to the finish, where it was greeted by jeers and a hail of stones and bottle tops.

Skibby never did win Flanders and the Koppenberg was dropped from the race route until 2002.

6 April

Ellen van Dijk wins Tour of Flanders
(2014)

Held on the same day and using some of the same climbs as the men's event, the Women's Tour of Flanders has grown to become one of the most important races in the women's world cup calendar.

First held in 2004, the race shares many of the characteristics that define the men's race, with steep cobbled climbs and stretches of shuddering pavé. At the time of writing Mirjam Melchers-Van Poppel of the Netherlands and Judith Arndt of Germany are the only riders to have won the race more than once, Melchers-Van Poppel picking up back-to-back victories in 2005 and 2006 and Arndt collecting wins in 2008 and 2012.

This 2014 edition was won by the Netherlands' Ellen van Dijk. Van Dijk, a world time-trial champion, put her soloing skills to good use, breaking away on the Kruisberg and riding the last 27km alone to win by just over one minute.

'I wanted to win three races in my career: the world title, the Tour of Flanders and the Olympics. Now only one remains,' she said after the win, confirming in one simple sentence the high regard the female peloton hold for the race.

7 April

Grégory Baugé wins 7th world title

(2012)

One of the greatest track sprinters in French cycling history, in 2012 Grégory Baugé claimed his seventh world title when he won the sprint at the world championships held in Melbourne.

Already the possessor of six rainbow jerseys, having won the team sprint world championships four times (2006–2009) and the individual match sprint twice (2009 and 2010), Baugé entered the 2012 worlds on the back of a twelve-month retrospective ban for missing competition doping tests. The ban was dated from December 2010 meaning Baugé's 2011 results were wiped out, including what had been a third individual sprint world title.

That 2011 title went to Britain's Jason Kenny, who had finished second to Baugé.

It was to be the start of a fascinating eighteen-month-long duel between the two. At the 2012 worlds Baugé prevailed, dominating Kenny who, having lost the opening race of the three-race final, was forced to go for broke right from the start of the second race. While Kenny actually crossed the line first, he was judged to have hindered Baugé's final sprint with the French star given the win and his seventh world title.

Four months on and the tables were turned. At the Olympic Games in London in 2012, it was Kenny's turn to stand on the top step, having overpowered the Frenchman in front of a raucous home crowd. In 2015, however, Baugé added world titles eight and nine.

8 April

First cycling event at modern Olympics held
(1896)

By the Gregorian calendar in universal use today, the first modern-day Olympic Games were held in Athens from 6 to 15 April. (Greece was still using the Julian calendar in 1896, meaning that some contemporary accounts have the dates as 25 March to 3 April.)

Day three of the Games had brought the first cycling action, which took place in a new velodrome specially built for the new Olympics in New Phaleron.

The first event on the cycling programme was the 100km race, equating to 300 times around the 333m-long track. Ten riders started the race on a cold and windswept afternoon. The official report describes the initial enthusiasm of the spectators waning as 'the spectacle of seeing the cyclists whirl by at full speed became rather monotonous'.

Only two men completed the race. Frenchman Léon Flameng survived a fall to win in a time of three hours and eight minutes, ahead of Greece's Georgios Kolettis, who was eleven laps behind. Flameng's win means that he was the first cyclist ever to claim an Olympic title. Four other races were held in 1896: one lap sprint, 2,000m sprint, 10km and a twelve-hour race. France's Paul Masson dominated those events, winning all but the twelve-hour race, which was claimed by Adolf Schmal of Austria. Just six riders started the 87km road race which was won by Aristidis Konstantinidis. Cycling's rich Olympic history was underway.

9 April

Jan Raas wins Amstel Gold
(1977)

Entering the final kilometre of the 1977 Amstel Gold race, Frisol-Gazelle-Thirion rider Jan Raas was very much the filling in a Ti-Raleigh sandwich.

Having dropped the last hanger-on during the climb of the Cauberg, Dutchman Raas was now left to duke it out with two compatriots, Gerrie Knetemann and Hennie Kuiper, who both rode for Ti-Raleigh. Knetemann had won the race in 1974; Kuiper was an Olympic and world champion. Raas had just won Milan–Sanremo. All three had proved they could win big races then, but Raas was outnumbered and surely the underdog.

Raas had ridden for Ti-Raleigh himself for the 1975 and 1976 seasons but had moved to Frisol for 1977. Now his former team-mates started to work him over, both Knetemann and Kuiper taking turns to attack. First one, then the other would accelerate, forcing Raas to react constantly, giving him no time to recover. But Raas held on and as soon as Kuiper made his final bid for glory, he was up and around him in a flash. Knetemann and Kuiper had nothing left as Raas crossed the line a length or two ahead

It was the first of a record five Amstel Gold wins for Raas, who also added wins at the Tour of Flanders, Paris–Roubaix and the world championships during an eleven-year career.

10 April

Boonen wins his first Flanders/Roubaix double
(2005)

From the mid-2000s, Belgium's Tom Boonen has been one of the world's best one-day classic riders. While he has also claimed a world championship title (2005) and the green jersey at the Tour de France (2007), it is for his performances at the Tour of Flanders and Paris–Roubaix that he earned his nickname, Tornado Tom.

Boonen moved to the Quick Step team in 2003 and has been with the various incarnations of that set-up ever since. In 2004 he took his first significant wins, claiming E3 Prijs Harelbeke, Ghent–Wevelgem and a couple of Tour stages. Then, in 2005, Boonen exploded.

First he won the Tour of Flanders, attacking with nine kilometres to go and staying away to win by thirty-five seconds. One week later he headed to the start line of Paris–Roubaix. He'd already stood on the Roubaix podium, having come an impressive third in his debut in 2002. Now, with his Quick Step team fully behind him, Boonen was well placed to go even better

Which was exactly what he did. With 40km to go, Boonen was at the head of the race along with four others: Magnus Bäckstedt, Juan Antonio Flecha, Lars Michaelsen and George Hincapie.

And so began the war of attrition. Over the course of the next hour Bäckstedt and Michaelsen fell away, leaving Boonen, Flecha and Hincapie to sprint it out in the Roubaix velodrome. Boonen timed his sprint to perfection, diving down the banking on the penultimate bend and holding on for the win. It was only the ninth time a rider had completed the Flanders/Roubaix double. At just twenty-four, Boonen had achieved something the likes of Eddy Merckx and classics legend Johan Museeuw never managed in their own stellar careers.

Seven years later, in 2012, Boonen became the first rider in history to repeat the double, a feat since matched by his greatest rival, Fabian Cancellara (2008 and 2013).

At the time of writing Boonen shares the record for most wins at both Paris–Roubaix (four, with Roger De Vlaeminck) and Flanders (three, with five others including Museeuw and Cancellara).

11 April

A Sunday in Hell is filmed
(1976)

'Year after year this hell is the setting for a veritable Dante's inferno with incredible torture and even martyrdom. Sometimes the roadside is transformed into a quagmire and the cobblestones into a skating rink. And this hell has become the home ground of the Flemish supermen. An exclusive affair reserved only for the strongest.'

So narrates David Saunders, a British cycling journalist, over black and white footage of riders skidding and sliding, falling and crashing. Muddied and bloodied racers are shown hoisting their bikes on to their shoulders or taking to verges and gutters to avoid the soul-shaking cobblestones.

This is A Sunday in Hell, a documentary film shot in 1976 that followed the seventy-fourth edition of Paris–Roubaix. Directed by the Dane Jørgen Leth, the film shows every aspect of the race. From its opening minutes depicting a mechanic painstakingly preparing a bicycle, to Eddy Merckx and Roger De Vlaeminck arriving to check equipment, shave legs and have massages, the film is an intimate portrayal of all that happens during one of cycling's biggest days.

The film contrasts the silence of a breaking dawn over the square from where the riders will depart to the frenzy of an afternoon following the peloton as they do battle on the pavé.

And the ordeal isn't over when the race is run, for the cameras keep rolling, even following the riders into the legendary (and antiquated) Roubaix velodrome showers.

It's an iconic piece of film-making that has its own place in cycling history.

12 April

Hinault wins Paris–Roubaix and declares it Bullshit
(1981)

'Paris–Roubaix, c'est une connerie' (Paris–Roubaix is bullshit), so Bernard Hinault famously declared after the 1981 edition of the race. A surprising statement, perhaps, given that he had just won it.

Hinault had entered the race wearing the rainbow jersey of world champion. It wasn't the first time he'd raced on the cobblestones to Roubaix: he'd finished thirteenth in 1978, eleventh in 1979 and fourth in 1980. It had been twenty-five years since Louison Bobet had won Roubaix, the last Frenchman to have done so. It was time for France to grab its race back from the Belgians and Italians, who had dominated it for the past quarter of a century.

Hinault had prepared well and carried good form into the race, having won the Amstel Gold ten days earlier. But it's hard to prepare for everything Paris–Roubaix throws at you: Hinault fell seven times during the race. At one point he was forced to shoulder his bike and run through a field.

Despite all his crashes and diversions, Hinault entered the Roubaix velodrome at the front of the race with five others, including former winners Roger De Vlaeminck, Francesco Moser and Marc Demeyer. It was the man in the rainbow jersey who prevailed, winning the sprint and ending France's long wait for another Roubaix champion.

13 April

50th edition of Paris–Roubaix
(1952)

Perhaps one of the greatest contests Paris–Roubaix has ever seen came as the race celebrated its fiftieth edition in 1952. It featured two very different champions: the graceful Fausto Coppi, more at home in the Grand Tours and the Italian classics (although he had won the race two years previously), and Rik Van Steenbergen, by contrast better suited to the classics of northern Europe, having already claimed the Tour of Flanders twice and the 1948 edition of Roubaix.

With just over 50km to go Coppi was at the head of the race with four others. Van Steenbergen trailed far behind. Then the Belgian launched a furious pursuit. For his part, Coppi just drove harder, shelling the remnants of the break off his wheel until he was alone.

But Van Steenbergen, showing immense strength of both limb and will, bridged the gap to the Italian. There was now less than 20km to go. Coppi had to get rid of Van Steenbergen before they reached the velodrome. He knew a sprint would be a formality for the Belgian.

Time and again Coppi attacked but somehow Van Steenbergen clung on. Coppi threw everything he had at the Belgian but it wasn't enough. They entered the velodrome together, where Van Steenbergen won the sprint. Afterwards the Belgian, clearly in some distress, with dead eyes peering out from a dirt-encrusted face, admitted that just one more burst from Coppi would have ended his race.

As cycling joiurnalist Pierre Chany later wrote, it was a titanic battle between two champions and a race more than fit to celebrate its fiftieth edition.

14 April

Formation of the UCI
(1900)

Cycling's international governing body was formed in 1900 after several nations broke away from the International Cycling Association (ICA). The ICA had been established in 1892 and was a predominantly British-run institution. With the continental racing scene blossoming, many member nations felt that Britain, which combined the voting power of England, Scotland, Wales and Ireland, enjoyed unwarranted power in the administration of the sport. And so they decided to do something about it.

On 14 April 1900, representatives of the national cycling Federations of France, Italy, Belgium, Switzerland and the United States founded the Union Cycliste Internationale, or UCI, with the aim of 'justly representing the interests of cycling countries'.

Belgium's Emile de Beukelaer was the UCI's first president, a post he held until his death in 1922 (see 23 January). At the time of writing only nine men have followed de Beukelaer during the institution's 115-year history, with Italian Adriano Rodoni the longest-serving, holding the position from 1958 until 1981.

In 2002 the institution moved from Lausanne to its current headquarters in Aigle, Switzerland.

15 April

Luperini wins first La Flèche Wallonne Féminine
(1998)

While the men's edition of the Flèche Wallonne classic has been held since 1936, a women's race didn't appear on the race calendar until more than sixty years later.

In 1998 the first Flèche Wallonne Féminine was held. More than a hundred riders started the 84km-long race that used the same circuit as the men's race, finishing on top of the murderously steep Mur de Huy, a 1.3km-long climb that averages over 9.5 per cent but with stretches of over 18 per cent.

The race was won by Italy's Fabiana Luperini. Luperini dominated women's cycling during the mid to late 1990s and carried on winning big races until 2008. In total she claimed five Giro d'Italia Femminile and three Tour de France Féminine titles.

Luperini won the inaugural Flèche Wallonne Féminine by distancing Finnish rider Pia Sundstedt on the final climb, winning by just nine seconds. The following year the race became a part of the UCI World Cup and has remained so ever since. Luperini would win three of the first five editions. That record was first matched by Nicole Cooke and then bettered by Marianne Vos, who, at the time of writing, has five wins to her name.

16 April

Phil O'Shea is born
(1889)

Dubbed the Wizard on Wheels, Phil O'Shea ruled New Zealand cycling for twenty years. Born in 1889, despite a youth blighted by ill health O'Shea developed into a cricketer of some promise. But cycling was his first love and he followed the sport through newspaper race reports.

In October 1909 he entered his first ever race, winning new tyres for his bike. Just one week later he was on the start line of the 180km-long Timaru to Christchurch classic, one of the biggest races in New Zealand.

This was a handicap race and O'Shea was an unknown quantity so the future Wizard was granted a head start over the better-known riders. Big mistake. Despite it being his first serious contest, O'Shea entered the final moments with four others at the head of the race and easily won the sprint. If that alone seems remarkable, it becomes even more so when you consider that he sprinted with a buckled wheel, courtesy of an earlier coming together. Clearly here was a rider of unusual ability.

And so began an era of O'Shea dominance. Two years later he won the race again. Once more he suffered a crash on his way to victory and this time finished the race with his head bandaged. The reward was a chance to ride at the Australasian Championship. O'Shea travelled to Melbourne and beat the favourites in front of 20,000 spectators. He had become the best rider in Australasia.

Hailed in 1929 as the greatest cyclist New Zealand had ever produced, O'Shea continued winning national and Australasia titles throughout his career. He retired from racing in 1932 at the age of forty-three.

17 April

De Vlaeminck wins fourth Paris–Roubaix
(1977)

From 1970 until 1981, Belgium's Roger De Vlaeminck finished on the podium of Paris–Roubaix nine times.

Dubbed Mr Paris–Roubaix by *L'Equipe* because of his stranglehold on the race, on four of those nine visits to the podium he stood on the top step, setting a record for most wins not matched until Tom Boonen's victory in 2012.

The 1977 Paris–Roubaix saw a number of changes to the route as the organisers looked for new cobblestones to throw at the peloton. They included six new sections of pavé, moving the start to Compiègne to accommodate their new finds.

It may have been a new route but the result was the same as it had so often been.

De Vlaeminck, supremely comfortable on the cobblestones, was in a class of his own. While others crashed or punctured, De Vlaeminck simply rode his own race before escaping 25km from the finish and riding alone into the Roubaix velodrome to win by a minute and a half. Eddy Merckx later observed that it was as if De Vlaeminck knew every cobble. *La Stampa* simply called him 'irresistible'.

De Vlaeminck would never win Roubaix again. He finished second in 1978, 1979 and 1981. He last rode the race in 1982, finishing sixth.

18 April

Denis Verschueren dies
(1954)

Born in 1897 in Berlaar, Belgium, Denis Verschueren was a classics and track specialist who turned professional in 1923. During his career he won some of the biggest races of the era, picking up two Paris–Tours titles (1925 and 1928) and the Tour of Flanders (1926).

His 1928 Paris–Tours win came as he held off a comeback by Charles Pélissier. Pélissier, who was trying to match his brothers Henri and Francis, both of whom had won the race previously, had been dropped by a leading group of six, including Verschueren, but had fought his way back into the hunt with four kilometres

to go. In the sprint Verschueren, a tough and gritty rider, held on to take the win by half a wheel. A photograph from the race shows the Belgian crossing the line in full sprint mode, crouched low over his handlebars, elbows out. Behind Pélissier looks on exhausted, mouth gaping wide, resigned to his efforts coming to nothing.

Nicknamed the Giant of Itegem, Verschueren retired from cycling to run his bike shop. His personal life was beset by tragedy with the deaths of two of his children and a grandchild. He died in 1954 at the age of fifty-seven.

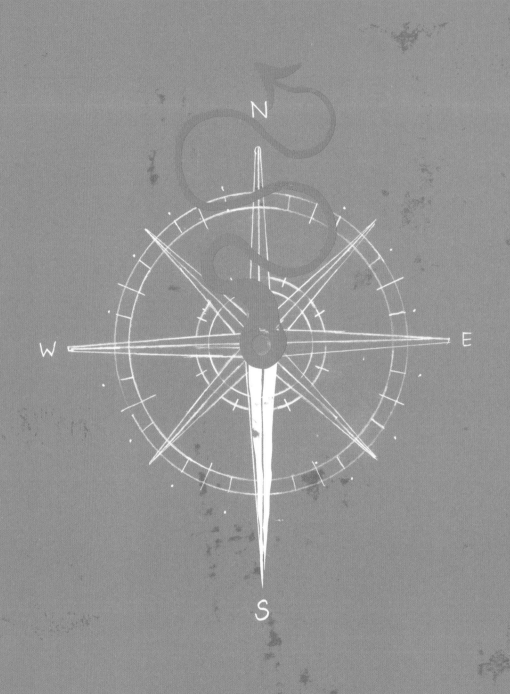

19 April

Fischer wins first Hell of the North
(1896)

Dubbed *l'Enfer du Nord*, the Hell of the North, because of the menacing stretches of cobblestoned roads known as pavé that punctuate the second half of the race, Paris–Roubaix is the biggest one-day classic on the racing calendar today.

The first edition was held in 1896 when textile merchants Théodore Vienne and Maurice Perez, keen to capitalise on the burgeoning popularity of cycle racing, hit upon the idea of a race from Paris to the velodrome they had built in Roubaix. Having convinced the management team behind the sports paper *Paris-Vélo* to back the project, and with handsome prizes on offer, fifty-one riders assembled before dawn on 19 April for the 280km race.

Initially billed as a warm-up for the Bordeaux–Paris classic, the race was won by Germany's Josef Fischer. Fischer had joined Arthur Linton at the head of the race after he'd completed a furious pursuit of the Welshman, having been four minutes behind at Beauvais. Linton was then brought down by a runaway dog at Amiens, leaving the way clear for Fischer to win by twenty-five minutes.

Also known as the Queen of the Classics, or *La Pascale* (the Easter race), after Fischer's win Paris–Roubaix grew into the most prestigious of all of cycling's one-day races. Having had to wait until the thirteenth edition for its first win (Cyrille Van Hauwaert in 1908), Belgium currently holds the record for most wins, having claimed fifty-five of the 112 editions contested at the time of writing.

20 April

Hinault wins Liège–Bastogne–Liège
(1980)

Known as *la Doyenne*, or the Old Lady, Liège–Bastogne–Liège is the oldest of all the classics, with 1980 bringing the sixty-sixth edition of the race (see 8 November for more on its first edition).

It would go down in history as one of the toughest one-day classics ever held, with conditions rarely seen at the race, either before or since, greeting the 174 riders who started in Liège.

The race began amid snow and freezing temperatures. Soon riders were abandoning in their dozens. After only an hour, half the field had packed it in. Bernard Hinault, the winner of the race in 1977 and already a two-time Tour champion, had had enough. As the snow fell harder and the temperature dropped still further, he told his team-mates he was quitting but was persuaded to tough it out until Bastogne and then to reconsider.

As the race hit the halfway mark, less than sixty riders remained in the race, Hinault still among them, having opted to carry on at Bastogne.

Ahead of him was Rudy Pévenage, who was being chased by a small group of other riders. If Hinault had spent the preceding three-quarters of the race just trying to decide whether to keep going, now he decided the time was right to start racing. He accelerated up the climb of the Stockeu, passed those chasing Pévenage, and then caught the Belgian. On the next climb, the Haute Levée, he attacked again. No one went with him. It was still bitterly cold, there were still 80km to go and Hinault was alone. So he simply put his head down and got on with things.

Braving some of the toughest conditions ever faced in a bike race, Hinault continued on alone. He survived the perilously icy roads to finish in Liège a little over seven hours after he had set out, to win by over nine minutes. Only twenty-one riders finished the race.

Hinault's team-mates had watched on aghast at the performance of their leader. They had a bath waiting for him back at their hotel. So numbed had Hinault been by the cold that it took him weeks to recover. It is said that he still has no feeling in one of his fingers.

21 April

Fermo Camellini wins La Flèche Wallonne
(1948)

Entering its twelfth year, La Flèche Wallonne brought a new race route to the table in 1948. The previous year the race had been 276km from Mons to Liège. Now part of the newly introduced Weekend Ardennes (see 10 May for more), the start had been moved to Charleroi and the distance cut to 231km.

The change suited Fermo Camellini. Born in Italy in 1914, Camellini would later adopt French nationality. He was a talented climber who had won the 1946 Paris–Nice stage race and then claimed the first of two Tour stage wins in 1947 among the peaks of the Alps, leading over the Croix de Fer and the Galibier and into Briançon, finally finishing seventh in Paris.

He entered the 1948 edition of La Flèche Wallonne in good form, having recorded top five placings at Milan–Sanremo and Paris–Brussels in the preceding weeks. As the race progressed Camellini found himself in a group of seven riders that energised the race. Soon his fellow escapees fell behind until, on the climb of the Malchamps, he found himself alone.

At the top he had a lead of over two minutes. By the time he reached Verviers, just over 30km from the finish, he'd stretched it to five. On the run-in to Liège, Briek Schotte got some of that time back but the race was effectively over.

Camellini won by over three minutes to become the first non-Belgian to claim the race. A trained builder, with his winnings from La Flèche Wallonne he built himself a house on the Côte d'Azur. It would remain his biggest one-day victory.

22 April

Hippolyte Aucouturier dies
(1944)

With a handlebar moustache and often wearing a thickly striped jersey and flat cap, the splendidly named Hippolyte Aucouturier was a racing cyclist in the early to mid-1900s who bore more than a passing resemblance to the archetypal circus strongman.

Nicknamed *le Terrible* by Henri Desgrange, Aucouturier was a long-distance specialist and one of the favourites for the first Tour de France in 1903. He abandoned the first stage but in those days riders were allowed to continue to go for stage wins (although they were no longer eligible for the overall win). Aucouturier stayed and picked up two stages. He was among the riders disqualified from the 1904 race (see 2 December), and finally recorded a spot on the Tour's podium in 1905, when he finished second and claimed three more stage wins. It was to be his best performance at the world's biggest race.

Away from the Tour, Aucouturier won Paris–Roubaix twice in a row (1903 and 1904), as well as claiming two wins at Bordeaux–Paris, at the time a more prestigious race than Roubaix.

23 April

The Florist wins Paris–Roubaix
(1905)

Louis Trousselier, dubbed the Florist because of his family's flower business, enjoyed the best year of his career in 1905 when he won both Paris–Roubaix and the Tour de France, the first time a rider had won both races in the same year. If that doesn't sound particularly remarkable given that the Tour was only in its third year at the time, it takes on new meaning when you consider that only three riders have achieved the same feat since: Octave Lapize (1910), Eddy Merckx (1970) and Bernard Hinault (1981).

Trousselier's win at Roubaix came ahead of René Pottier and Henri Cornet. Cornet had attacked early on and at one point had gained four minutes. Just after the race had reached Doullens, there were four leading the way, with Cornet and Pottier joined by Trousselier and the 1903 and 1904 winner, Hippolyte Aucouturier. It was Trousselier who would prove to be the strongest. He finally took a grip on the race and led into Arras, going on to win by seven minutes. Three months later he took five stages and the overall at the Tour.

The Florist would go on to win another seven stages at the Tour and, while he never again won in Roubaix, he did add Bordeaux–Paris to his palmares in 1908. The onset of war in 1914 brought an end to Trousselier's professional cycling career. He died in 1939.

24 April

André Darrigade is born
(1929)

Frenchman André 'Dédé' Darrigade is one of the finest sprinters ever to grace the Tour. From 1953 until 1966 he started every race, only failing to finish once, in 1963. In that time he won twenty-two stages, at the time placing him second on the all-time list behind André Leducq, with twenty-five. Eddy Merckx, Bernard Hinault and Mark Cavendish are the only riders to have since won more.

Darrigade was born in the Landes department of south-west France. He first came to the public's attention in 1949 when he won on the track at the Vél d'Hiv, but it was on the road, more specifically on the roads of France in July, where he made his name.

At the Tour, Darrigade worked as a super-domestique for some of the best riders of the day – Bobet, Anquetil and Bahamontes – but that didn't stop him racking up the stage wins, including claiming the opening stage of the race five times (a record).

While he often experienced triumph at the world's biggest race, he also saw tragedy. In 1958, as he wound up for the sprint at the Parc des Princes in Paris, he collided heavily with Constant Wouters, the General Secretary of the venue. Darrigade managed to pick himself up and finish but Wouters died eleven days later in hospital.

Away from the Tour, Darrigade became national champion in 1955, then won the Tour of Lombardy in 1956 before claiming the world championships in 1959.

25 April

Alejandro Valverde is born
(1980)

Born in Murcia, Spain, Alejandro Valverde combines strong climbing abilities with a terrific turn of speed to great effect, making him one of the most rounded riders in the peloton with a career that has brought him wins in one-day classics, a Grand Tour and one-week stage races.

Valverde, who started riding at nine years old, signed professional terms with the Kelme-Costa Blanca team in 2002. His first win came the following year when he won a stage at the Vuelta al País Vasco, later finishing third overall and claiming a first stage at the Vuelta a España, a race he would later go on to win (see 20 September).

Ideally suited to the hilly Ardennes classics, at the time of writing Valverde has won La Flèche Wallonne a record breaking three times and Liège–Bastogne–Liège three times, only needing to add the Amstel Gold to his palmares to join the likes of Eddy Merckx, Bernard Hinault and Philippe Gilbert as a winner of all three Ardennes races (his best result to date has been second in 2013).

In 2010 Valverde was handed a two-year suspension for his connection with Operación Puerto (see also 7 March), the Spanish anti-doping investigation into Eufemiano Fuentes, a former doctor with the Kelme team.

He returned to the peloton in 2012 as the leader of the Movistar team, where he has remained ever since, now sharing leadership duties with Nairo Quintana.

26 April

28th edition of Vuelta a España starts
(1973)

By the time April 1973 rolled around, Eddy Merckx was firmly established as the most successful road cyclist ever to have turned over a pedal.

He'd already won four Tours, three Giro titles and every Monument (most more than once). He also had two world championships. Of course, more would come over the coming years but as the 1973 Grand Tour season started there was one gap on his CV left to plug – the Vuelta a España.

The twenty-eighth edition of the Vuelta was the first and only time the Cannibal started the race. That was probably a relief to the rest of the Vuelta peloton, for Merckx went to Spain and did what Merckx did everywhere else. He won. Or, rather, he dominated.

He took the leader's jersey on the opening day before letting it out on temporary loan. He won two more stages before claiming the jersey back on stage eleven. This time it was to stay on his shoulders for the duration of the race. By the time the race ended in San Sebastián, Merckx had led the race for nine straight stages. In doing so, he became only the third rider to have won the Tour, Giro and Vuelta, joining Jacques Anquetil and Felice Gimondi (since matched by Bernard Hinault, Alberto Contador and Vincenzo Nibali).

After his win Merckx left Spain and promptly went to Italy, where he won the Giro for the fourth time – the first time anyone had achieved the Vuelta/Giro double.

27 April

Graeme Obree reclaims the hour record
(1994)

Scotsman Graeme Obree was an individual pursuit specialist who revolutionised racing against the clock, experimenting with bicycle design and riding posture in order to achieve the most aerodynamic position possible.

With little funding, in 1993 Obree targeted the hour record. He designed his bike himself, which he named Old Faithful. In July of that year he travelled to Norway to try to break the record that had been set nine years earlier by Italy's Francesco Moser. Adopting his unique tuck position, he failed initially but the next day took to the track again and bettered the mark by 445m. 'Because of my sense of failure and worthlessness at the day before, I was willing to die on that track instead of failing again,' Obree later reflected. 'It changed me as a human being.'

Obree's benchmark lasted just six days as Chris Boardman launched his own attempt one week later in Bordeaux, taking the record from the Scot.

Nicknamed the Flying Scotsman, Obree wasn't done. Having beaten Boardman in August 1993 to claim his first pursuit world championship, in April 1994 he went to Bordeaux and set about reclaiming his record. Again he used the tuck position and again he took the record, setting a new best mark of 52.719km. This time his mark stood for a little over four months before Miguel Indurain improved it.

Obree's tuck position was subsequently banned by the UCI. Not to be outdone, he adopted the 'Superman' position. With arms outstretched in triumph, he won the 1995 pursuit worlds before the UCI banned that position as well.

28 April

The circuit of the battlefields starts

(1919)

On the second page of its 28 April 1919 edition, the Paris-based newspaper *Le Petit Journal* ran a preview of its latest race: 'This morning, at 6 a.m., the participants of the Circuit des Champs de Bataille took to the start line of the first stage, Strasbourg–Luxembourg, 275km,' it said.

The Circuit of the Battlefields. The name says it all. Just months after peace at last fell after four years of conflict, *Le Petit Journal* brought bike racing back to the area that had witnessed the very worst of the war. It was meant to be a race of rehabilitation and of respect. Some of the best riders took part, including Tour of Flanders winner Marcel Buysse, Swiss national champion and Paris–Tours winner Oscar Egg and multiple Tour stage winner Jean Alavoine. Famous names that will 'assure that the Circuit des Champs de Bataille is an immense sporting success,' claimed the preview.

In fact the seven-stage, 2,000km race was anything but a success, whatever positive noises the paper made. To ride such huge distances over ground that had been destroyed beyond all recognition, across a landscape battered and scarred by the guns and shells that had fallen silent only months earlier, to cross the fields of the Somme and Ypres, where so many had perished, would have been more than enough for many. But April 1919 brought terrible weather: ice, sleet and snow and freezing winds. The hardy souls who took on the enormous physical and psychological challenge also had to battle the elements.

The race nearly folded after the stage from Brussels to Amiens. So bad were the conditions and the terrain that it took stage winner Charles Deruyter nearly eighteen and a half hours to complete the 323km. 'This rider is more than a champion. He is better than the winner. He is, in the true sense of the word, a MAN,' ran *Le Petit Journal*'s stage report. It would be thirty-six hours before the last-placed rider on the stage finished.

Deruyter would go on to win the overall race, riding back into Strasbourg on 11 May with a winning margin of over two hours and twenty minutes.

29 April

The birth of Vélocio
(1853)

Paul de Vivie was a silk factory owner who in the 1880s became obsessed with the bicycle. Born in Pernes-les-Fontaines, so smitten was he that he sold up, moved his family to St-Etienne, opened a small bike shop importing cycles from Britain and started a magazine called *Le Cycliste* celebrating all things cycling. The magazine, most of which he wrote himself, signing off as Vélocio, encouraged people to get out on the bike and grew increasingly influential. But it is his invention of the derailleur in the early 1900s that is his lasting legacy.

Amazing as it may seem today when new technology is embraced, the cycling world was stubbornly resistant to de Vivie's newfangled device. Henri Desgrange labelled it as something artificial, saying it was 'better to triumph by the strength of your muscles' and deriding it as being something for grandparents.

But de Vivie persevered, demonstrating the efficiency of his invention on the Col de la République, just to the south of St-Etienne, and his invention gradually took hold. Unfortunately for him, he neglected to obtain a patent for his invention, meaning the financial rewards never came.

Through his magazine de Vivie published lots of advice for the cyclo-tourist, including his seven golden rules of cycling;

1. Keep your rest short and infrequent to maintain your rhythm.
2. Eat before you are hungry and drink before you are thirsty.
3. Never ride to the point of exhaustion where you can't eat or sleep.
4. Cover up before you are cold, peel off before you are hot.
5. Don't drink alcohol, smoke, or eat meat on tour.
6. Never force the pace, especially during the first hours.
7. Never ride just for the sake of riding.

De Vivie died in 1930 when he was hit by a tram in St-Etienne while pushing his bike.

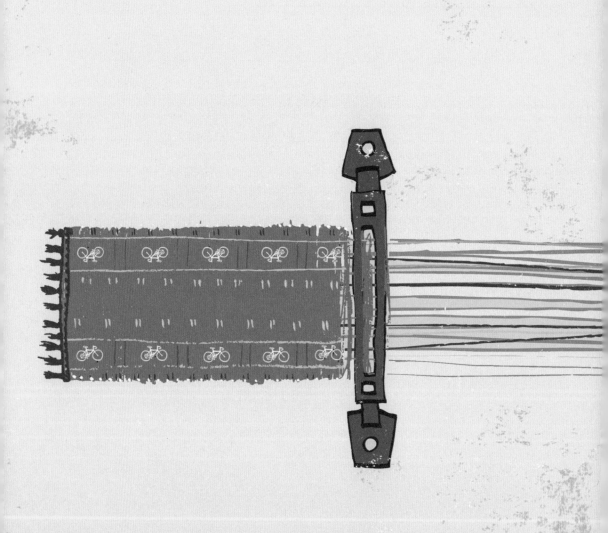

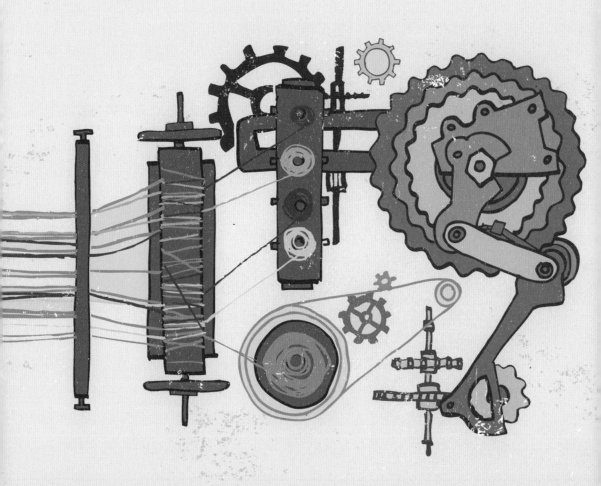

30 April

Poulidor starts Vuelta for the first time
(1864)

Best known for his rivalry with Jacques Anquetil at the start of his career and then for standing on the podium of the Tour eight times but never winning it, a feat for which he became known as 'the eternal second', Raymond Poulidor started the Vuelta a España for the first time in 1964.

His nickname was more than a little harsh. Poulidor was a classy rider whose career just happened to fall in a period ruled first by Anquetil and then by Merckx, two of the greatest riders of all time. And regardless of the moniker, he did actually win; by the time of the 1964 Vuelta he had already been a champion of France and won Milan–Sanremo – more than most ever achieve.

It was in Spain, though, that he won his only Grand Tour. The 1964 edition took in 2,860km across seventeen stages (two were split). Eighty riders started with forty-nine, making it to the finish in Madrid. At the top of the classification sat Poulidor. He had taken over the race lead just two days before, having won the stage into Valladolid. His final margin was just thirty-three seconds over Luis Otaño.

Poulidor would go on to win Paris–Nice and the Critérium du Dauphiné before retiring from racing at the end of the 1977 season.

MAY

1 May

Henri Pélissier, convict of the road, is shot dead
(1935)

Henri Pélissier was one of France's first great riders but his life both on and off the bike was mired in controversy. (See 22 January and 5 October for details of his cycling achievements.) He was a prickly character who repeatedly took issue with what he saw as petty officialdom. And on occasion you could say he had a point. In 1924, along with his brother Francis and a team-mate, he abandoned the Tour during its third stage after being quizzed by officials over how many jerseys he had started the race with – the rules being that you had to finish with exactly the same equipment and clothing that you had started with.

The abandoning of Pélissier was big news. He had won the race the year before and was French cycling's biggest star. The three riders set up court in a café and told their story to journalist Albert Londres. The resulting article was a revelation and lifted the lid on how riders dealt with the terrible conditions and the formidable examinations of human stamina they faced.

The riders showed Londres the contents of their bags: 'That, that is cocaine for our eyes and chloroform for our gums ...' Henri told Londres.'... we run on dynamite,' said Francis.

The article itself was dynamite. Splashed on the front page of the next day's Le Petit Parisien, it became one of the most explosive pieces of cycling journalism of the age. The article was later dubbed les forçats de la route – the 'convicts of the road'.

Less than eleven years later, the 'convict' was shot dead. Pélissier's wife had committed suicide in 1933 and by 1935 he was in a relationship with Camille Tharault, a woman twenty years his junior. During a violent row with Tharault and her sister, Pélissier pulled a knife and cut Tharault's face. Tharault told the subsequent investigation that she feared for her life when she grabbed the gun Pélissier's wife had used on herself two years earlier and shot her lover dead.

'The tragic end of a champion,' ran the headline in Le Petit Journal.

2 May

Vuelta a España climbs to Lagos de Covadonga
(1983)

At just over 14km in length and with an average gradient of nearly 7 per cent, the climb to Lagos de Covadonga is often likened to l'Alpe d'Huez. Lagos de Covadonga can't match the Alpe's legendary hairpins but still has much to celebrate. The climb starts at the striking Basílica de Santa María la Real de Covadonga and winds its way skyward against a backdrop of the Picos de Europa, towards the Enol and Ercina lakes. A third lake, the Bricial, sometimes appears after heavy rain or snow.

The climb was introduced in 1983, when the race was in search of its own legendary ascent. The Tour had the Alpe, the Galibier, the Tourmalet and the Ventoux; the Giro had the Stelvio. The Vuelta needed a climb on which stories could be written and history crafted.

It brought results immediately. Marino Lejarreta exploded up the road to win by over one minute on Bernard Hinault. It was a sensational finale, said Spanish newspaper *ABC*. Hinault would have the last laugh, though, going on to win the race (see 8 May).

At the time of writing the race has visited the climb eighteen times. Pedro Delgado and Luis Herrera both won there on the way to overall victory (in 1985 and 1987 respectively) and, along with Frenchman Laurent Jalabert, are the only men to have won the stage more than once, all three having recorded two wins apiece.

3 May

Armand Desmet wins first E3 Harelbeke
(1958)

Originally called Harelbeke–Antwerp–Harelbeke, the E3 Harelbeke is a Belgian semi-classic race that is today part of twelve days of cobbled racing in Belgium that culminates in the Tour of Flanders.

First held in 1958, the inaugural edition was won by Armand Desmet, a fourteen-year professional who went on to win the Tour of Belgium and secure top five placings at the Tour and Vuelta. Desmet won in a sprint finish ahead of Lucien Demunster and Briek Schotte.

Important in its own right, and with a route that takes in many of the same cobbled climbs as the Tour of Flanders (but around 50km shorter), the race is vital preparation for those seeking to add Flanders to their palmares.

Over the years the race has changed its name. In 1979 it became the E3 Prijs Harelbeke in recognition of the new E3 motorway. Since 2011 it has been known simply as the E3 Harelbeke.

Now part of the WorldTour, the record for most victories at the E3 Harelbeke is held by Tom Boonen. Tornado Tom has claimed five wins to date, with Rik Van Looy next on the list with four.

4 May

Achiel Buysse wins Flanders
(1941)

In 1941 Achiel Buysse became only the second rider to defend his Flanders title successfully when he won a shortened 198km-long race, beating Gustaaf Van Overloop and Odiel Van Den Meersschaut.

Buysse had turned professional in 1938. His was a famous name but Achiel was in fact no relation to the Buysse brothers, Marcel and Lucien, winners of the Tour of Flanders and the Tour de France respectively in 1914 and 1926.

Achiel Buysse's first major win as a professional came at the 1940 Tour of Flanders when he attacked his two remaining breakaway companions in the run-in to the finish at Wetteren, winning by twenty seconds.

Twelve months on, his successful defence of that 1940 win meant he joined Romain Gijssels as the only men to have won the race two years in a row – Gijssels claiming the 1931 and 1932 races.

Buysse won again in 1943, becoming the first to record three Flanders' victories.

5 May

Gino Bartali dies
(2000)

A deeply religious man, Gino Bartali had his first yellow jersey blessed by a priest and used to attend Mass during races. He was given the nickname Gino the Pious but his fellow riders, impressed by his strong constitution and his ability to ride well in all conditions, dubbed him the Iron Man.

Born in Tuscany in 1914, Bartali worked as a bike mechanic before he turned professional in 1935. Immediately he started winning important races, claiming the national championship road race (the first of four titles). The following year he won his first Giro, claiming the race lead on stage nine and holding it to Milan. Bartali would finish with a winning margin of nearly two and a half minutes. He would go on to claim a further two Giro titles.

In 1938 he went to the Tour and won, taking over the lead on stage fourteen with a barnstorming ride over the Allos, Vars and Izoard. His overall margin in Paris was more than eighteen minutes. He won the race again in 1948. The ten-year gap between wins is the longest in history (see 15 July).

His post-war career was defined by a fierce rivalry with Fausto Coppi that divided Italy. The two men couldn't have been more different – Bartali religious and conventional, blessed by the Pope; Coppi spirited and instinctive, denounced by the Pope over his love affair with the 'White Lady' (see 2 January). From 1938 until Bartali's retirement in 1954, the two raced head-to-head, their battles on the roads and mountains of Europe captivating Italy and the cycling world.

Away from the Grand Tours, Bartali took four wins at Milan–Sanremo and won the Tour of Lombardy three times.

He was eighty-five when he died from a heart attack after months of ill health. 'Farewell Bartali,' ran the headline in *La Stampa*. 'With him Italy climbed the post-war [era].' (See 31 May for Bartali's work during the Second World War.)

6 May

The narrowest ever Grand Tour win is recorded
(1984)

When Frenchman Eric Caritoux stood on the top step of the final podium at the 1984 Vuelta it was with the narrowest margin of victory recorded in Grand Tour history.

Prior to his six-second win, over Alberto Fernández Blanco of Spain, the record had been shared by Fiorenzo Magni and José-Manuel Fuente, who had both recorded eleven-second victories in the 1948 Giro and 1974 Vuelta respectively. The narrowest win at the Tour at that point was Jan Janssen's thirty-eight-second win in 1968, later usurped by Greg LeMond (see 23 July).

It was by far the biggest win of Caritoux's career, although he did later claim back-to-back national championships (1988 and 1989). Caritoux took over the race lead on the stage to the Lagos de Covadonga and managed to hold it until Madrid despite Fernández Blanco coming back at him over the course of the final time trials.

Nicknamed the Biscuit (he lived in a town famous for its biscuits), the year before he had finished third in the Giro. He also had a top-ten finish at the Tour behind him. Aged thirty, it seemed he was now a genuine Grand Tour contender. Sadly his life was cut short just seven months after this narrow defeat when he and his wife were killed in a car accident.

He is remembered by the race he so nearly won, with a prize, awarded to the first over the highest point of any Vuelta, named in his honour.

7 May

Paul Kimmage, cyclist, author and journalist is born
(1962)

Born in Dublin in 1962, Paul Kimmage won Ireland's amateur national championships in 1981, claiming a title his father, Christy, had also won, later turning professional with the RMO-Meral-Mavic team.

Irish cycling was experiencing a boom. This was the era of Sean Kelly and of Stephen Roche, riders who operated at the very top end of the sport. Kimmage was not in the same class, however; he was a domestique, destined to spend his days at the front of the bunch in the wind when the TV cameras hadn't yet come live, or fetching water for the leaders on his team.

Kimmage possessed a talent for writing and quit cycling for a career as a sportswriter in 1989. The following year his book, *Rough Ride*, was published, telling the story of his career and revealing the extent of doping in the sport.

No one, not even Kimmage, could have predicted the ensuing fallout which saw him ostracised by his former fellow professionals. Reflecting on the book's impact in 2012, Kimmage told *Bicycling* that it was essential for him to have written it so that he could avoid being labelled a hypocrite during his career as a journalist.

Along with David Walsh and Pierre Ballester, Kimmage was among the few writers who worked to expose Lance Armstrong. At one point he was the subject of a lawsuit brought by the UCI and its former presidents Pat McQuaid and Hein Verbruggen. The case was later dropped.

8 May

Hinault wins his second Vuelta
(1983)

The 1983 edition of the Vuelta was the second time the Frenchman had claimed the top spot in Spain's national tour. Hinault had first won the race in 1978, claiming his first Grand Tour win. A couple of months later he would ride the Tour for the first time, going on to win the world's biggest race at his first attempt (see 29 June).

By May 1983 Hinault was the biggest star in cycling. In just five years he had amassed a staggering number of wins including four Tours, two Giri, a clutch of Monuments and a rainbow jersey. He was well on the way to his place as second only to Eddy Merckx in terms of Grand Tour wins.

But at the 1983 Vuelta, Hinault managed something that set him apart from even the great Merckx. When he took over the race lead three days from Madrid and held it until the end of the final day, he became the first rider in history to win all three Grand Tours more than once.

No other rider matched Hinault's achievement until 2015, when Spain's Alberto Contador won his second Giro title. At the time of writing, Contador has two Tours, two Giros, and three Vueltas to his name to join Hinault as the only men to have won all three more than once.

9 May

Svein Tuft is born
(1977)

Born in Langley City, British Columbia, Canadian road cyclist Svein Tuft was twenty-three when he signed his first professional contract with the Mercury-Viatel team in 2001.

Tuft is a strong time-trial rider and at the time of writing is a nine-time national champion at the discipline, just one win behind the record holder, Jocelyn Lovell. He also took second place at the 2008 worlds despite suffering a puncture.

It was in 2013 that Tuft rose to wider recognition. That year's Tour started in Corsica and for the first time in his twelve-year-old career Tuft was on the start line. At thirty-six, he was also the oldest Tour rookie of the modern era, a statistic that garnered him more column inches than he had ever had before.

Tuft went on to become the 100th Tour's *lanterne rouge* (see 23 December for more), the first time a Canadian had taken the title. Afterwards he told the *Globe and Mail* newspaper:'… it was just survival. The General Classification meant nothing to me … The whole last week was so difficult. I'm still in a bit of shell-shock.'

10 May

Ferdi Kübler wins La Flèche Wallonne
(1952)

At the time of writing only seven riders have won both La Flèche Wallonne and Liège–Bastogne–Liège in the same year, a pair of races known as the Ardennes double. The first to achieve the feat was Swiss rider Ferdi Kübler. Kübler was one of the foremost riders of the 1940s and 1950s, although all of his important wins came in a five-year period between 1948 and 1952. (See 23 June and 7 August for more on his career.)

After claiming his first Ardennes double in 1951, and thus securing his place in history, Kübler returned to La Flèche Wallonne in 1952. Only one rider had successfully defended that title (see 3 June) but, remarkably, Kübler won, beating Belgium's Stan Ockers in a desperate sprint to the line. Such was the extent of his efforts that Kübler tumbled from his bike after crossing the finish line.

Today four days separate the two races, but back in 1952 Liège–Bastogne–Liège came the day after La Flèche Wallonne. If Kübler was worried that his efforts the previous day could deny him a 'double-double', he didn't show it. The Swiss followed Louison Bobet's attack on the newly introduced Côte de Wanne, and then pounced when the Frenchman punctured.

On the run-in to Liège, Kübler proved to be the strongest of the three riders left at the head of the race, winning the final sprint. To date he is the only rider in history to have claimed the Ardennes double twice.

11 May

First hour record set by Henri Desgrange
(1893)

Currently enjoying a surge in interest after the UCI standardised the required equipment specifications in May 2014, the first hour record recognised by the UCI is the mark achieved by the future father of the Tour, Henri Desgrange, in 1893.

In May of that year, at the Buffalo velodrome in Paris, Desgrange set a distance of 35.325km. His record stood for a little under eighteen months before Jules Dubois bettered it by nearly three kilometres.

Over the coming decades the record grew in importance, with such greats as Fausto Coppi, Jacques Anquetil and Eddy Merckx all claiming it during their careers. With the development of better technology in the 1980s and 1990s, however, the UCI was moved to act to prevent the record becoming a technological race rather than one of human endeavour. In 2000 they split the record into the 'athletes' hour,' performed on a machine similar to the one Merckx used in 1972, and the 'absolute hour', where no such restrictions were in place.

The result was a confused mess that led to the hour record falling out of fashion. In 2014 the UCI again changed the rules, unifying the record and paving the way for modern-day track bikes to be used, a move that sparked renewed interest in the record. In the space of nine months from the UCI's announcement the record was broken three times, with more attempts planned at the time of writing.

12 May

Beryl Burton is born
(1937)

It is September 1967. Beryl Burton has just won the world championship road race for the second time. She has returned from that race in the Netherlands to barely a suggestion of the coverage that such an achievement would receive today. Now she is back in her home county of Yorkshire and at the start line of the Otley CC's twelve-hour time trial.

Burton sets off two minutes after Mike McNamara, the last competitor in the men's event. Despite preparing well she doesn't feel her best and over the next twelve hours will suffer mechanical problems and stomach pains. Later she will say that when

she started she had doubts as to whether she could finish.

But Burton would do more than finish. After steadily gaining on McNamara throughout her ride she finally passes him. As she does so, Burton reaches into her pocket, pulls out a stick of liquorice and offers it to McNamara. His reported response? 'Ta, love.'

McNamara set the record for the best performance by a man in a twelve-hour time trial that day: 276.52 miles. Burton beat it. She covered 277.25 miles before climbing off her bike at the foot of a hill with nearly a minute of her twelve hours still to go. It

was the only time the women's record had outstripped the men's.

But, then, Burton was special. Born in Leeds, she went on to dominate the domestic racing scene for over a quarter of a century. Her achievements over the course of her thirty-year career are staggering: seven world titles (two on the road, five on the track), seventy national time-trial championships (distances ranging from ten to a hundred miles), thirteen pursuit and twelve road race national titles and every national time-trial record from ten miles to twelve hours. For twenty-five years in a row she won the Best British All-Rounder title, awarded to the nation's most complete time-trial rider.

Even more remarkable is the fact that all the above was accomplished as an amateur, with Burton combining cycling with her work on a rhubarb farm. She was made an MBE in 1964 and an OBE in 1968. Such was the longevity of her career that she has two entries in Britain's *Golden Book of Cycling* – one from 1960, the other from 1991.

Beryl Burton died of heart failure in 1996 at the age of fifty-eight while out riding her beloved bicycle. Today a cabinet at the national cycling centre in Manchester holds many of her trophies and jerseys – a memorial to arguably Britain's greatest ever cyclist.

13 May

The first Giro d'Italia starts
(1909)

Buoyed by the success of one-day races Milan–Sanremo and the Tour of Lombardy, and fearful of rival publication *Corriere della Sera*'s own plans to launch a national tour, in August 1908 *La Gazzetta dello Sport* hastily, but boldly, announced a new bicycle race. There, on its front page, were the details of the new Giro d'Italia. It would take place the following spring. It would take in 3,000km. It would offer 25,000 lire in prize money. It would, in short, be 'one of the biggest, most ambitious races in international cycling'.

The *Gazzetta* had been pushed into declaring the race. Now it had to arrange it. And that responsibility fell to Armando Cougnet, a cycling writer and senior executive at the *Gazzetta*. Initially sponsorship was hard to come by and at one point the race was postponed but eventually funds began to trickle in and on the morning of 13 May 1909, 127 riders set off from Milan for an eight-stage race.

It was decided on a points system. One point for first on a stage, two for second and so on, with the rider with the fewest points at the end of the race being declared the winner. Luigi Ganna was that man. He finished with three stage wins and twenty-five points overall to win by just two points over Carlo Galetti.

14 May

Gerbi starts the Giro aged forty-seven years
(1932)

The oldest rider ever to contest the Giro d'Italia is Giovanni Gerbi. The Red Devil rode his final Giro in 1932, aged forty-seven, an incredible twenty-three years after he took his place on the start line of the inaugural race.

Gerbi had turned professional in 1902 and, despite possessing rather modest palmares in comparison with other riders of the era, he was one of the most popular with both the *tifosi* and Italy's sports journalists. He had a reputation for mischief and cunning. If Gerbi was around a good story was never far behind.

Gerbi never won the Giro, never even won a stage. His best placing was third overall, which he achieved in 1911, but in 1932 he entered the race's history books as its oldest rider when he rode as an *indépendant*.

The race did not go well for him. The first stage started in Milan and finished in Vicenza, 207km away. Learco Guerra won it in under six hours. Gerbi finished nearly an hour later, outside of the time limit. Day one done and he was out of the official race already.

But Gerbi had promised to finish the race in Milan and finish it he would. Three weeks later he rolled into Milan. He wasn't classified, and he was so far behind the others that only his wife was there to greet him, but the tenacious Gerbi had finished. His wife gave him flowers. His name went down in history.

15 May

Evans wins on white roads while wearing a rainbow
(2010)

In 2007 a new race in Italy entered the cycling calendar. Initially called the Monte Paschi Eroica, today it is known simply as Strade Bianche, named after the stretches of 'white' unpaved gravel roads that punctuate the race's route through Tuscany. It was an instant hit – Italy's answer to the cobbled classics of Belgium and northern France.

With that race so capturing the cycling public's imagination, in 2010 Italy's national tour decided to pay a visit to the same roads. Stage seven was 222km from Carrara to Montalcino, with 20km of the stage's final 30km on white roads.

Unhelpfully for the riders (but helpfully for the race's history) rain fell heavily during the stage, turning the gravel roads into a festival of mud. Riders came to the finish dressed head to toe in suits of grime, resembling miners more than professional athletes.

Australia's Cadel Evans, wearing the rainbow jersey, won the stage, prevailing in a three-man sprint. It was only the second time since Moreno Argentin's 1987 stage win that a reigning world champion had won a stage at the Giro. A famous winner for a famous stage.

The stage was immediately hailed a classic, a Giro day that would still be talked of years later. 'As tough as Roubaix,' said Alexandre Vinokourov, wearer of the pink jersey, after the stage.

16 May

Tour of California moves to May
(2010)

If the Giro was busy crafting new legends in 2010 (see 15 May), they couldn't have come at a more vital time. With the race in Italy about to enter its second week, over in the USA the Tour of California was starting, with the two races going head-to-head for the first time.

The 2010 Tour of California was only in its fifth edition. Previously it had been held in February but the move to May was designed to help the race grow in popularity. The organizers wanted better weather and sold the race as ideal preparation for July's Tour de France.

The change of date was spun as a battle between the two races; the young pretender looking to take on the elder statesman. The truth, of course, is that few riders with eyes on the Tour choose to ride the Giro, it's just too hard to ride both in the space of two months, and the Tour of California was never going to supplant the Giro and its 100 years of history in terms of prestige. But rarely does reality get in the way of a good story.

The move to May was a success. Australia's Michael Rogers won the race, ending Levi Leipheimer's three-year winning streak in the process. The race has remained in its May slot ever since with Leipheimer's three wins still a record.

17 May

First Paris–Tours is held
(1896)

Initially a 250km race for amateurs, organised by the publication *Paris-Vélo* and designed to promote a newly built velodrome in Tours, the first Paris–Tours was announced by the magazine on 22 March 1896.

Just under two months later 151 riders started the race. Eugène Prévost was one of the pre-race favourites and he proved why, riding to the finish alone, winning from Emile Ouzou, who arrived in the velodrome over ten minutes later.

Paris-Vélo had planned for the race to become an annual fixture but for the next ten years there was only more race, with Jean Fischer winning in 1901.

Known as the sprinters classic, in reality the race is often won by an escape. From 1988 until 2010 the finish was on the 2.7km-long and dead straight Avenue du Grammont. A new tramline put a stop to that but the finish line remains on the famous avenue, albeit with a finishing straight now 800m long rather than nearly three kilometres.

Four riders hold the record for victories, with Gustaaf Danneels, Paul Maye, Guido Reybrouck and Erik Zabel all claiming three wins each.

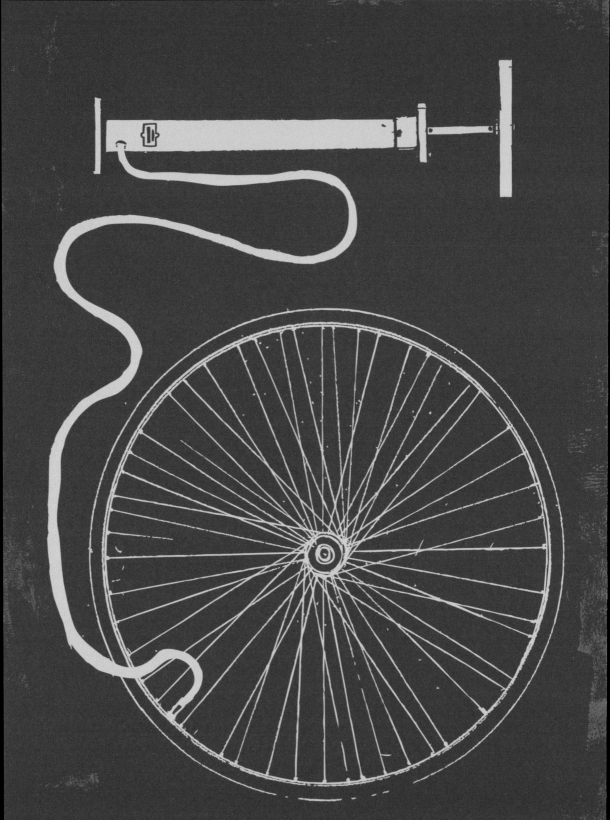

18 May

Willie Hume wins in Belfast and changes cycle racing
(1889)

In 1889 the penny-farthing was still the steed of choice for those wanting to win bicycle races. It was considered to be much quicker than the then new 'safety bicycle', the fundamentals of which went on to give us the bike as we know it today.

Willie Hume was a cyclist in Belfast. He wasn't the best in the city but he had something that others didn't – a bit of vision. A few years earlier John Boyd Dunlop had invented the pneumatic tyre. At the time, racers used solid tyres and weren't convinced by the new development. Dunlop's invention had been laughed at and dubbed sausage tyres.

That all changed on 18 May 1889. Hume fitted Dunlop's pneumatic tyres to his safety bicycle and entered four races at the North of Ireland Cricket Club in Belfast. He won all four. Then he went to England and won there.

All of sudden people understood that inflatable tyres were not to be sneered at and that they not only made riding easier and more comfortable, but made you faster as well. Soon the pneumatic tyre was the tyre of choice for racers everywhere.

19 May

The Giro heads to the Galibier
(2013)

One of cycling's most famous mountains, the Col du Galibier, has borne witness to many a daring deed over the past hundred years or so. The climb is synonymous with the Tour de France but in 2013 Italy's national race decided to cross over into France and pay its first visit.

Stage fifteen took the riders out of Italy via the Mont Cenis Pass before hitting the classic one-two punch that is the Télégraphe and the Galibier, passing the monument to Italian legend Marco Pantani that stands on the Galibier's slopes, marking the spot where he launched his bid for Tour glory in 1998 (see 27 July).

On the day of the stage the Galibier lay under a thick coat of snow as wintry conditions continued to pervade the Alpine spring. The stage finish had to be moved four kilometres down the mountain.

On Mont Cenis a break formed. In the group was Giovanni Visconti, a former three-time national champion of Italy. Visconti stayed away with the group and then, on the Télégraphe, struck out alone.

At the bottom of the Galibier Visconti had a lead of just one minute. Then the weather closed in: rain turned to sleet, which turned to snow. Visconti reached deep into his reserves. He kept his bike going ever forwards, ever upwards. He held to take his first Giro stage by forty-two seconds. Fittingly the line was in front of Pantani's monument – the Italian winning under the gaze of *Il Pirata*. 'I gave everything in my heart for this victory,' Visconti said afterwards.

20 May

Last Peace Race finishes
(2006)

When Italian rider Giampaolo Cheula stood on the top step of the podium at the end of the 2006 edition of the Peace Race in Hanover, courtesy of a narrow victory over compatriot Andrea Tonti, he stood as the final winner of what had arguably been the most important of all bike races.

The race is known as Wyścig Pokoju in Polish, Závod Míru in Czech and Friedensfahrt in German. As the Iron Curtain was drawn across Europe after the Second World War, its impenetrable weight dividing east from west for decades to come, it was these three countries that turned to a humble bike race in an attempt to build unity and identity after the ravages of war had ripped them apart.

The first race was in 1948, a five-stage affair from Warsaw to Prague won by a Yugoslavian, August Prosenic. With no professional sport in the Eastern Bloc, the race was for amateurs only; however, with peace and solidarity central to its ideology it was open to all nationalities, regardless of political persuasion.

That spirit of openness was severely tested in 1950. It was the year it took the name of the Peace Race for the first time and adopted the dove as its symbol, but when the German Democratic Republic (GDR) asked to send a team it wasn't well received. The scars of war were still raw; Germany was the pariah of Europe. Millions had been expelled from Poland and Czechoslovakia. In short, Germany was still very much the enemy.

But the GDR did send a team. It was a small but important step in the process of reconciliation. In *The Race Against the Stasi* (2014), Herbie Sykes recounts the story of the GDR's mechanic forced to share a car with a Polish counterpart. The Pole spent the first day full of hostility, repeatedly insulting the mechanic to the point where the German told his GDR team he was leaving. Persuaded to continue, he spent the rest of the race in the same car. At the end of the final day he went missing only to be found hours later in a bar, drunk and happy with the Polish mechanic. The Peace Race was starting to build bridges.

Heralded as the Tour de France of the East, over its fifty-eight-year history the race brought millions out on to the streets, a welcome distraction from the hardships of their daily lives as they cheered on their sporting heroes.

With the fall of the Iron Curtain, the race turned professional in the 1990s and by the time of its last edition was part of the UCI calendar. Steffen Wesemann of Switzerland holds the record for most wins with five victories but the race's most noteworthy winner is Täve Schur, who recorded the GDR's first win in the race in 1955 and was the first to record a second victory (in 1959).

On the back of his wins Schur became the GDR's biggest sporting star. He was, in the words of Sykes, 'Karl Marx and Gino Bartali, Elvis Presley and Roy Rogers … all things to all men'.

21 May

Mark Cavendish is born
(1985)

Nicknamed the Manx Missile for his furious turn of speed as the finish line approaches, Isle of Man-born Mark Cavendish is the most successful sprinter in Tour history.

With twenty-five stage wins to his name at the time of writing, he is third on the all-time stage wins list, behind only five-time race winners Eddy Merckx and Bernard Hinault.

Cavendish is also the only rider in history to have won the Tour's final stage on the Champs-Elysées four times. From 2008 until 2012 he was unbeatable in a Tour sprint. He also claimed the green jersey in 2011. (See 22 July for more on his Champs-Elysées wins.)

Away from the Tour, Cavendish has won eighteen stages across the Giro and Vuelta and taken the points jersey at both. In 2009 he won his only Monument to date, Milan–Sanremo. Two years later he took the world championships. Cavendish's rainbow jersey-winning ride saw him at the peak of his power and was the culmination of a long-term plan devised by British Cycling to deliver a British winner at the worlds. Dubbed 'Project Rainbow', the plan worked to perfection.

Currently riding for the Etixx-Quick Step team, Cavendish remains in his prime with Hinault's twenty-eight stage wins now in his sights.

22 May

Simoni conquers Zoncolan
(2003)

With only five visits to date, what the now legendary Giro climb of Monte Zoncolan lacks in history it more than makes up for with its vital statistics. This is a climb that boggles the mind, as well as murders the legs. From Ovaro, over the course of its 10km distance the climb averages a gradient of nearly 12 per cent with stretches that near a soul-destroying 22 per cent.

'The Gates of Hell' proclaimed a banner strung above the road at the foot of the climb when the race last visited in 2014. A warm welcome to what is surely one of the toughest climbs faced by the professional peloton.

It all makes for a terrific spectacle. Riders are reduced to the pace of cyclo-tourists, emerging blinking from darkened tunnels, teeth bared in pain as they slowly grind their way to the summit.

The race first climbed the Zoncolan in 2003 (the Giro d'Italia Femminile visited in 1997 but with a finish line before the summit). Then Gilberto Simoni won while wearing the pink jersey on his way to his second Giro victory. 'It got so steep that I wanted to put my foot down and push,' he said later.

Simoni won on Zoncolan again the next time the Giro visited, in 2007. With Ivan Basso, Igor Antón and Michael Rogers the only other stage winners on Zoncolan, Simoni is currently the only rider to have twice tamed these particular precipitous slopes.

23 May

Brits conquer the first Bordeaux–Paris
(1891)

If a 572km, one-day race seems crazy in the modern age, just imagine what it must have been like back in the 1890s on single-geared machines that weighed about the same as a small house. That's what faced the twenty-eight riders who set out from the Place du Pont in Bordeaux at five o'clock on the morning of 23 May 1891. Organised by *Le Véloce-sport*, a Bordeaux-based cycling periodical, the new Bordeaux–Paris race was designed to test the staying powers of that age's greatest riders. Long-distance racing on the relatively new invention of the bicycle was en vogue. This race was designed to push the limits of what was possible.

It was won in twenty-six hours, thirty-four minutes by George Pilkington Mills. A twenty-four-year-old from London, Pilkington Mills was a long-distance specialist who gathered an armful of records that seem quite incredible even today, but considering the bicycles he was riding and the road conditions he faced, they seem almost impossible – Land's End to John O'Groats in three days and sixteen hours? In 1893? On a tricycle? It seems barely plausible.

British riders dominated that first Bordeaux–Paris, claiming the top four places. It soon became a fixture on the cycling season's calendar. While the route remained relatively consistent, the format varied slightly through the years, with pacing variously provided by bicycles, tandems, motorcycles and cars.

The race continued until 1988 when Jean-François Rault won the final edition in a time of eighteen hours and five minutes. The record for most victories is held by Belgian rider Herman van Springel, who won the race seven times from 1970 to 1981.

24 May

Start of the toughest Grand Tour in history

(1914)

'The numbers of the 6th Giro are easily done: 80 starters, eight finishers. Ninety per-cent withdrawn. A huge proportion. How did it come to this disastrous result?'

That was the question posed by *La Stampa* on 8 June, the day after the 1914 Giro finished in Milan with Alfonso Calzolari the overall winner, a rider who had started the race with just one win at the Giro dell'Emilia to his name. How indeed?

The race had started two weeks earlier in Milan. Cut from the previous year's nine stages to eight, there was no corresponding reduction in distance. Quite the contrary. The distance went up, from 2,932km to 3,162km. Divide 3,162km by eight stages and you get an average stage distance of 395km. The longest was 430km, the shortest 328km. It was, in short, a brutal route.

Stage one was 420km from Milan to Cuneo over the 2,000m-high climb of Sestrière. The torrential rain that would blight most of the race started when the riders left Milan in the dead of night. The countryside flooded and soon the roads of northern Italy were little more than mud tracks. In the Alps the rain turned into a blizzard. Riders abandoned in their dozens, including pre-race favourite and two-time Tour winner Lucien Petit-Breton, who was driven into a rage by the conditions before giving up.

If the weather and the route weren't enough for the riders to deal with, then they also faced sabotage. Nails and tacks were laid on the route by those hoping to 'assist' their favoured riders or by those who saw the still relatively new bicycle as a threat to their traditional livelihoods.

The stage winner was Angelo Gremo, who took over seventeen hours to complete the stage. Just thirty-seven riders finished. One day done and over half the field gone.

And so it went on. On stage three, from Lucca into Rome, Lauro Bordin undertook the longest breakaway in Giro history – 350km. He was caught some 60km before the finish and ended up losing more than sixteen minutes.

The weather continued its abysmal assault. On the stage to L'Aquila, the overall race leader, Giuseppe Azzini, disappeared in a blizzard. A search party was sent out and he was eventually found huddling in a barn, nursing a fever.

The route. The weather. The sabotage. All had taken their toll. Just eight riders crossed the finish line in Milan. And still it wasn't over. There was a legal challenge to Calzolari's win: he had, it was claimed, taken a tow from a car during the stage to L'Aquila for which he had been given a three-hour penalty. Now the Italian cycling federation wanted him disqualified.

In the end the result of the toughest Grand Tour in history stood. Two months later war came to Europe and it would be another five years before the Giro returned.

25 May

Inaugural Tour of Flanders
(1913)

Founded by Karel Van Wijnendaele and Léon Van den Haute, editor and correspondent respectively of a new Belgian sports paper, *Sportwereld*, the first edition of the Tour of Flanders took place in 1913. The newspaper was new. Launched in 1912, Van Wijnendaele became its editor at the beginning of 1913 and along with Van den Haute set about establishing a race around Flanders that the paper could both promote and report on.

Only thirty-seven riders started the first race with the quality of the field hampered by the largest French teams' refusal to let their riders start, a situation that would be repeated the following year.

'Gentlemen, go!' shouted Van Wijnendaele at 5.45 a.m., sending the first edition of the race that would become known as Flanders' Finest on its way.

Twelve hours later seven riders entered the velodrome at Mariakerek, where the track encircled a large fish pond. Two collided and fell, leaving a five-man sprint to the line. The dash was won by future Paris–Roubaix winner Paul (Pol) Deman. Just sixteen riders finished in all.

An inauspicious start it may have been but the people of Flanders had flocked to the roadsides (if not to the track, where they were required to pay) to watch the race. The Tour of Flanders had started to write its history, one that over the coming decades would take the race to its place at the very top table of cycling's classics.

26 May

Alfredo Binda wins the first of 41 Giro stages
(1925)

When Alfredo Binda won an eight-man sprint into Bari on stage six of the 1925 Giro, it was the start of a remarkable run for the Italian that would see him established as Italy's second *Campionissimo* and its first five-time Giro champion.

It was Binda's first Giro and he was already leading the race, having taken advantage of Costante Girardengo's puncture on stage five. On the 314km stage from Naples to Bari, Binda found himself in a leading group of fifteen that, by the time they had reached the outskirts of the finishing city,

had been whittled down to eight, including Girardengo. Binda took the stage on the line ahead of Gira and the then two-time Giro winner Giovanni Brunero (Brunero would go on to win his third Giro in 1926).

When Binda called time on his own Giro career ten years later he had amassed a startling record of forty-one stage wins. It was a record that would stand for sixty-eight years before Mario Cipollini took his forty-second win in 2003. (See 11 August for more on Binda's career.)

27 May

Freddie Grubb is born

(1887)

Born in Kingston, Surrey, Freddie Grubb was Britain's first road-racing Olympic silver medallist. He was also its first Grand Tour rider.

Grubb rode for the Vegetarian Cycle & Athletic Club. He set a number of records on the domestic scene before heading to his one and only Olympic Games in 1912. Hosted by Stockholm, Sweden, the 1912 Games featured only two cycling competitions, both decided by a single 318km race around Lake Mälaren. The 123 riders were sent off at two-minute intervals for an extraordinary solo test against the clock, with the fastest individual rider being awarded the gold medal in the individual competition. The times of the four best-placed riders from each nation were then combined to calculate the result of the team classification.

Grubb paced his ride perfectly. He was ninth fastest after 120km and steadily moved up the standings. Fifth at 165km became fourth at 200km, third at 265km and, finally, second at the finish. His time of ten hours, fifty-one minutes and twenty-four seconds placed him just over eight minutes behind winner Rudolf Lewis of South Africa. Grubb's performance helped the British team secure silver in the team competition as well.

By 1914 Grub was a professional. He went to ride the Giro, becoming Britain's first Grand Tour rider. Unfortunately for him he picked probably the hardest edition in history (see 24 May) and lasted only one day. He quit cycling shortly afterwards, going on to form a bicycle manufacturing business that carried his name until the 1950s.

28 May

The Devil in a Dress wins Giro hearts
(1924)

Many of the leading riders of the era stayed away from the 1924 edition of the Giro d'Italia following a dispute with the race organisers over appearance fees. Costante Girardengo, Gaetano Belloni and Giovanni Brunero, who between them had won the past five editions of the race, all opted to sit it out. The organisers needed something, or someone, to ignite interest in the race. Step forward Alfonsina Strada.

Strada was born in 1891 into a large peasant family. She started riding against her family's wishes but was immediately successful, reportedly winning her family a pig in one race at the age of thirteen. She was obsessed by cycling, asking for a bicycle as a wedding gift when she married Luigi Strada, a cyclist who became her coach.

By the time of the 1924 Giro, Strada, dubbed the Devil in a Dress, was used to racing against men, having ridden the Tour of Lombardy. But the Giro was something else. It comprised twelve stages over twenty-three days. It totalled 3,613km. The shortest stage was 230km, the longest 415km. It was a severe test of endurance.

Accounts vary as to whether Strada conned the organisers into thinking she was a man on her application, or whether she was invited by them to ride for the increased publicity. However she came to be there, Strada was among the ninety riders who started the race in Milan.

A gifted athlete, she kept pace with the peloton over the opening stages. She didn't win or feature in any top tens, but she finished each stage within the mandated time limit, impressive enough in such a gruelling race.

On stage eight her race unravelled. On a day of heavy rain and strong wind she fell from her bike repeatedly. She was forced to make hasty repairs and, ignoring the pain screaming from her injured knee, rolled into Bologna more than fifteen hours after starting and well outside the time limit.

Now the organisers were faced with a dilemma. Strada had brought the Giro a huge amount of badly needed attention, but she had to be thrown off the race. A compromise was reached. Strada would no longer be officially classified, but she was allowed (and funded) to continue riding.

On 28 May the race faced its toughest day. From Bolgna to Fiume (now Rijeka, Croatia), the riders battled for 415km. At the end of the stage Strada had spent more than twenty-one hours in the saddle. Crying with exhaustion, she was lifted from her bike by the crowds and into a special place in their hearts, heralded as the true heroine of the race.

Thirty riders would finish the 1924 Giro. With them was one unclassified woman. Alfonsina Strada: the first and last woman to have ridden the Giro d'Italia.

29 May

Jacques Anquetil wins Dauphiné Libéré ....
(1965)

In 1965 Jacques Anquetil's *director sportif*, Raphaël Geminiani, set his star rider a seemingly impossible challenge: to win the stage-race Dauphiné Libéré and then hotfoot it across southern France to take on the Bordeaux–Paris long-distance classic, which started just seven hours later.

At first Anquetil thought the idea insane. If nothing else, just getting to Bordeaux in time for the start was going to be a major logistical challenge. And Bordeaux–Paris was tough enough without more than a week's hard racing in the legs. Nevertheless, Geminiani finally convinced his charge, telling him it would capture the imagination of the public. The challenge was on.

At the Dauphiné he was up against his biggest rival, Raymond Poulidor, who had finished second the year before and the man that Anquetil was fighting for the love of the French public. Anquetil won three of the ten stages, took the race lead on stage three and held it until the finish in Avignon.

After the ceremonials Anquetil grabbed some steak tartare, washed it down with a beer or two and dashed to the airport to get on the plane that was waiting to take him to Bordeaux, his every move followed by journalists recording every moment. Phase one was in the bag. France could barely wait to see how phase two would go.

30 May

... and then wins Bordeaux–Paris
(1965)

At midnight Anquetil was on the start line of the 557km-long Bordeaux–Paris. He had barely slept since his win in Avignon; now he was about to take on one of the toughest one-day races in cycling.

Due to the distance there was an understanding that the early part of the race would be ridden at a reasonable pace but with no attacks. One rider, Claude Valdois, decided to do things his way and sprinted off, prompting Anquetil to send one of his team-mates, Vin Denson, after him.

Anquetil was suffering. It was cold and there was a strong headwind. He couldn't breathe and his legs were already hurting. Dawn was still to break. He'd had enough and wanted to quit. It was only the words of Geminiani that kept him going.

The riders collected their derny-riding pacemakers at Châtellerault. François Mahé rode into a lead of six minutes. Riders were now attacking Anquetil constantly, but he bided his time. Then, when his team-mate Jean Stablinski started a pursuit of Mahé, Anquetil latched on.

After a furious chase Stablinski and Anquetil passed Mahé. Joined by Britain's Tom Simpson, the three rode towards Paris until Anquetil dropped them around 20km from the finish.

Anquetil rode into the Parc des Princes alone. Twenty thousand people were waiting there to see him complete a remarkable double, chanting his name for minutes after he crossed the finish line.

'This may be my best win,' he said. 'In any case it gives me immense pleasure.'

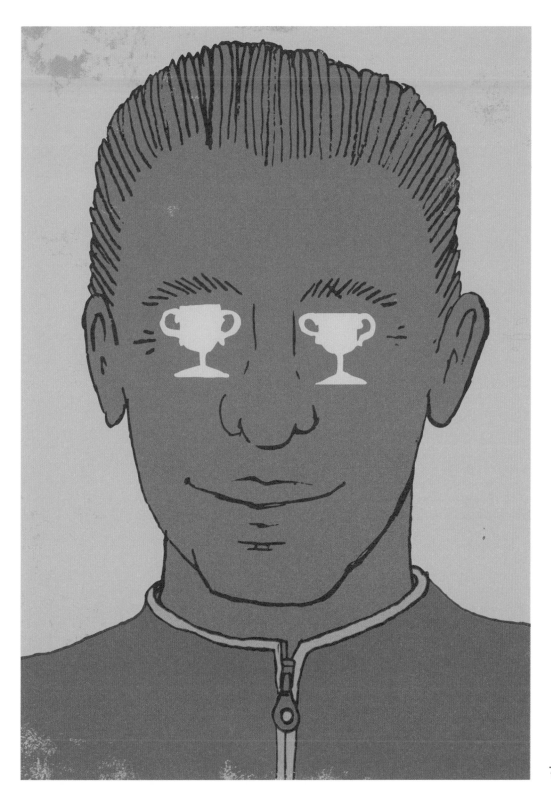

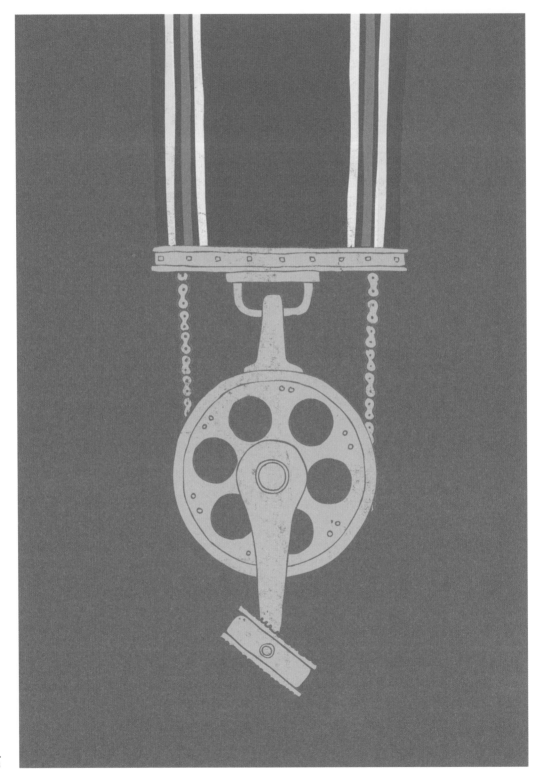

31 May

Gino Bartali awarded Medaglia d'Oro al Merito Civile
(2005)

Italian Gino Bartali enjoyed a hugely successful twenty-year career (see 5 May), but his life's greatest work came during the Second World War when the racing calendar was all but cancelled.

By the early 1940s Bartali was one of the most famous sportsmen in Europe. In Italy he was already a legend, with two Giri d'Italia titles and one Tour de France win to his name (his third Giro and second Tour would come after the war). Gino the Pious was well known and well loved.

Bartali still rode during the war years – he won a national title in 1940, as well as recording top-five finishes in the Tour of Lombardy and Milan–Sanremo in 1942 and 1943 respectively. So when the Italian champion was stopped and searched by members of the Fascist party while he was out covering kilometre after kilometre on his bike, he was able to explain his presence on the roads as part of his training. He was also able to ask them to leave his bicycle untouched as it was exactly set to his measurements.

It was crucial to Bartali that soldiers and police left his bike alone, but not just because he would then have to readjust his saddle height. Often hidden in the bike's frame and under its saddle were counterfeit papers that Bartali was smuggling to help the Jews of Italy escape persecution.

Bartali was working with a Jewish resistance group operating in Italy, transporting forged papers between Florence and a convent where Jews were in hiding. And his actions went beyond the vital courier work – he sheltered one Jewish family in his cellar for nearly a year. In all it is estimated that Bartali helped save 800 Jews.

The full extent of his actions only came to light after his death. Later research revealed that the authorities were closely monitoring Bartali and his 'training rides'. In fact he was imprisoned for just over a month in 1943 for his support of the Vatican but released without charge.

In May 2005 Bartali was awarded Italy's Medaglia d'Oro al Merito Civile for his 'wonderful example of great spirit of sacrifice and human solidarity'. In 2013 the state of Israel awarded him the honour of Righteous Among The Nations – given to those who risked their own lives to save the lives of Jews.

For his part Bartali never spoke of his actions nor courted recognition for them, saying only: 'Some medals are pinned to your soul, not to your jacket.'

1 June

Michael Rasmussen, aka the Chicken, is born
(1974)

Michael Rasmussen was a world champion mountain bike rider who turned to the road in 2001. He won the polka dot jersey at the Tour in 2005 and 2006.

It was in 2007 that Rasmussen really rose to prominence. Rasmussen was always a talented climber: he truly soared where others faltered, but for all his prowess in the mountains he was never a real challenger for the overall. He wasn't good enough in time-trials.

But in 2007 something was different. Rasmussen climbed into yellow in the Alps. Nothing odd there. But on stage 13's time-trial he posted a terrific time, ahead of riders who had previously been much stronger against the clock.

Rumours started circulating: Rasmussen had missed out of competition drugs tests; Rasmussen had lied about his whereabouts to the authorities.

He protested his innocence. Nobody believed him. He rode to a stage win on the Aubisque and was booed by the crowds. That evening his team withdrew him from the race while still in yellow.

In 2013, Rasmussen, who was nicknamed the Chicken, admitted to doping throughout his career.

2 June

Coppi wins his fifth Giro d'Italia
(1953)

In 1953 Fausto Coppi had entered the Giro with high expectations of adding the 1953 race to the four titles he already had in the bag.

But it hadn't gone to plan.

Also in the Giro peloton in 1953 was Hugo Koblet, a handsome Swiss rider who, like Coppi, was an artist on the bike. In 1950 Koblet had become the first non-Italian to win the Giro. After a lean 1952 he was back and ready to challenge.

Koblet took the race lead on stage eight and kept it until the final week. With two stages left Coppi was two minutes down. Over the past fortnight he'd tried all he could to shake Koblet but couldn't. With the race seemingly over he congratulated the Swiss and talked only of aiming for the next stage win.

That next stage was over the Stelvio. It was the first time the race had visited the fearsome climb. Coppi's lover was coming to watch and he wanted to impress.

On the Stelvio Coppi attacked and left an unsuspecting Koblet for dead. The Swiss knew Coppi wanted the stage but the Italian powered away with such force that Koblet's jersey was now in danger. He had no answer. Coppi won in front of his lover and took nearly three and a half minutes from the Swiss.

Coppi had stolen the pink jersey with one stage to go. The following day, 2nd June, he sealed his fifth Giro win in Milan.

3 June

Marcel Kint wins third Flèche Wallonne
(1945)

Born in Kortrijk, Belgium, Marcel Kint was a professional cyclist from 1935 until 1951. He won stages at the Tour, the 1938 world championships and the 1943 Paris–Roubaix.

While world championships, Tour stage wins and Monument victories would obviously remain the high points of any palmares, in 1945 Marcel Kint achieved something no rider had managed before, and that none has managed since. As well as winning Paris–Roubax in 1943, Kint had also won La Flèche Wallonne for the first time. Then, in 1944, he won it again, becoming the first rider to win the race twice. In 1945 he went one better, powering away with four other riders and outsprinting them to take his third win in a row.

While Eddy Merckx, Moreno Argentin, Davide Rebellin and Alejandro Valverde have all since triumphed three times in La Flèche Wallonne, Kint was the first to reach that mark and he remains the only rider to have won in successive years.

4 June

The Stelvio becomes the first Cima Coppi at the Giro

(1965)

Mountains have long played an integral part in Italy's national tour. In 1933 the organisers introduced a prize for the best climber, and in 1965 they decided to introduce a prize in honour of Italy's greatest ever cyclist.

The Cima Coppi was to be awarded to the first rider over the highest point of the race. In 1965 that meant the Stelvio, the very mountain on which Coppi had sped away to win his fifth Giro (see 2 June). The Stelvio is a monstrous climb: it reaches up to 2,758m, and has a maximum gradient of 14 per cent with an average of 7 per cent. And it is long: 22km from Bormio, 24km from Ponte di Stelvio.

In 1965 stage twenty finished at the top of that brutish climb. Not only would the winner claim one of the Giro's most storied climbs, but he would be forever known as the winner of the first Cima Coppi.

One of the problems with climbing high mountains in late spring is that snow still often falls. Lots of it. And 4 June was one such day. Snowploughs were employed to clear the way but snow still blocked the final metres. So it was that the riders had to dismount, shoulder their bikes and run to the top of the Stelvio. Graziano Battistini became the Giro's first winner of the Cima Coppi, but, ironically, he did it on foot.

5 June

Pantani scales the Mortirolo
(1994)

Unlike the Stelvio, the Mortirolo is a fairly recent addition to the Giro's array of mountains. It first featured in 1990 when Venezuela's Leonardo Sierra was the first over the top of the climb on his way to the biggest stage win of his career. The climb was a hit and returned in 1991 and then again in 1994.

At 12.5km the Mortirolo is not long, neither, at 1,852m, is it particularly high. At an average of 10.5 per cent, with long stretches well above that and a maximum gradient of 18 per cent, it is, however, very steep.

Some have said that makes the Mortirolo the hardest climb in cycling.

On 5 June 1994, Marco Pantani, riding only his second Giro, launched himself up the Mortirolo. He'd already won a tough mountain stage the day before and now he was about to repeat that feat. Riding through dappled shade, Pantani left the pink jersey group standing. In front of enormous crowds, he conquered the Mortirolo alone and rode on to his second straight stage victory, stunning even the established cycling order.

6 June

Gianni Bugno leads Giro from start to finish
(1990)

Only four riders have held the race lead in the Giro d'Italia from the first stage to the last: Costante Girardengo (1919), Alfredo Binda (1927), Eddy Merckx (1973) and, in 1990, Gianni Bugno.

Bugno was a versatile rider, a rare cyclist who could win classics, world championships and Grand Tours. The best years of his career were from 1990 to 1992, when he won Milan–Sanremo, the Clásica de San Sebastián and back-to-back road races at the world championships.

Bugno's most dominant performance, however, came in the 1990 Giro, when he took the first pink jersey of the race, a 13km time trial in Bari. He came within one second of losing it the next day but managed to cross the line in the nick of time to stop Thierry Marie stealing the jersey. Over the next week he steadily increased his margin without really disappearing out of sight.

Until stage ten. A dominant performance in the 68km time trial secured him a lead of over four minutes. After winning his second time trial on the penultimate stage, Bugno's winning margin grew to over six minutes, securing his place in history.

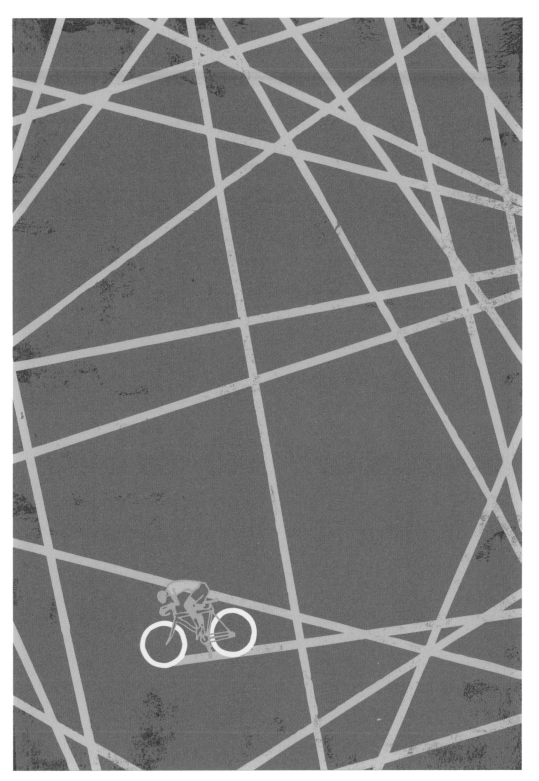

7 June

Albert Zweifel is born
(1949)

Switzerland's finest cyclo-cross rider, Albert Zweifel was born in Rüti, near Zurich. He won the world championships five times between 1976 and 1986.

Zweifel turned professional in 1973. Three years later he won the cyclo-cross world championships in Chazay d'Azergues, France. Thereafter, the nine-time Swiss national champion would win the worlds four years on the trot. This was a period of Swiss control; a period when they claimed first and second place at every world championship from 1976 until 1979, always with Zweifel taking the top spot.

In the early 1980s, however, Zweifel had to content himself with lower podium positions. Until 1986 that is. That year the worlds took place in Lembeek, Belgium. The week leading up to the race had seen heavy rain: the course was a quagmire, the mud calf-deep. Cycling was virtually impossible. It looked like the race might be cancelled but cyclo-cross riders are made of stern stuff. In atrocious conditions, Zweifel took advantage of his ability to run with the bike, winning ahead of compatroit Pascal Richard. His ten-year gap between first and last wins remains a record.

8 June

Cameron Meyer wins Suisse stage on brother's birthday
(2013)

The Australian Cameron Meyer shares his profession with his younger brother Travis. Of the two, it is fair to say that Cameron has so far enjoyed the more successful career, with a handful of world titles on the track and stage wins at the Tour and Giro in team time trials.

A multiple junior world champion on the track, Travis's biggest win to date on tarmac is at the 2010 Australian national championships. He has won the U23 Tour de Berlin and the Tour de Perth.

Both Meyers first rode professionally for the Garmin team, Cameron first in 2009 and Travis in 2010, before they left to ride for Australia's Orica-GreenEDGE in 2012. At the time of writing Cameron is still with Orica, but Travis has dropped down a level to ride for Drapac, an Australian Pro-Continental team.

In 2013 Cameron celebrated his brother's twenty-fourth birthday by winning the opening stage of the Tour de Suisse, taking the famous leader's jersey for the first time.

9 June

Coppi prepares to ride into history

(1949)

On 9 June 1949, stage sixteen of the Giro ended in Cuneo. In a bunch sprint won by Oreste Conte, the race's overall leaders were conspicuously absent at the front end of the stage. Who could blame them? They knew full well what was to come the following day. Stage seventeen was a monster – 254km over five huge Alpine passes: the Maddalena, Vars, Izoard, Montgenèvre and Sestrière .

That evening Fausto Coppi plotted his next move. He was second on GC, forty-three seconds behind Adolfo Leoni, but more than nine minutes ahead of his great rival, Gino Bartali. The pair would go head-to-head the next day. Both had to ride aggressively if they were to try to win the race, Bartali even more so than Coppi. The two men engaged in their usual sparring, each telling reporters to inform the other that tomorrow they would wreak havoc, grind their rival into the ground en route to victory. If it all whetted the appetite for the race's Queen Stage, as the Giro circus turned in for the night no one could have expected what would unfold over the next twenty-four hours.

The next day and the peloton reaches the first climb, the Maddalena. There are more than 200km still to go; rain is falling; snow still lines the roadsides. No matter. Coppi attacks and is gone. No one goes with him.

Bartali had predicted this move and was not worried. There was a long way to go and he was confident he could pass Coppi before the day was out. But Bartali had underestimated his rival.

Coppi stayed alone at the head of the race and cemented a legend that had been forming for nearly ten years.

Coppi had three minutes at the top of that first climb and he never looked back. This was to be the moment that defined him, that elevated him beyond all others: the greatest of all solo escapades through cycling's harshest terrain.

After nine hours and nineteen minutes of majestic mountain climbing, Coppi glided into Pinerolo. Bartali followed nearly twelve minutes later. The next rider took another eight minutes to arrive. Coppi had destroyed everyone to take pink. He was now over twenty-three minutes ahead.

'Il capolavoro di Coppi,' proclaimed the headlines the next day, Coppi's masterpiece.

It truly was the master's greatest work of art.

10 June

Wiggins completes historic treble
(2012)

With a history as long and varied as professional cycling's, there are precious few true 'firsts' these days. However, for Bradley Wiggins, 2012 brought more than one.

Of course, that was the year he became the first Briton to win the Tour de France (see 1 August) but before Wiggins had even started the Tour he had already entered the record books. Apart from the three Grand Tours, there are a handful of stage races that have genuine prestige: Paris–Nice, Tour de Romandie and the Critérium du Dauphiné are three of them.

Until 2012 – until Wiggins – no one had won all three in a single season.

In March he took Paris–Nice. In April he claimed Romandie. And then, in June, he won his second consecutive Dauphiné. Only cycling legends Eddy Merckx and Jacques Anquetil had won Paris–Nice and the Dauphiné in the same year, but no one had won Romandie as well. There Wiggins stands alone.

11 June

LeMond storms back after two-year absence
(1989)

On 20 April 1987, Greg LeMond was spending time at a family-owned ranch in the foothills of the Sierra Nevada Mountains in California. He was out hunting with his uncle and brother-in-law when an accident occurred that nearly cost the reigning Tour champion his life.

His brother-in-law, Patrick Blades, mistakenly shot LeMond. The cyclist was airlifted to hospital and newspaper reports the next day told the world that LeMond had lost a great deal of blood and had undergone emergency surgery. Trauma specialists said he would be back to normal in a couple of months.

In fact it took LeMond a couple of years.

In May 1989 he went to the Giro. During a torrid three weeks he had to use every ounce of strength and determination simply to survive. Then, on the final stage, a 54km time trial, LeMond stunned everyone, coming second and putting over one minute into pink jersey Laurent Fignon.

As Fignon would soon discover, LeMond finally was back (see 23 July).

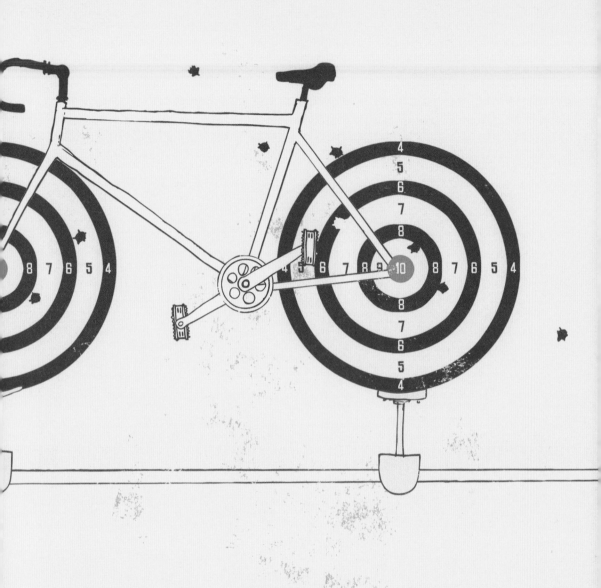

12 June

The Bernina Strike
(1954)

The penultimate stage of the 1954 Giro d'Italia was a mountainous affair into St Moritz. The previous year's race had been a classic showdown between Fausto Coppi and Hugo Koblet and the Giro's organisers were hoping for a repeat performance. Unfortunately things didn't quite work out that way.

Italy was suffering a heatwave and the race was long (4,337km) and hard. With the riders arguing among themselves and with the organisers, Coppi himself was ill and distracted – his life away from the bike was under intense media and public scrutiny.

On stage six a breakaway formed and won by a huge margin. Koblet's team-mate, Carlo Clerici, took the lead – thirty-five minutes over Koblet, forty-five over Coppi.

Koblet announced he would now work for Clerici. Coppi remained uninterested.

The race became a procession. With no one inclined to take on Clerici, Italy's biggest race turned into nothing short of a farce. Fans and media were incensed and Coppi bore the brunt of their ire.

A strike was called. The stage over the Bernina Pass and into St Moritz, the one designed to be action-packed and intended to decide the Giro, was instead ridden at the peloton's leisure, much to the disgust of organisers and fans. The go slow meant that it took the peloton over nine hours to ride the 222km stage.

And so 1954 became the Giro of the Bernina Strike.

13 June

Klabinski takes lead in inaugural Critérium du Dauphiné
(1947)

Now considered one of the most important races on the annual calendar, the first edition of the Critérium du Dauphiné was held in 1947.

Founded by the daily newspaper Le Dauphiné Libéré the first race took the peloton on a 967km loop from Grenoble and back, via Vienne, Annecy, Geneva and Annemasse.

The first stage, on 12 June, 265km into Vienne, was won by Fermo Camellini. Second on the stage was Polish rider Eduoard Klabinski.

Klabinski was a second-year professional with the Mercier team who had won only a handful of criteriums. However, the next day, 13 June, he rose to the top of the overall classification, and there he stayed. Klabinski held on to the overall race lead despite not winning a stage himself. He recorded a time of 27 hours, 59 minutes, 52 seconds, winning by just ten seconds ahead of Italy's Gino Sciardis.

Later the same month Klabinski became the first Polish rider to start the Tour de France, leading over the Col du Glandon – the first time the climb had been used.

14 June

Ottavio Bottecchia dies after a training ride 'accident'
(1927)

Born into a large family in 1894, Italian Ottavio Bottecchia, nicknamed the Butterfly by Henri Desgrange, joined the Automoto team in 1923, after finishing fifth in that year's Giro as an independent rider.

Bottecchia was thrown straight into the Tour, riding for Henri Pélissier. He was an instant hit, winning the second stage and wearing yellow for six days. Pélissier won the race, Bottecchia came second, with his leader tipping him as a rider who would one day win the Tour.

The Italian didn't take long to justify Pélissier's faith in him. The following year, 1924, he won the opening stage, slipping on the first yellow jersey of the year. He didn't remove it until the race returned to Paris, some fifteen stages and 5,425km later. Bottecchia had become the first Italian winner of the Tour.

The following year he won the Tour again. Once more he won the opening stage, again he took yellow. This time he relinquished it for five days but won it back in plenty of time for Paris. His winning margin was even more impressive than before – fifty-four minutes this time around.

But then the tale turned dark.

Having abandoned the 1926 race, Bottecchia was determined to return in 1927. On 3 June he went out training early. He would never return home. He was found, hours later, by the roadside, with head injuries and broken bones. A priest was called and he was given the last rites before being taken to hospital, where he remained until he died. Sources vary on the date of death, some stating 14th June, others 15th.

Theories abounded as to what had happened. Some pointed to a crash that caused him to fall, though his bike bore no evidence of any such incident; others to the farmer who had summoned the priest and who had, it was alleged, caught Bottecchia eating grapes from his vines and thrown a rock to scare him off, only for it to hit him. Others talked of a Fascist plot to kill the great champion after his failure to fully support their cause.

The truth was never uncovered. The death of Ottavio Bottecchia, Italy's first Tour champion, remains shrouded in mystery to this day.

15 June

The Giro's post-war era starts
(1946)

Having been interrupted by war, the Giro returned in 1946. It was the first that witnessed Coppi and Bartali riding for different teams.

Coppi had won the 1940 race while riding on Bartali's Legnano team. Bartali had crashed early on, leaving the newly arrived Coppi to take the win. Now, six years on, Coppi had moved to Bianchi and the rivalry resumed.

While Coppi would win a stage early on, Bartali landed a blow on the 244km stage to Naples, coming in more than four minutes ahead of his rival. Coppi won stage fifteen, but on the same stage Bartali inherited the race lead for the first time, ahead of Coppi by those four minutes gained in Naples.

Gradually Coppi came back. He won stage sixteen and came second on stage seventeen, whittling Bartali's lead down to forty-seven seconds. But he could do no more: Bartali's final margin remained forty-seven seconds. The Giro's post-war era had started just as the pre-war years had ended: with Bartali and Coppi as Italy's foremost riders.

16 June

First Tour de Luxembourg starts
(1935)

Now fully established on the road race calendar, the first Tour de Luxembourg started on 16 June 1935 and, war years apart, has been held every year since.

The first edition was an eight-stage race, with a total distance of 1,128km. The stage distances were fairly short for the period – the longest just 165km – in contrast to that year's Tour de France, where the longest was 325km.

Luxembourg lends itself to short, punchy stages over rolling terrain. Rarely is a stage pan-flat, but then neither does the country have huge mountains; rather, stages are punctuated by snappy but testing climbs.

The timing of the Tour de Luxembourg, after the Giro but before the Tour, means the race is sometimes used as a warm-up by those with their sights set on the Tour. Some of the biggest names in cycling have won the race, Bobet, Gaul, Maertens and Hinault among them.

Matthias Clemens won the first three editions of the race and then added the 1939 and 1947 titles. He still holds the record for the most victories.

17 June

One second! Moreau wins Dauphiné by a single second
(2001)

The 2001 Critérium du Dauphiné was a mountainous affair. The climbs of Mont Ventoux, Chamrousse, Glandon/Croix de Fer, Télégraphe and the Galibier all featured. That's an A-list line-up of mountains to climb. Many of the favourites for the Tour stayed away that year: only Christophe Moreau and Francisco Mancebo from the previous year's Tour top ten were on the start list for the 2001 Dauphiné.

Stage five, 151km over the Chamrousse, was won by Andrei Kivilev. Moreau, who had chased hard, trailed in thirty-three seconds down, enough to take the race lead by one second ahead of Pavel Tonkov.

One second. Two stages and the Croix de Fer, Télégraphe and Galibier to come. The scene was set for a classic showdown.

The next day Moreau decided attack was the best means of defence. He was first over the Galibier. But hot on his wheel? Tonkov. The two matched each other pedal stroke for pedal stroke over the remaining kilometres, and once again the next day. Tonkov did what he could, but at the end of it all, Moreau still had his single second advantage, recording the closest of possible outright stage race wins.

18 June

Pierre Chany, master of cycling journalism, dies
(1996)

'With the TV people think they see, but it is also an illusion.' So said Pierre Chany, the master of cycling journalism.

Chany was born in Langeac, Haute-Loire, in 1922, later moving to Paris, where he became obsessed with the stories and photographs he saw of racers like René Vietto and Antonin Magne.

During the Second World War he joined the Resistance, ending up in North Africa. He returned to France with the restoration of peace and started writing cycling articles for *La Marseillaise* and *Le Soir*. In 1953 he joined *L'Equipe* as their head of cycling.

He remained with the newspaper for thirty-five years.

In all, Chany covered forty-nine Tours and earned the respect of the riders – Jacques Anquetil in particular held Chany dear and once said he'd wait for Chany's race report to see what he'd done and why.

Chany was a cycling historian without parallel. He wrote a number of authoritative accounts of the sport, including the *La Fabuleuse Histoire* series, three volumes on the history of cycling that are essential reading for any student of the sport.

19 June

Francesco Moser is born
(1951)

Only two men have won Paris–Roubaix three years in succession: Octave Lapize (1909, 1910 and 1911), then Italy's Francesco Moser, who started his own run on Roubaix in 1978.

Nicknamed the Sheriff, Moser was wearing the rainbow jersey when he claimed his first Roubaix cobblestone trophy. He had won the world championships the previous year in San Cristóbal, Venezuela, a race that confirmed Moser as a rider of pedigree and staying power. The morning had brought a tropical storm to the streets of San Cristóbal, making conditions for the 255km race even more testing. But in a field that included Eddy Merckx, Freddy Maertens, Felice Gimondi, Bernard Hinault and Hennie Kuiper, Moser triumphed. He escaped with Dietrich Thurau and then outsprinted the German to the line.

Seven months later, Moser entered the Roubaix velodrome alone. He escaped 20km from the finish, and rode into Roubaix more than one and a half minutes up.

Moser's solitary entrance would be something he would repeat in 1979 and 1980.

Moser was one of twelve children who grew up in Palù di Giovo in the Trentino-Alto Adige region of Italy. Three of his brothers, Diego, Aldo and Enzo, would also turn pro although none would have anything like Francesco's success.

While Roubaix was Moser's favourite hunting ground he took many other important wins. He won twenty-three stages at the Giro over the course of his fifteen-year career as well as winning the pink jersey in 1984. He also won the Tour of Lombardy, Milan–Sanremo, Tirreno–Adriatico, La Flèche Wallonne and Ghent–Wevelgem. He only rode one Tour, in 1975. He took two stage wins, wore yellow for a week and came seventh in Paris, but never returned. Away from the road Moser also won national and world titles on the track.

He retired in 1988 with over 300 victories on road and track to his name.

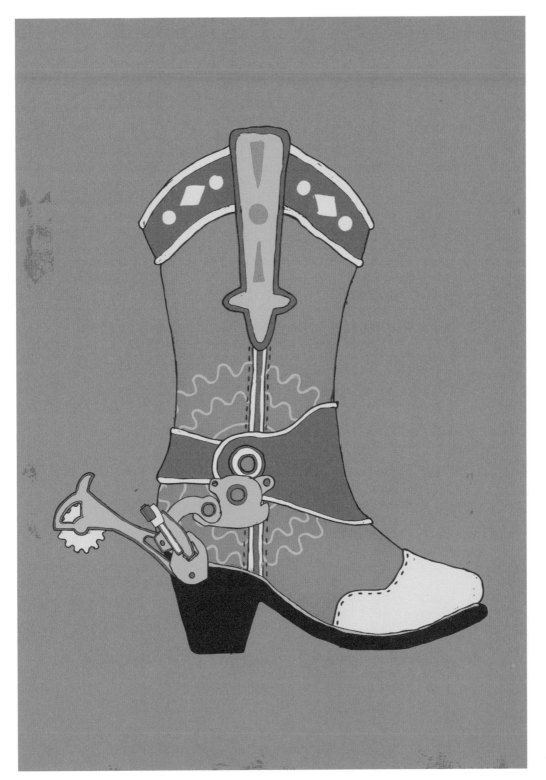

20 June

The longest Tour starts
(1926)

Henri Desgrange famously liked his races long and hard. In 1926 he devised a route that would be the longest in history.

The race started in Evian, the first time it had done so outside Paris, and the lakeside town was the flavour of the month: three and a half weeks after it hosted the Grand Départ, the race returned for a stage fifteen's finish and the start of stage sixteen.

The total race distance was 5,745km over seventeen stages, making the average stage distance a whopping 338km. The longest was 433km, from Metz to Dunkirk, won by Gustaaf Van Slembrouck.

The race's first yellow jersey was worn by Jules Buysse, after a 160km solo escape into Mulhouse left him thirteen minutes ahead of the rest, but it was his brother, Lucien, who would eventually prevail, taking yellow into Paris after a tremendous performance in the Pyrénées (see 11 September).

21 June

Merckx wins it all at Tour du Suisse
(1974)

Rarely has a rider dominated a race quite so emphatically as Eddy Merckx at the 1974 Tour de Suisse. He was riding the race for the first time, tempted by a sizeable appearance fee from the race organisers. The Cannibal (so-called for his insatiable appetite for winning) had just completed a narrow win at the Giro and in the weeks to come would go on to win the Tour (see 25 August for more on Merckx's 1974 season).

Merckx was fully focused on giving the Tour de Suisse value for money. He won the opening prologue, claimed stage three and then took the final stage into Olten. He held the jersey of race leader from the first to the final stage, but that wasn't all. He won the mountains prize, the points classification and, naturally enough, the combination classification. His final winning margin was just under one minute ahead of Sweden's Gösta Pettersson, but such was his power you have the feeling Merckx could have won by any margin he chose.

22 June

Thomas Voeckler is born
(1979)

'When I saw all the emotion and excitement that surrounds this jersey, I understood what it meant to people … and for me too.' So said Thomas Voeckler, reflecting on the moment in 2004 that he went from journeyman cyclist to national hero.

That year Voeckler was riding his second Tour de France. Expectations were suitably modest: maybe a stage win if he was lucky. On stage five he got himself in a break that would stay away, crossing the line over twelve minutes ahead of the bunch. Voeckler finished fourth but he was the best placed on GC of the breakaway, and that meant one thing: yellow.

Voeckler's performances over the next ten days of that race have entered Tour history. The Frenchman turned himself inside out to hold on to the golden fleece. He put in a heroic ride to Plateau de Beille in the Pyrénées to keep the jersey by twenty-two seconds. 'I did it on guts alone,' he said. Finally, Voeckler surrendered the lead in the Alps. He finished eighteenth in Paris but had secured his place in history.

In 2011 Voeckler repeated his 2004 heroics, again taking yellow early, again defending it for ten days. Perhaps no other rider in the Tour's modern era has encapsulated so perfectly the power of the yellow jersey.

23 June

Kübler and Koblet go toe to toe in the Tour du Suisse
(1951)

In the 1950s Switzerland had two riders at the top of the sport: Hugo Koblet and Ferdinand Kübler.

While each would win at least one Grand Tour and national title they would also often clash in their own national tour, the Tour de Suisse.

Kübler, the eldest of the two by six years, had won the race in 1942 and 1948. Koblet had taken his first in 1950. Going into the 1951 race the question was whether Koblet could win to match Kübler's haul, or if Kübler would exert himself and take a third win.

Early on the two traded stage wins but the defining day was the 249km stage into Lugano. Koblet was best placed on GC but Kübler came second in Lugano, more than eight minutes ahead of Koblet, who punctured four times, and taking over the race lead.

Koblet tried to strike back on the penultimate stage to Davos, winning by nearly a minute ahead of his great rival, but it wasn't enough. Kübler prevailed and won his third title. Koblet finished second overall, more than four minutes back, those punctures costing him the win.

Koblet would return to win the race in 1953 and 1955 and he ended his career with three Tour de Suisse wins, the same number as his great rival Kübler.

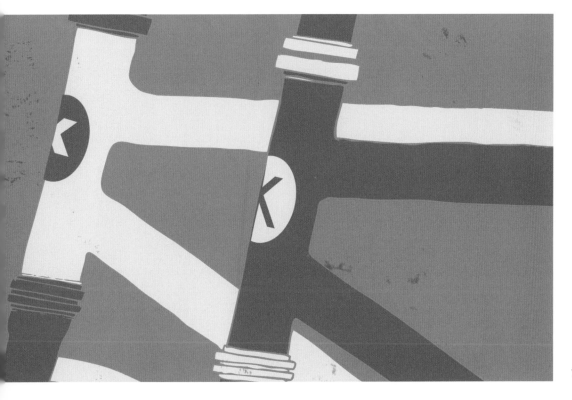

24 June

Gustaaf Deloor, first winner of Vuelta a España is born
(1913)

It wasn't until 1935 that Spain held its first national tour. Organised by Clemente López Dóriga, a former cyclist, and Juan Pujol, editor of the Spanish daily *Informaciones*, the first race took in fourteen stages, starting and finishing in Madrid. Gustaaf Deloor, a Belgian professional, won three stages of the race and the overall classification. His aggregate time of 120 hours and seven seconds put him over twelve minutes ahead of second-placed Mariano Cañardo.

Despite impending civil war, the following year the race was held once more. Again the race started and finished in Madrid but this time the route was expanded to twenty-one stages, three of which Deloor won on his way to a second straight win. Also on the list of stage winners was one Alfons Deloor, Gustaaf's elder brother, who ended up coming second overall. It was the first time brothers had stood on the top two steps of the podium at a Grand Tour, a feat that would be repeated in the 1950 Vuelta by Emilio and Manuel Rodriguez.

25 June

'Shay' Elliot wins a stage and wears yellow
(1963)

A photograph, taken during stage four of the 1963 Tour de France, shows three team-mates sitting on a step filling their bidons. On the right is Jacques Anquetil, Saint-Raphaël's team leader and the rider who would go on to win the race. In the middle is Jean Stablinski, wearing the rainbow jersey of world champion. And on the left is Seamus 'Shay' Elliott, the first Irishman to ride the Tour in 1956, the first to win a stage, and, as shown in the photograph, the first to wear the yellow jersey.

The day before that photo was taken, Elliott and Stablinski had escaped on the 223km stage to Roubaix. Five kilometres from the stage finish, Elliott left the escape group and soloed to the stage win. It was his and Ireland's first Tour stage victory. And it was enough to propel him to the top of GC. Elliott became Ireland's first yellow jersey, holding the lead for four days.

26 June

Greg LeMond is born
(1961)

Once described by *Sports Illustrated* as a 'Huck Finn with steel thighs', Greg LeMond blazed a trail from the USA to France, breaking down the door to European cycling.

In 1984, the year LeMond started his first Tour, he was one of only two Americans on the race (the other being Jonathan Boyer). By 1986 there were ten, including the 7-Eleven team, the first American team to take to the Tour's start line. LeMond was the main reason for the surge in popularity.

Born in Lakewood, California, LeMond's entrance into European cycling brought him almost instant success. A junior world champion (see 13 October), he turned professional in 1981 and never looked back. In his first two years he recorded wins in the Tour de l'Avenir, Critérium du Dauphiné and the world championships (see 4 September).

His first Tour ride brought him a podium place – third behind Laurent Fignon and Bernard Hinault – and a year later he moved one step up but still remained behind Hinault. Then, in 1986, he finally made the top spot.

That 1986 Tour was a legendary battle between LeMond and Hinault, rivals who happened to be on the same team. LeMond felt he was held back in 1985 to allow Frenchman Hinault's fifth win. Hinault had said he'd help LeMond win in '86 but then repeatedly attacked the American, even when LeMond was in yellow. LeMond held on, though, to become the first American to win the Tour.

Though his career was interrupted by a hunting accident (see 11 June), when he retired in 1994 LeMond had three Tour wins and two world championships to his name (see 23 July for his 1989 Tour win). After retiring he returned to the USA and turned his attention to business. Today his interests include a successful bicycle company.

27 June

Federico Bahamontes abandons the Tour
(1960)

Nicknamed the Eagle of Toledo, and already a two-time winner of the Tour's mountains classification, Federico Bahamontes won the yellow jersey in 1959. He was Spain's first Tour champion but his win wasn't universally acclaimed. French media believed him to be the beneficiary of infighting among the French riders. *Miroir-Sprint* derided the win, calling it the 'most curious and disappointing Tour since the war'.

His relationship with the Tour's media didn't improve the following year. A temperamental character, as prone to threatening to throw his bike or shoes off a mountain as to cycle up it, he quit the 1960 race on 27 June, just three days in. He was pictured dressed in a suit, sitting on his suitcase at Malo-les-Bains station, bike propped against a sign, waiting to go home.

Having famously once stopped for an ice cream at the top of a climb, it was in the mountains that Bahamontes made his name. He ended his career with six mountain prizes at the Tour, two at the Vuelta and one at the Giro, the first rider to win the classification at all three Grand Tours.

28 June

The last pre-war Tour starts
(1914)

In the early hours of 28 June 1914, with the French capital still shrouded in darkness, 147 riders rode out of Paris. It was the start of what would turn out to be the last Tour for four years. Hours later, Austria's Archduke Franz Ferdinand was assassinated in Sarajevo. While Philippe Thys was taking the race lead, across Europe all hell was breaking out.

The peloton continued to race, Thys holding the lead for the entire race. He started with an advantage of over thirty-one minutes on Henri Pélissier. Thys broke a fork. It was against race rules to obtain assistance but Thys knew the consequences and was happy to take them. Less than twenty minutes later he was back on the road. The Tour organisers slapped a thirty-minute penalty on him. It meant that going into the final stage Thys's lead was under two minutes. Pélissier attacked remorselessly but couldn't shake Thys, the Belgian holding on to win his second Tour.

Two days later, Austria-Hungary declared war on Serbia. Many of the riders in the 1914 Tour joined up. Like millions of others, some would never return, among them Tour champions Lucien Petit-Breton, Octave Lapize and François Faber.

29 June

The Badger starts the Tour for the first time
(1978)

By the time of the 1978 Tour, Bernard Hinault was already a force in world cycling. He'd won the Dauphiné, Liège–Bastogne–Liège and, just six weeks earlier, the Vuelta a España. Now it was time to tame the biggest race of them all.

Known as the Badger for his aggressive style, Hinault proudly wore the jersey of the French national champion and was considered one of the favourites, along with Joop Zoetemelk, Hennie Kuiper and Michel Pollentier. But this was Hinault's first Tour. How would he fare against the world's best? Three weeks later the cycling world had its answer.

Hinault won stage eight's time trial, and then rode impressively in the Pyrénées to exit the mountain range second overall. Equally noteworthy rides in the Alps, including second on l'Alpe d'Huez, meant that, going into the final time trial, he was just fourteen seconds off the yellow jersey, now worn by Joop Zoetemelk.

He annihilated Zoetemelk in the 72km race against the clock, to take yellow by nearly four minutes. Two days later Hinault was crowned in Paris. In an ominous warning for the future he said: 'I feel so good I could race another three months like that.' Hinault would win the Tour four more times.

30 June

Phil Anderson becomes first Australian to wear yellow
(1981)

In 1981 Phil Anderson was the only Australian on the start line of the Tour in Nice. Five days later, he found himself in the top ten overall, just a couple of minutes behind yellow jersey Dutchman Gerrie Knetemann.

Stage six was 117km to Pla d'Adet, the ski station that sits high above St-Lary-Soulon. Anderson had told the world's media he felt good but surely even he couldn't have known just how good. Entering St-Lary-Soulon, Anderson was at the head of the race with Bernard Hinault, Alberto Fernandez, Lucien Van Impe, Claude Criquielion and Marino Lejarreta.

Three kilometres into the climb Van Impe escaped, on his way to a second win on the climb.

Behind, Hinault rode hard. He shelled everyone out the back, apart from Anderson, who matched him all the way. At one point Anderson, the rookie, offered Hinault, the then two-time winner, a swig of Coke. Hinault swiped the bottle to the ground.

Hinault ultimately beat Anderson to the line but the Australian's ride had been enough to give him the overall lead, making him the first Australian and the first non-European to wear yellow.

JULY

1 July

The first Tour de France starts
(1903)

In January 1903 the sports paper *L'Auto* ran a front page that would change the face of cycling: 'The Tour de France,' it announced, 'the greatest cycle race in the world.'

Initially a six-stage race was designed, starting and finishing in Paris, calling in on Lyons, Marseilles, Toulouse, Bordeaux and Nantes. It was to start on 31 May and finish on 6 June. Many felt the race was ridiculous, including most of the riders of the day. Just weeks before the start, the Tour's first peloton numbered just fifteen. The itinerary was too hard and the rewards not great enough.

Back to the drawing board: the race was put back a month, rest days were included, entrance fees halved, prize money increased, daily expenses paid. Suddenly the first Tour was looking more attractive.

On the afternoon of 1 July, sixty riders assembled in Paris at a café called Au Réveil Matin for the start of the first Tour. Only twenty-one would make it back. Maurice Garin (see 3 March) won three stages and held the lead for the entire race.

'I have dreamed many sporting dreams in my life but never have I conceived of anything as worthy as this reality,' wrote Henri Desgrange after the final stage.

Cycling would never be the same again.

2 July

Chris Boardman wins in Lille
(1994)

By the summer of 1994 Chris Boardman, Olympic gold medallist in Barcelona two years earlier, was just ten months into his professional career. Riding for the Gan team, Boardman had boldly announced his main aim as a pro – to claim yellow on the first day of his first Tour.

On 2 July 1994 the Tour's circus descended on Lille for a 7.2km-long prologue and Boardman was there. This was the day he had talked about. This was his time. He'd won three stages at the Dauphiné a few weeks earlier, including the prologue, but this was a different proposition. On the start line were Miguel Indurain, Tony Rominger and Alex Zülle, all highly fancied for the Paris podium and all wanting to put down a marker.

But Boardman was in fine form. He blasted around the course at an average of over 55km/hr, stopping the clock in 7:49. The next best was Indurain, fifteen seconds down.

On his first day in the race, Boardman had taken cycling's most sacred jersey. He would wear it for three days before losing it to Johan Museeuw.

Boardman would win Tour prologues again in 1997 and 1998.

3 July

The Tour takes to the skies
(1971)

Look at the map of the 1971 Tour published by *L'Equipe* and you will notice something never before seen on the traditional Tour carte. Towards the top of the map, punctuating a line drawn from Le-Touquet-Paris-Plage to Rungis, is a drawing of an aeroplane, denoting the use of an air transfer. It was the first time the Tour's organisation had taken the peloton to the skies.

While the first Tour transfer had taken place as early as 1906, prior to the 1970s transfers between the finish of one stage and the start of the next were few and far between. Riders dislike nothing more than long transfers, so hosting both a stage finish and start in the same town alleviated at least a little of the pain of a long race.

But in the 1970s all that changed as the Tour organizers sought to take the race into areas of the country not visited before.

On 3 July, therefore, the Tour ensemble boarded a plane at Le Touquet and flew south to Paris for the start of the next day's stage. It was a first that would soon become commonplace as the race continued to evolve.

4 July

Coppi Christens the Alpe
(1952)

Stage ten of the 1952 Tour was the first time a Tour stage had finished at the top of a climb. This was a new kind of mountain stage – the Arrivée, placed not in a valley town following a long descent, but on a summit. And what a summit – the l'Alpe d'Huez. Who knew what to expect?

Going into the 266km stage Fausto Coppi who, having already won the Giro, was bidding to repeat his 1949 Giro/Tour double, was lying five minutes behind his team-mate, Andrea Carrea.

As the stage approached the first of the Alpe's twenty-one hairpins, Coppi was with France's Jean Robic. The 1947 Tour winner, and no slouch in the mountains himself, Robic attacked early, briefly distancing the Italian before Coppi got back to his wheel. Over the mid-part of the climb the two matched each other until Coppi decided enough was enough and gracefully took off. In six kilometres Coppi gained over one minute on Robic. It was enough for him to take the yellow jersey from Carrea. By the end of the next stage that lead had become nearly twenty minutes. Coppi had secured his second Tour win.

5 July

Carnage on the Passage du Gois
(1999)

There is only one thing worse than riding over cobblestones on a sleek and slender racing bike and that is riding over cobblestones that are wet. So quite what possessed the Tour's organization to take the 1999 peloton over to the Ile de Noirmoutier via the Passage de Gois, a cobbled causeway off the Vendée coast that is submerged twice a day at high tide, is anyone's guess. It was the first time the 4.5km-long passage had been used. It would certainly prove to be memorable.

The peloton was together as it hit the causeway at speed. It made for terrific television footage: the speeding peloton blasting over cobbles, flanked by boats resting dormant on the sand.

Then all hell broke loose. Riders lost their front wheels on the slippery surface and down they went, smashing into cobblestones, bikes entangled. Soon dozens were sprawled all over the road. For those caught in the crash it would have a dramatic effect on their race. As the front end of the race powered on those held up lost minutes.

One massive loser was Alex Zülle. Second in 1995, Zülle lost six minutes, effectively ending his chances after just three days (though he would again finish second in Paris).

The Tour wasn't put off, though. It returned to the passage in 2005 and 2011.

6 July

Teutenberg wears pink for first time
(2008)

The longest stage of the 2008 Giro Donne (formerly Giro d'Italia femminile) was stage two, 131km from Asola to Lendinara. It was won by the German powerhouse Ina Teutenberg, who also took the pink jersey.

Teutenberg, an eight-year pro in 2008, had already won two stages of the race in 2007 but until now had never pulled on the leader's jersey. 'It's pretty cool,' she said after receiving it. Teutenberg continued her impressive form, taking the next two stage wins while wearing pink, but she knew her time at the top of the standings was coming to an end as the mountains loomed.

Italy's Fabiana Luperini, wearing the jersey of national champion, powered to a solo win on Monte Serre, taking over the race lead. She defended the jersey before winning the penultimate stage to secure the overall win.

It was Luperini's fifth Giro Donne title, coming ten years after she had won her fourth straight race. She still holds the record for most wins in women cycling's most prestigious race.

7 July

Super Mario wins first of four straight Tour stage wins
(1999)

If there's one thing Italian stallion Mario Cipollini is known for, even more than his flamboyant taste in time-trial apparel (tiger or zebra print skinsuit, anyone?), then it's sprinting towards the finish line of a flat stage, ready to raise his arms into the air in celebration as everyone else trails in his wake.

Super Mario was the premier sprinter of his generation and took more than 190 road victories over the course of his career, including the road race world championships and forty-two stages of the Giro (a record haul).

Also known as the Lion King, Cipo rode eight Tours but never finished one. The high mountain passes of the Alps and Pyrénées were not for him. However, in that time he amassed twelve stage wins.

On 7 July he took his first win of the 1999 race on stage four into Blois. Three days later his tally stood at four. All were bunch sprints (although his stage six win came only after Tom Steels was controversially disqualified).

It was the first time the same rider had claimed four Tour stage wins in a row since Charles Pélissier in 1930.

8 July

Luis Ocaña takes yellow
(1971)

If there was one rider whom Eddy Merckx genuinely feared during his reign at the top of cycling's tree, it was Luis Ocaña. And the events of 8 July 1971 tell us why.

Ocaña had won the Vuelta in 1970 and had put Merckx in difficulty at the 1971 Dauphiné. Held back by injury and sickness at previous Tours, he was now ready to take the fight to Merckx. He won on the Puy de Dôme and going into stage eleven he was second on GC, one second behind Joop Zoetemelk but fifty-nine ahead of Merckx.

That was when Ocaña showed what he was truly made of. On stage eleven, to Orcières Merlette, he ripped the race to shreds. Having followed an earlier breakaway, at the foot of the Col de Noyer, Ocaña attacked and left everyone standing. For 60km he rode alone through the Alps. At the finish he had the yellow jersey by more than eight minutes.

The Tour's writers went to town, calling it an historical day. Even Merckx agreed: 'What he did was extraordinary,' he said.

Ocaña held the jersey for just three days when a dreadful crash in the Pyrénées forced him to abandon, leaving Merckx to inherit the race lead. The Spaniard would finally win the Tour in 1973.

9 July

Eugène Christophe snaps forks on the Tourmalet
(1913)

Eugène Christophe never won the Tour de France but he is one of the race's most renowned riders because of the events of 9 July 1913.

The day started in Bayonne and finished in Luchon; 326km over four of the most terrible passes in the Pyrénées – the Aubisque, Tourmalet, Aspin and Peyresourde. Christophe was second in the overall standings heading into the stage and the day began well for him when the race leader, Odile Defraye, started to fall behind. Defraye had lost over an hour after the climb of the Aubisque, giving Christophe the virtual lead. Defraye finally abandoned at Barèges, halfway up the Tourmalet. By then, though, Christophe's day had taken a significant turn for the worse.

Having topped the Tourmalet just behind Philippe Thys, Christophe noticed a problem with his bike. What happened next has entered Tour legend.

Christophe watched his forks fold under him. 'I didn't crash,' he told *Sport et Vie* some forty-seven years later. 'I had time to see my forks bend before me.' As Christophe

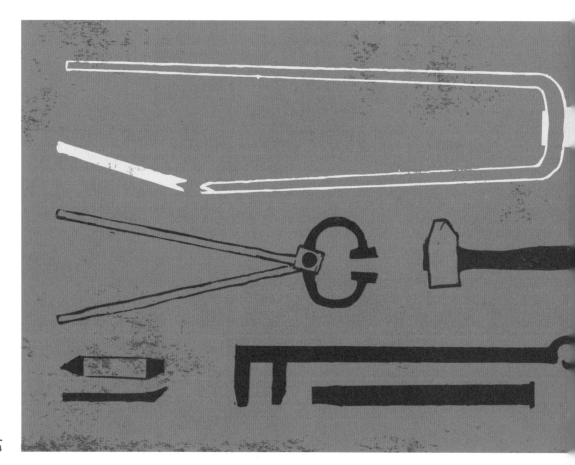

stood alone on the side of one of the Tour's mightiest mountains with a broken bike, his rivals sped by one by one. With little option he shouldered his machine and set off down the mountain on foot.

Eventually, after walking 12km, he made it to Sainte-Marie-de-Campan. There he was directed to a forge, where he set about repairing his bike, refusing all help from the blacksmith, such assistance being against race rules.

With his bike repaired, Christophe set off again, bound for Luchon. Over the Aspin and Peyresourde the Frenchman rode, ignoring his exhausted body screaming at him to stop.

He made it to the finish line three hours and fifty minutes after stage winner Philippe Thys had crossed it. Incredibly, Christophe was not last on the stage. That dubious honour went to Henry Fontaine and Celidonio Morini, who came in together more than seven hours down.

But Christophe's pain was not quite over. Race organizers decided to dock him a further three minutes because a boy at the forge had operated the billows for him.

Christophe had lost the Tour but his tale of broken forks and village forges had secured his spot in Tour history.

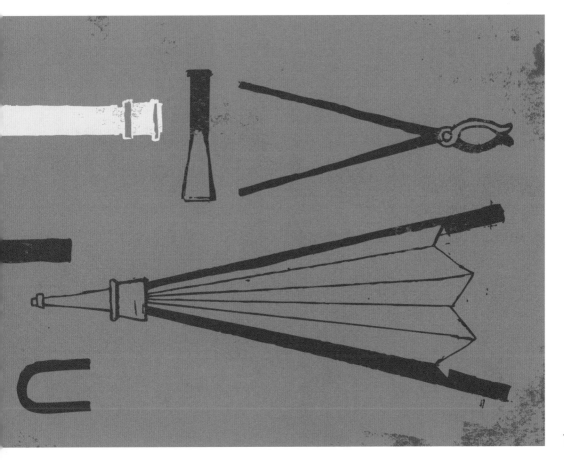

10 July

The Tour's first ascent of the Galibier
(1911)

In 1910 the Tour had introduced the high mountains to the Tour route for the first time by heading into the Pyrénées (see 21 July). In 1911 Henri Desgrange decided to go a step further and take his riders to the Alps. Looking to top the fearsome Tourmalet, he opted for the Galibier as the high point of his first foray into the Alps.

Emile Georget was the first to scale the Alpine giant, going on to win the stage in Grenoble. The introduction of the climb did not sit well with the riders of the day.

Eventual 1911 winner Gustave Garrigou spoke of the 'tasteless prank of slipping mountains under the roads of our beautiful country', and called Desgrange a thug.

But Desgrange did not care. He was smitten by the Galibier, writing: 'all one can do before this giant is doff one's hat and bow.' The climb returned every year until 1949 and remains one of the most-visited mountains by the Tour. A monument to Desgrange now stands on its southern slopes.

11 July

Merckx is punched by a fan
(1975)

By stage fourteen of the 1975 Tour, Eddy Merckx had been in yellow for nine days. One and a half minutes ahead of Bernard Thévenet, it was looking as though a sixth Tour title was a formality.

Stage fourteen was 173km to the summit of Puy de Dôme. As the race approached the climb that year's main riders, Merckx, Thévenet, Van Impe and Zoetemelk, were together. When Van Impe attacked, Thévenet responded, but neither Merckx nor Zoetemelk could answer and the two rode away, Van Impe going on to take the stage.

Merckx was working hard trying to limit the time he would lose to them both. Then, with about 100m to ride, a fan broke from the masses at the roadside and punched the Belgian in the kidneys, striking out against the Cannibal's continued dominance. Merckx, winded and all but prostrate in pain, somehow managed to finish and keep yellow by just under a minute.

But the effect was long-lasting. Still suffering, Merckx lost the jersey to Thévenet on the next stage (see 10 January for more on Thévenet). Merckx would never wear yellow again.

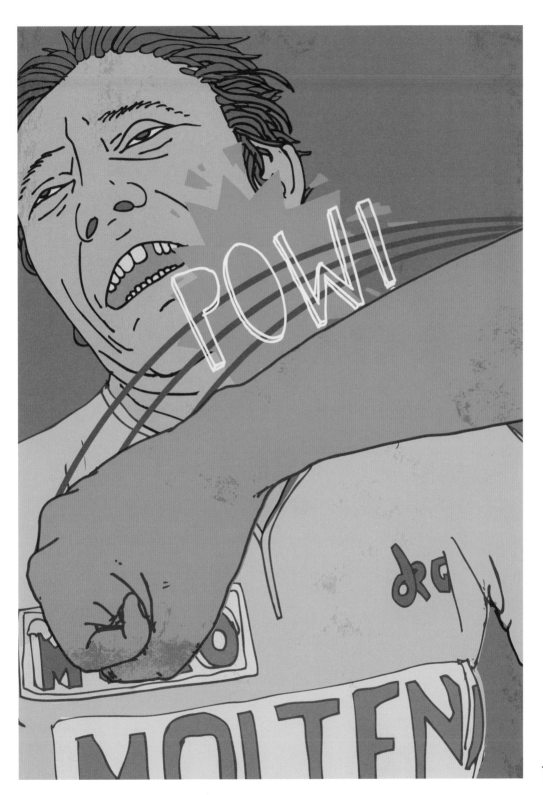

12 July

Anquetil and Poulidor go shoulder to shoulder
(1964)

One of the most iconic photographs in Tour history was captured forever on 12 July, the day the Tour de France visited Puy de Dôme for the third time in its history.

By the time the 1964 Tour rolled around, Jacques Anquetil and Raymond Poulidor had divided France. The country's affections were split between the handsome but calculating winner and the loveable nearly man. Anquetil had four Tours to his name; Poulidor had one podium spot.

As the race developed it took on a familiar form. Anquetil took yellow as it entered its final, definitive days. Poulidor was second. By the time the stage to Puy de Dôme came around, just two days from Paris, Poulidor was fifty-six seconds back. This was the only day left for Poulidor to seize the moment, finally to wrest the jersey from his great rival. They hit the climb together, with Federico Bahamontes and Julio Jiménez, two of the greatest climbers in history. With five kilometres to go, Jiménez, and then Bahamontes, danced away.

But the real action was with Anquetil and Poulidor. This was a personal battle, not just for yellow but for honour. For more than three kilometres they rode alongside one another, neither ceding an inch. Shoulder-to-shoulder, head-to-head, toe-to-toe, they rode the Puy de Dôme. Chased by press and cameramen on motorcycles, at one point they came together: eyes fixed in downward stares, shoulders and elbows clashed, bikes wavered. The cameras whirred and the Tour's most famous image was in the bank.

Eventually, Poulidor left his nemesis trailing. He crossed the line alone, much to the delight of his fans. As the seconds counted down, where was Anquetil?

Eventually, an exhausted but focused Anquetil arrived in the final straight, crouched over his handlebars, glancing up in a desperate search for the line.

In one of the greatest duels the Tour had seen Anquetil had managed to save the jersey by fourteen seconds.

'That's thirteen more than I need,' he said.

13 July

Tom Simpson falls on Ventoux
(1967)

In 1967 Britain's Tom Simpson headed to the Tour with hope in his heart but a weight on his shoulders. Among the world's greatest cyclists, he had won a clutch of classics as well as the world championships. At the Tour, though, things hadn't quite worked out. He'd worn yellow for one day in 1962 – the first British rider to do so, appearing in the next day's papers wearing the jersey and a bowler hat, holding an umbrella and sipping tea – on his way to finishing sixth in Paris, but so far that had been as good as it got for Simpson at the world's greatest race.

He'd abandoned in 1965 and 1966 and he entered the 1967 race determined to put in a stronger showing. Too determined, it would turn out.

Simpson was lying seventh going into the stage over the Ventoux. In infernal heat he found himself on the early slopes of the climb in a group with the yellow jersey, Roger Pingeon, chasing Julio Jiménez and Raymond Poulidor, who were up the road.

With three kilometres to go Simpson slowed dramatically and fell to the ground. The crowds picked him up and helped him back on to the bike. Simpson, riding in a daze, carried on for another 300m before collapsing again. Something was very, very wrong.

The Tour's doctor performed heart massage and gave the fallen cyclist an injection. He worked on Simpson for over an hour. Finally, a helicopter took him to hospital but Simpson was pronounced dead on arrival. The cause of death was cardiac arrest. Evidence of amphetamine was found in his bloodstream. 'A decent chap who probably simply feared defeat,' wrote Jacques Goddet.

Today a monument to the rider stands on the Ventoux near the spot where Simpson fell. Cyclists pass and leave small offerings – bidons or caps – to the man known simply as Mr Tom.

14 July

Robic wins in Luchon on Bastille Day
(1953)

For a Frenchman to win a stage of the Tour de France is a career-changing moment. But to win a Tour stage on Bastille Day, when the eyes of France are looking for the day to be crowned with a home winner? That is truly something special. And if that win brings with it the yellow jersey? Well, life can't get any better. And that is exactly what happened to Jean Robic in 1953.

Bastille Day in 1953 took the riders to Luchon from Cauterets. It was a short stage, 115km, over the Tourmalet, Aspin and Peyresourde. Robic was fourth on GC, over five minutes behind leader Fritz Schaer. The Frenchman rode strongly from the start. He led over all the mountains, building his lead over the entire stage. Schaer could do nothing, losing time on every climb to Robic.

Robic crossed the line after three hours and fifty minutes. Louison Bobet came in second, nearly one and a half minutes down. Schaer came in fourth.

Robic's win was enough to propel him up the standings and into the yellow jersey. A stage, gained after a superb ride over three legendary climbs, and yellow, on Bastille Day. Perfection indeed.

15 July

Bartali rampages through the Alps and saves a nation
(1948)

The day before stage thirteen of the 1948 Tour was the race's third rest day. Sitting at the top of the classification was the darling of France, Louison Bobet. Italy's own legend, Gino Bartali, was more than twenty-one minutes down, even if he did have three stage wins to his name.

Over the border in Italy revolution was in the air. Bartali's homeland was in chaos. In April 1948 elections had propelled the Christian Democratic Party of Alcide de Gasperi to power. A period of stability after years of turmoil finally seemed possible but then, as Bartali rested in Cannes, on 14 July the popular leader of the Communist Party, Palmiro Togliatti, was shot.

Within hours, with Togliatti fighting for his life, strikes and demonstrations were called. Togliatti's supporters soon occupied key facilities – tram lines and communication hubs. De Gasperi was in dire need of something to prevent the country slipping into violence so he called Bartali and told him he could make a difference; his country desperately needed him to win.

The next day, 15 July, Bartali answered his nation's call in emphatic style. From Cannes to Briançon, 274km over the Allos, Vars and Izoard, Bartali put on a one-man show. Bobet was left standing. By the time he reached the top of the Izoard, Bartali's lead over the Frenchman was a staggering eighteen minutes. Bartali was now second overall. But he wasn't done.

The next day the two went head-to-head. Bobet, fearing for his jersey, matched the Italian pedal stroke for pedal stroke over the Lauteret, Galibier and Croix de Fer, two men locked in combat.

Finally, though, the Italian proved too strong. On the Col de Porte, Bartali powered away as Bobet cracked. He won his second straight stage to rip the yellow jersey from Bobet's back. In two unbelievable days Bartali had taken a twenty-one-minute deficit and turned it into an eight-minute lead.

The French press lamented Bobet's fall. 'Tonight, all the girls in France are crying,' wrote one correspondent. In Italy De Gasperi was delighted. As Bartali had stormed through France so his countrymen had stopped their own rampaging and turned on their wirelesses. Instead of revolution, celebration was in the air. Bartali had won his second Tour and brought Italy back from the brink of civil war.

16 July

Gaul triumphs in the rain to set up his only Tour win
(1958)

Formidable against the clock and terrific riding up a mountain, it is perhaps a little surprising that Luxembourg's Charly Gaul claimed only a single Tour win (though he would win the Giro twice).

Gaul, nicknamed the Angel of the Mountains, set the foundation of his 1958 Tour win on a monster of a day through the Alps and the Chartreuse, from Briançon to Aix-les-Bains.

It was a day blighted by freezing rain, but Gaul loved the wet and the cold. He was well down overall but even so sought out Louison Bobet, his biggest rival, and told him he was going to attack on the Luitel. And that was exactly what he did. Through the Chartreuse, in driving rain, Gaul flew, opening up a huge margin. By the finish he had more than fourteen minutes on race leader Raphaël Géminiani. It wasn't quite enough to give him yellow but the foundation was in place. Of the top three riders he was by far the best against the clock, and with a 74km time trial to come his anointment as race leader was just a matter of time.

17 July

Roche dons a skinsuit for summit finish on the Aubisque
(1985)

Wednesday, 17 July 1985 featured two Tour stages. In the afternoon the riders faced an 83km race from Laruns to Pau, but before that they had a short blast to the top of the Col d'Aubisque to handle.

It was just 53km from Luz-Saint-Sauveur to the top of the Aubisque and the director of Stephen Roche's La Redoute team, Raphaël Géminiani, had a special plan up his sleeve. He gave Roche a present – a handmade silk skinsuit. Roche wasn't happy and told his director he wouldn't be seen wearing it in a road stage.

But Géminiani argued his case convincingly, telling his rider that the stage was so short that he should ride it as if it was a time trial. Roche eventually agreed, but kept the suit under wraps until the Aubisque. Then he took off his racing jersey and sprinted away. He caught and passed the lone leader and rode to the stage win by over one minute. It was his first Tour stage win. He would finish third in Paris.

18 July

The rainbow jersey tames the Ventoux
(1955)

In 1955 Louison Bobet was going for his third Tour title in a row as the reigning world champion. At the start of the stage he was over eleven minutes down on the race leader, team-mate Antonin Rolland. With intense Provençal heat burning down on the peloton, Bobet decided the time was right to launch his bid for overall victory.

Bobet's great rival Charly Gaul was suffering so Bobet attacked. He caught and passed earlier escapees Ferdi Kübler and Raphaël Géminiani. Through the lunar landscape of the climb's final kilometres Bobet soared, passing the top of the climb with an advantage of one minute. He retained his lead all the way to Avignon. Rolland finished over five minutes back, Gaul nearly six. Bobet had halved his deficit in just one day, starting a chain of events that would lead to him becoming the first rider to win three Tours in a row.

Behind Bobet the peloton had suffered. Jean Malléjac collapsed and had to be treated on the mountainside before being whisked to hospital. Ferdi Kübler finished the stage in a state of delirium, abandoned and never rode the Tour again.

19 July

Van Impe buckled
(1977)

After sixteen stages of the 1977 Tour, Lucien Van Impe was just thirty-three seconds behind leader Bernard Thévenet. With the l'Alpe d'Huez to come, the stage was set for the 1976 winner Van Impe, perhaps the greatest climber of all time, to launch his bid for another Tour victory.

On the Glandon, Van Impe mounted his offensive. No one went with him. At the foot of the Alpe he had over two minutes on Thévenet. He was riding into yellow. Then, with less than five kilometres to go, disaster struck a tiring Van Impe when he was knocked from his bike by a TV car. He quickly remounted but his rear wheel was buckled. Van Impe called forward his team car just as Hennie Kuiper rode past. Van Impe's hopes of the stage victory were gone.

Kuiper himself had started the day only forty-nine seconds off Thévenet. As he was riding to the stage win, down the road Thévenet was turning himself inside out, trying to retain his lead. As Kuiper crossed the finish line so Thévenet emerged into the final straight. This was a last-ditch, furious effort to keep hold of yellow. And it worked. Thévenet finished forty-one seconds behind Kuiper, keeping the jersey with just eight seconds to spare. Van Impe finished a further 1:25 down, his Tour dreams as buckled as his rear wheel.

20 July

Landis romps home, later tests positive
(2006)

In 2006 former mountain biker and Lance Armstrong lieutenant Floyd Landis was riding the Tour as the leader of the Phonak team. He had spent three days in yellow but had lost the race lead on stage sixteen to La Toussuire. There he had been nothing short of embarrassed, losing more than eight minutes on the final climb. His quest for yellow in Paris was surely finished.

But Landis thought otherwise. On stage seventeen, a day of five classified mountain climbs, he attacked with nearly 130km still to go. Showing no sign of the fatigue that had drained him less than twenty-four hours earlier, Landis romped through the northern Alps. By the top of the final climb of the day his lead was more than five minutes.

He descended like a daredevil into the stage finish in Morzine. The next rider, Carlos Sastre, trailed in nearly six minutes later. Landis was back in contention. He would take back yellow two days later to stand on top of the Paris podium.

It later emerged that Landis had tested positive for performance-enhancing drugs after that finish in Morzine, which led to him being stripped of his win.

21 July

First high mountain stage of the Tour de France
(1910)

The Tour's first ascent over 1000m was the Col de la République but it wasn't until 1910, seven years after the inaugural race, that the Tour's organisers felt bold enough to send the peloton over France's truly high mountain passes.

Surprisingly, given his penchant for making his riders suffer, it wasn't Henri Desgrange's idea but that of his assistant Alphonse Steinès. It took some effort to convince Desgrange, but Steinès eventually managed it (see 29 November for more) and so it was that the 1910 edition of the Tour included two stages in the Pyrénées. It was the second of these that would enter into legend. While stage nine took the riders from Perpignan to Luchon over the Portet d'Aspet, stage ten brought four huge passes that would soon become known as *le cercle de la mort* – the circle of death.

Peyresourde. Aspin. Tourmalet. Aubisque: four names to strike fear into even the strongest of riders. Ride them east to west, or west to east: either way you're in for a torrid time. At least today we know what to expect. Back in 1910 they had no idea.

The start time for the fifty-nine riders brave enough to turn up was 3.30 a.m. First up was the Peyresourde. Octave Lapize, riding with Gustave Garrigou, was first over. As he was the Aspin and the Tourmalet.

At the top of the Tourmalet, Lapize had a lead of 500m over Garrigou and plenty of time on everyone else.

Desgrange, fearful of the riders' reaction to this new initiative, had stayed away so it was left to Steinès and another *L'Auto* employee, Victor Breyer, to monitor the race. Having watched Lapize and Garrigou scale the Tourmalet, they motored to the Aubisque to wait.

Hours passed. Increasingly concerned, they were grateful to see a cyclist emerge at last. They could see he was in some distress and were shocked, not just by the rider's appearance but also by the fact it was neither Lapize nor Garrigou. When they asked the rider his name he just groaned: François Lafourcade.

It was another fifteen minutes before Lapize appeared. He looked at Steinès and Breyer and uttered a single word: 'Assassins.'

It was a moment that would enter Tour legend.

There were still 150km to go. Lapize won the stage after over fourteen hours of racing and would go on to win the race overall but the stars of the 1910 Tour were the mountains. The race would never be the same again.

22 July

Cavendish makes history on Champs-Elysées
(2012)

In recent years no rider has been more at home on the Champs-Elysées than Britain's Mark Cavendish. He has dominated the end-of-Tour sprint-fest like no other rider before him. In 2009 Cavendish started what would turn out to be an unprecedented streak of four consecutive wins on Europe's most famous boulevard.

Cavendish's victory in 2012 took him into the record books for two reasons. He was the reigning world champion and so his win not only made him the first rider to have won the stage four times in succession, but it was also a first for the rainbow jersey.

If the sight of Cavendish's team-mate Bradley Wiggins, resplendent in yellow, leading out the rainbow jersey to win on the Champs-Elysées really rammed home the message that British cycling had arrived at the Tour, perhaps Cavendish's most astonishing victory in Paris came in 2010.

Then, with the side-view camera showing Thor Hushovd and Alessandro Petacchi sprinting to the line, Cavendish, who was out of shot, emerged from behind and showed an astonishing turn of speed. Suddenly it looked like Hushovd and Petacchi, two of the fastest men in the world, were mere tourists as Cavendish simply blasted past them as if he was a rocket launched into space. Untouchable.

23 July

Eight seconds
(1989)

The most exciting Tour in living memory reached its infamous conclusion on this day in 1989, when a final day time trial on the Champs-Elysées brought the closest finish in Tour history.

It had been a see-saw race, with yellow passing between Greg LeMond and Laurent Fignon, but going into the last stage Fignon had a fifty-second lead. In any other year in the modern era that would have been that, but for the first time in eighteen years the final stage of the 1989 race was a time trial, giving the opportunity for LeMond to get the time back.

It was Fignon vs LeMond in the race of truth. Fignon, with his metal-rimmed glasses and flowing ponytail, cut a distinctly old-school figure against LeMond, with his Oakley sunglasses, custom time-trial helmet and tri-bars.

As Fignon, last out, desperately sprinted to the line, with motorcycles and cars in hot pursuit, the TV cameras swung to watching LeMond. The American didn't know what to do with himself, first listening to French radio, then ripping the headphones off and trying to peer down the road.

The clock ticked on, past the all-important time with Fignon still on the road. Then it was over. LeMond had beaten Fignon at the very last moment to record the narrowest-ever Tour win. Fignon, two-time Tour winner, became forever known as the man who lost the Tour by eight seconds.

24 July

Walkowiak springs a surprise and takes yellow
(1956)

Roger Walkowiak was a French rider who had started three Tours prior to 1956, finishing fifty-seventh and forty-seventh in 1951 and 1953 respectively and abandoning in 1955. His 1956 Tour would go better. Much better.

On stage seven Walkowiak found himself in a huge escape group of thirty-one riders. They crossed the line more than eighteen minutes ahead of the bunch. Walkowiak didn't win the stage but he was the best placed of the escape group overall and took yellow.

It was a huge surprise. The bunch had all but fallen asleep to let such a large group go. He held the jersey for three days before he lost it on the stage to Bayonne. And that looked to be that.

But then, on 24 July, on the stage to Grenoble, Walkowiak rode well over the Mont Cenis, Croix de Fer and Luitel to finish fifth on the stage. Wout Wagtmans, who had been in yellow by over four minutes, had a terrible day and finished over fifteen minutes down.

Surprisingly, Walkowiak had yellow back on his shoulders. This time he held it until Paris but the crowd's applause was only lukewarm, seeing his victory as something born of good fortune and bad tactics by others, rather than his strength. His name entered France's lexicon: 'à la Walko' is a reference to an undeserving winner.

25 July

Armstrong stands on the top step in Paris
(1999)

Lance Armstrong had only completed two three-week races as he took to the start line of the 1999 Tour. In 1995 he finished thirty-sixth in Paris. Then, in 1998, he came fourth in the Vuelta. In between those two performances he had been diagnosed with, and treated for, cancer. Now the man who had nearly died was back on his bike.

On 25 July, after three weeks of racing through France, Armstrong rode into Paris. He had won all three time trials and a mountain stage to Sestriére. He had yellow on his back. He had a winning margin of over seven minutes. He had achieved the impossible. He had turned the cycling world upside down.

As he stood on that Paris podium for the first time no one could quite believe what they had seen. Less than eighteen months earlier Armstrong, having had to fight for his life, was struggling to get a cycling team interested in taking him on. Eventually US Postal signed him. Now he had delivered them the ultimate prize. It was the greatest comeback in all of sport.

Armstrong's story is the best known in cycling. He went on to dominate the Tour, wearing yellow in Paris for seven straight years. He focused only on the Tour: everything else was just preparation for the big one. His team's only mission was to get Lance into yellow for Paris. And they were remarkably efficient at it.

Doubts were raised early. How could Armstrong be clean yet dominate in what was known to be a drug-riddled era? The Texan dismissed the doubters and was aggressive in his defence. He sued publications and individuals and ostracised riders and journalists who doubted him.

Then, in 2012, everything crashed down around him. USADA (the United States Anti-Doping Agency) brought charges against him and others, including alleged use, possession and trafficking of prohibited substances including EPO, testosterone and blood transfusion. Armstrong opted not to challenge the case, though still protesting his innocence. In August 2012 USADA imposed a lifetime ban and disqualified all Armstrong's results going back to 1998. Seven Tour titles gone in one swipe of the pen. Armstrong said: 'I know who won those seven Tours … and everyone I competed against knows who won those seven Tours.'

In January 2013 Armstrong finally confessed. He told talk show host Oprah Winfrey that the greatest story in sport, the story that had started on 25 July 1999, was all a lie. 'It's just this mythic perfect story, and it wasn't true,' he admitted.

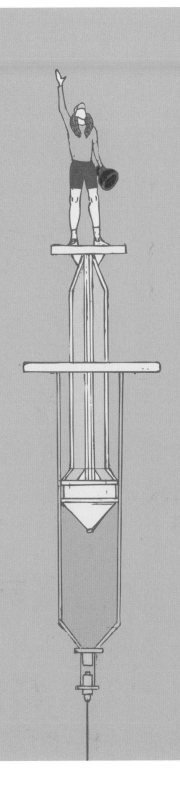

26 July

Geoff Cooke is born
(1944)

If you want to examine a case in cycling longevity you could do a lot worse than look at the career of Geoff Cooke. Born in Manchester, Cooke took his first title at senior level in 1963 as an amateur when he won the sprint discipline at the nationals.

In 1972 Cooke went to the Munich Olympics, where he competed in both the sprint and the 2,000m tandem sprint but failed to trouble the medal table. He fared better two years later when he travelled to New Zealand for the Commonwealth Games and won gold in the tandem with Ernie Crutchlow.

Cooke raced on until 1978 and then became national sprint coach in 1979, a position he held for ten years, taking the team to three Olympic Games. But it is as a veteran that he truly reigned supreme. He is a multiple masters champion, winning more than twenty-five titles. Since 1996 he has won fifteen masters world champions sprint titles, failing to win on only four occasions. At the time of writing his last win came in 2014, more than fifty years after that first national title.

27 July

Pantani takes flight to Tour victory
(1998)

The 1998 Tour was a troubled one. Hit by the Festina affair, when doping products were found in the car of the Festina team masseuse Willy Voigt, leading to the arrest of team officials, the race was rocked by police raids and rider protests. The entire race was in jeopardy. But on the rocky road to Paris one rider lit up the Tour. The little Italian Marco Pantani danced his way up the Alps on a day of tumbling temperatures and drenching rain to slip yellow on for the first time and then wear it all the way to Paris.

Pantani had trailed leader Jan Ullrich by more than three minutes going into the 189km stage from Grenoble to Les Deux Alpes. He lit the afterburners halfway up the mighty Galibier and the German never saw him again. A three-minute deficit was turned into a near four-minute lead by the end of the day as Pantani put in one of the great rides of the modern era.

Today Pantani's stunning escape is marked by two monuments. On the Galibier, at the spot where he began his initial surge, stands a simple metal and glass structure, etched with Pantani's outline, while at the entrance to Les Deux Alpes stands a stone carving of Pantani hunched over his bicycle, riding to glory.

28 July

Big Mig wins his first *maillot jaune*
(1991)

Big Mig, aka Miguel Indurain, would ride twelve Tours in a row, from 1985 until 1996. At first he rode in the service of his team leader, Pedro Delgado, but stage wins in the mountains (Cauterets, 1989; Luz Ardiden, 1990), as well as a top-ten finish in 1990 pointed to a rider who was about to move on to better things.

In 1991 Indurain won his first Tour. History has depicted Indurain as a rider who won races because of his time-trialling. That's not an unfair analysis – despite those mountain wins in 1989 and 1990 he would never again win a Tour stage that wasn't a time trial – but he wore yellow for the first time in 1991, thanks to a terrific ride in the Pyrénées, over the Aubisque, Tourmalet, Aspin and up to Val-Louron, where he came second but put minutes into pre-race favourite Greg LeMond. He held yellow for ten days and took it into Paris on 28 July.

And so began the era of Indurain (see 2 September for more).

29 July

Tommy Prim is born
(1955)

Born in Svenljunga, Sweden, Tommy Prim turned professional with the Bianchi-Piaggio team in 1980. A multiple national champion by the time he entered the professional ranks, Prim had a decent first season with Bianchi, picking up a stage win in Paris–Nice and a stage and the best young rider's competition at the Giro as he rode to fourth overall.

His best years were between 1981 and 1983, during which he won the Tour de Romandie, the Tour of Sweden twice, and came second in the Giro on two occasions.

After a disappointing Giro, where he finished fifteenth, in 1983 he became the first Scandinavian to win a major classic when he won Paris–Brussels in a three-way sprint ahead of Daniel Rossel and Ralf Hofeditz, since Denmark's Charles Meyer won Bordeaux–Paris in 1895.

Paris–Brussels was Prim's biggest win. In the early 2000s he returned to the sport for a few years to manage the U-23 squad, Team Crescent. He remains one of only two Swedish riders to have won a major classic – Magnus Bäckstedt, who won Paris–Roubaix in 2004, is the other.

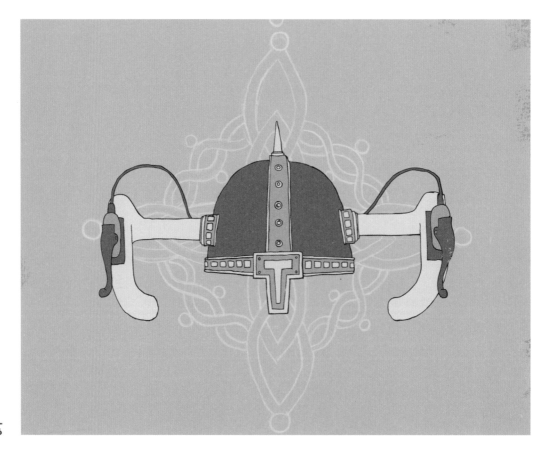

30 July

Paolo Pezzo wins first Olympic gold
(1996)

Mountain biking didn't make its entrance at the Olympic Games until Atlanta 1996. The women's race took place on 30 July at the Georgia International Horse Park. The three-lap, 32km race was held in intense heat. It was won by Italian Paolo Pezzo, who crossed the finish line in 1:50.51, one minute and seven seconds ahead of Canada's Alison Sydor.

By the time of her Olympic triumph Pezzo had already amassed a world championship, two European titles and three national championships. Her 1996 win in Atlanta started a remarkable run for her. She went on to win the World Cup in 1997, claiming eight wins in ten races, as well as a second world championship. Late in 1997 it was revealed she had tested positive for the anabolic steroid Nandrolone, but she was later cleared, partly because of flaws in the testing procedure.

Pezzo won a third European title in 1999 and then successfully defended her Olympic crown in 2000. She took her final national championships in 2005.

31 July

Rémy Di Grégorio is born
(1985)

A junior national champion, Rémy Di Grégorio entered the professional ranks as a gifted climber. In his second year he won a stage in the Alps at the Tour de l'Avenir and followed that in 2007 with the climber's jersey at the Critérium du Dauphiné.

The Frenchman picked up his biggest win to date in 2011 – a stage victory in Paris–Nice – but it was in 2012 that he hit the headlines. At the 2012 Tour, Di Grégorio was arrested following a police raid on his Cofidis team's hotel. Two days later he was charged with possession of supposed doping products. Di Grégorio denied any wrongdoing, saying that he could look himself in the mirror. 'Justice will do the rest,' he said. Cofidis, meanwhile, suspended and then sacked him.

But Di Grégorio was later cleared. The 'supposed doping products' were found to be vitamins and he successfully sued his former team. Although exonerated, his career was badly affected. Di Grégorio spent the 2013 and 2014 seasons riding for Team Martigues SC – Vivelo and Team La Pomme Marseille 13 (France) as he sought a return to top-level racing. 'I'll come back one day and with ambitions. I'll do it for my family,' he said … when he was cleared.

AUGUST

1 August

Wiggins becomes Britain's most decorated Olympian
(2012)

Hampton Court, London. Bradley Wiggins sits on a throne. His British Cycling jersey is unzipped, revealing a tattooed chest; his fingers and hands cast in 'V for Victory' formation; his adoring public bow before him, some of them wearing paper cut-outs of his trademark sideburns. Having being crowned as the winner of the Tour de France just ten days earlier, Wiggins now sits in the grounds of King Henry VIII's former palace as British cycling royalty.

Wiggins had just blasted around the 44km Olympic time-trial course. He had destroyed the competition. Silver-medal winner, Tony Martin, the reigning world champion in the race of truth, was more than forty seconds back. Third-placed Chris Froome was more than a minute behind. Wiggins had reigned supreme over London, roared on by the hundreds of thousands lining the road. It was his seventh Olympic medal, making him Britain's most-decorated Olympian (see 20 August for Chris Hoy equalling him). He was the toast of the capital.

That win brought to a close a staggering year for the man born in Ghent to a British mother and Australian father. In July 2012 Wiggins had become the first British rider to win the Tour. He had taken the yellow jersey on stage seven at the top of La Planche des Belles Filles in the Vosges Mountains and held it all the way to Paris. That win came after an historic Paris–Nice, Romandie, Dauphiné treble (see 10 June). In the summer of 2012 no one in the cycling world could touch him.

It was some rise to the top of road racing for Wiggins. Until 2009 his major successes had come on the track and his first Olympic medal came at the Sydney Games with a bronze in the team pursuit. A world championship title in 2003 in the individual pursuit was followed by his first Olympic gold in 2004.

During his period of track domination he had also competed on the road, riding the Giro and Tour and picking up stage wins in the Tour de l'Avenir and Dauphiné. But it wasn't until the 2009 Tour and his surprise fourth place (he was later awarded third following Lance Armstrong's disqualification) that he emerged as a real contender, and if his 2010 and 2011 seasons were ultimately disappointing and affected by crashes and injuries, 2012 made up for it in spades.

'I don't think my sporting career will ever top this now. That's it. It will never, never get better than that. Incredible,' said King Bradley as he sat on his throne.

2 August

Fabio Casartelli wins Olympic gold

(1992)

Under a broiling Spanish sun, Italian rider Fabio Casartelli took the biggest win of his career when he won a three-man uphill sprint to take gold at the 1992 Barcelona Olympic Games.

Casartelli had been part of a breakaway that had successfully fended off repeated attempts by the peloton to reel them in over the concluding kilometres of the 195km race. As Casartelli, accompanied by Holland's Erik Dekker and Latvia's Dainis Ozols, entered the final 500m, it was clear the winner would be one of the trio. Casartelli, the superior sprinter of the three, bided his time, launched his sprint with around

150m to go and never looked back. He was mobbed as he crossed the line, becoming the first Italian Olympic road race winner since Pierfranco Vianelli in 1968.

Casartelli turned professional in 1993 but his life was cruelly cut short just two years later. Having married and recently become a father, he was called up to ride the 1995 Tour by his Motorola team just two days before it started in Lille. Descending the Col de Portet d'Aspet, he suffered a sickening crash. One of six riders to go down, Casartelli lay fatally stricken on the road. He had hit his head on a block of concrete and had suffered multiple cranial injuries.

3 August

Tom Danielson wins the first Tour of Qinghai Lake

(2002)

In 2002 the authorities in China's remote Qinghai province were looking for a way of promoting greater awareness of their region. Lying in the north-west of the country, and despite boasting the largest lake in China, Qinghai had virtually no tourism. Something was needed to promote it.

That something would turn out to be a bike race. Unperturbed, perhaps even encouraged, by the elevation of Qinghai – it sits on the Tibetan plateau with an average elevation of over 3,000m – the authorities introduced the Tour of Qinghai Lake to the cycling calendar in 2002.

It was no small undertaking. Hundreds of kilometres of new roads had to be constructed and hotels built, and all in ridiculously quick time. But built they were and in 2002 the race was on. It attracted seventeen teams and was won by America's Tom Danielson, who took two stages, including the pivotal penultimate leg into Xining, a stage that included a 30km-long climb.

The race has been held every year since and has grown in both popularity and category. It has now been given the same rating as the Tour of Britain.

4 August

Luc Leblanc is born

(1966)

Born in Limoges in 1966, Luc Leblanc's story is one of triumph over adversity, followed by a scent of scandal. When they were boys, Leblanc and his brother were hit by a car. His brother died while Leblanc was hospitalised and had to learn to walk again, with one leg left shorter than the other.

He turned professional in 1987 with the Toshiba team and he rode his first Tour in 1990, finishing seventy-third. The following year brought a huge leap up the standings with fifth place in Paris and a day in yellow.

A good climber, his best year came in 1994. Sixth place and the mountains jersey at the Vuelta was followed by fourth in the Tour and a stage win in the Pyrénées on the Tour's first ascent of Hautacam.

Then came the rainbow jersey. Leblanc won the 1994 world championships in Agrigento, Sicily, ahead of home favourite Claudio Chiappucci, and Richard Virenque. It was the biggest win of his career.

Leblanc retired in 1999 after being sacked by his Polti team before the end of his contract, leading to a successful action for unfair dismissal. He became embroiled in the fallout from the Festina affair and in 2000 admitted having taken performance-enhancing drugs during his time with the team but insisted his world title was won when he was clean.

5 August

Tour de Guadeloupe joins UCI America Tour
(2005)

First held in 1948, the Tour de Guadeloupe became part of the UCI America Tour for the first time in 2005. The 2005 edition comprised a prologue and nine stages for a total race distance of over 1,280km around the Caribbean island.

The race was won by Colombia's José Flober Peña, who took three stage wins en route to the victory. It was his second straight win in the race, having also triumphed in 2004. Peña would also go on to win the race in 2007 and 2008, to equal the record of four victories held by fellow Colombian José Daniel Bernal. Peña also holds the record for most stage wins, with thirteen.

The race continues to be held with the 2014 edition of the race attracting twenty-three teams to the island. It was won by Venezuela's John Nava.

6 August

Oakley's Overthetop trademark is registered
(2002)

In the mid-1980s Oakley revolutionised eyewear in cycling. Up to then the most famous pair of glasses in the peloton were Laurent Fignon's round spectacles that helped coin his nickname le Prof. But then came Greg LeMond and his Oakleys.

Jim Jannard, a scientist, formed Oakley in 1975, determined to bring a new approach to sports equipment. He started with motorcycle handgrips but in the 1980s, having successfully launched a new motocross goggle, he turned his attention to sunglasses. Never before had eyewear been specifically designed for cyclists. Greg LeMond wore Oakley's Eyeshades in the 1985 Tour. He finished third, bringing his Oakleys firmly into the public gaze.

LeMond was something of a trailblazer. He liked to do things differently and the brash-looking Eyeshades were certainly different. Initially, he was laughed at but the cycling community was soon convinced. Then Oakleys were everywhere.

In 2002 Oakley registered the trademark of perhaps its most innovative product – the OVERTHETOP sunglasses. Described within the registration certificate as 'protective hingeless eyewear without earstems', the glasses wrap around the top of the head rather than sitting on the ears and nose, giving the wearer a futuristic look.

Though worn only occasionally by cyclists, the design was brave and unique and defined Oakley as a dynamic organisation, willing to push the boundaries. 'Inventions wrapped in art,' in Jannard's own words.

7 August

Kübler wins his Tour
(1950)

In 1950 Ferdi Kübler became the first Swiss rider to win the Tour de France. On 7 August he rode into Paris and mounted the podium more than nine minutes ahead of Belgium's Constant 'Stan' Ockers. His victory, however, owed more than a little to the events of two weeks earlier on the Col d'Aspin.

The 1948 and 1949 Tours had been won by the Italians Gino Bartali and Fausto Coppi respectively. France was restless, fed up with watching their neighbours win their Tour. On stage eleven, over the Tourmalet and Aspin, Bartali was in the lead group with Frenchmen Louison Bobet and Jean Robic. Crowds spilled into the roads. At the top of the Aspin, Robic and Bartali touched. Both fell, Robic damaging a wheel. The crowd was incensed and started throwing stones and abusing Bartali.

Bartali, furious, remounted and rode to the stage win. His Italian team-mate Fiorenzo Magni took yellow. But Bartali was disturbed. That night he called his manager to his room and told him he was abandoning and that every Italian should follow his lead. 'No Italian will ride tomorrow,' he told reporters.

Sure enough every Italian abandoned, even race leader Magni. That left Kübler in yellow and the Swiss took full advantage. Now by far the strongest rider left in the race, he won two more stages (he'd already picked up one in the first week) and steadily increased his lead all the way to Paris.

8 August

Final Coors Classic starts
(1988)

This year brought the curtain down on what had once been the biggest cycling race held in the USA, first run in 1975 under the name the Red Zinger Race.

Six years before any American had even turned a pedal at the Tour de France, Mo Seigel, a businessman from Colorado whose company, Celestial Seasonings, was thriving in the herbal tea business, decided to inaugurate his own bike race. Named after one of Seigel's brands, the 1975 Red Zinger Race comprised three stages around Boulder, Colorado. It was won by John Howard.

The race soon started to draw significant crowds and attracted riders from around the country. By 1979 it had grown to eight stages, but the change that was to transform the event was still to come.

In 1980 Coors took over sponsorship and the race, renamed the Coors International Bicycle Classic, or the Coors Classic, expanded further. Stages were held in other states, including Hawaii. It became by far the biggest race in the USA and one of the first anywhere to hold both a men's and women's race.

Winners included Greg LeMond and Bernard Hinault. In 1988, however, Coors pulled their sponsorship and the race folded. The final winner was Davis Phinney, who also holds the record for most stage wins at the race with twenty-one.

9 August

Renato Longo is born
(1937)

Born in Vittoria Veneto, Italy, for a period in the 1960s Renato Longo was the world's premier cyclo-cross rider. A baker until he turned professional in 1960, Longo's first title of note actually came on the track when he won a national title in the 1958 Stayers Race. Then he switched to cyclo-cross and rewards immediately followed.

From 1959 until his retirement in 1972, Longo failed only twice to win Italy's national cyclo-cross championships. His haul of twelve national titles still remains a record.

It wasn't just in Italy that he triumphed. Slightly built for a cyclo-cross rider, Longo took his first world title in 1959, beating German Rolf Wolfshohl in Geneva. It was the first time that a non-Frenchman had won the official cyclo-cross world championships.

Longo and Wolfshohl would do battle throughout the early 1960s, sharing the world title between them. Longo would win a total of five world titles before passing on the mantle of world's best cyclo-crosser to the Belgian Erik De Vlaeminck.

10 August

Maris Strombergs defends Olympic BMX gold
(2012)

Latvia's golden boy Maris Strombergs is the only man to have won Olympic gold in BMX, an event first added to the Olympic programme in 2008. He won the inaugural gold ahead of Mike Day at the Laoshan BMX Field, and returned to the Olympic Games in 2012, hoping to repeat the feat.

Strombergs, nicknamed the Machine, has been winning BMX races all his life. His first world title came in Brighton, England, at a tender age when he won the nine-year-old-boy classification. National and European junior titles followed and in 2008 he took his first elite world championships ahead of the Beijing Games.

But heading into London 2012, Strombergs was far from a sure winner. A bad crash in 2010 meant he lost six months of riding and his form leading up to London was uncertain.

He left it late to show the world he was still the man to beat. Unconvincing in qualifying and the heats, Strombergs nevertheless secured his spot in the final and then let loose. Leading into the crucial first corner, he stayed there from start to finish to defend his Olympic title. It was only the third gold medal in Latvia's Olympic history. 'I think my country believed in me,' Strombergs said afterwards.

11 August

Alfredo Binda, first pro world champion, is born
(1902)

Throughout the late 1920s and the early 1930s, Italy's Alfredo Binda ruled the cycling world, winning the Giro five times and world championships three times in a spectacular career. Add to these four Tours of Lombardy, a couple of Milan–Sanremos and four national road race titles and you have a rider who dominated Italian cycling for more than eight years.

Binda took over Italian cycling from Costante Girardengo. Just as Gira's career was declining so Binda's was building. Binda, born in Cittiglio, near Varese, but raised across the border in Nice, first came to notice in the 1924 Tour of Lombardy. He finished fourth but had climbed the Ghisallo alone at the head of the race and mixed it with Italian cycling royalty in the closing kilometres. When it was discovered that Binda was Italian, the Italian cycling press suddenly sat up and took notice of this newcomer. Soon they would not be able to

miss him even if they wanted to. In 1925 he rode his first Giro, winning nearly five minutes ahead of Girardengo. Binda was only twenty-two, Girardengo ten years older. It was to be the passing of the torch.

Described by René Vietto as having such a smooth style that he could cycle with a cup of milk on his back and it would remain full, Binda would win the Giro again in 1927, 1928, 1929 and 1933. His five titles remain a record, now shared with Fausto Coppi and Eddy Merckx. To say that Binda dominated the 1927 race is to understate his superiority. He won twelve of the fifteen stages, recording a winning margin of over twenty-seven minutes. That

same year he won the inaugural world championships, again beating Girardengo.

In 1930, the Giro organisers, fearful that yet another Binda victory would dilute the public's interest in the race, paid the great man to stay away, giving him the same amount of money as he would have received had he won.

As he rode primarily for Italian teams, Binda's focus was always the Giro, hence he rode the Tour only once, in 1930. He won two stages in the Pyrénées and then abandoned. He would return to the race as a team manager, claiming wins with both Gino Bartali and Coppi.

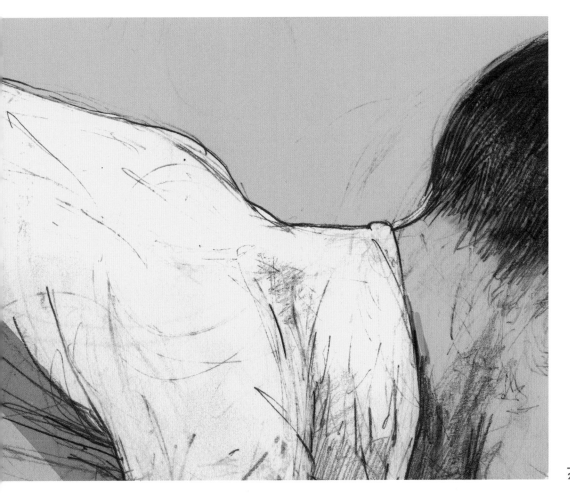

12 August

Laurent Fignon, le Prof, is born

(1960)

With a blond ponytail, headband and round, rimless glasses, Laurent Fignon cut a somewhat unorthodox figure in the professional peloton of the 1980s and early 1990s.

Born in Paris, as a boy Fignon first used his bike to cycle to his beloved football training sessions. Discovering he was a good deal quicker than his friends, he joined the cycling club, La Pédale de Combs-la-Ville. His first race was a 50km road race, which he won. Very soon he became the rider to beat on the local scene.

At eighteen he enrolled at the Université Paris XIII in Villetaneuse only to drop out to do his military service and continue cycling. It was this partial university education that, coupled with his glasses, led to him being nicknamed the Professor.

An impressive showing at the 1981 Tour of Corsica led to a professional contract with Bernard Hinault's Renault team. By 1983 he was riding his first Tour. Hinault was injured so the team leadership passed to Fignon.

His first yellow jersey came a little tainted, coming only because of the abandonment of Pascal Simon, who had captured the hearts of France by riding for six days with a broken shoulder. But Fignon won the penultimate stage and entered Paris the winner by over four minutes.

He repeated the win in 1984, destroying Hinault, who had by now left Renault for the new La Vie Claire team. That year's stage to the l'Alpe d'Huez has passed into legend, with Hinault repeatedly attacking but Fignon repelling each skirmish and then finally powering away on the final climb.

With two Tour wins in as many attempts, a period of Fignon dominance surely beckoned. But it was not to be. Injury cruelly robbed him of some of his prime years and, despite wins in classics, including Milan–Sanremo, it wasn't until 1989 that he returned to form at the Tour.

He'd won his one and only Giro that spring and entered the Tour confident of completing the fabled Giro/Tour double. In the end he came second in the closest Tour finish in history (see 23 July). What took place that year on the roads of France followed him for the rest of his life.

Fignon died in 2010 from stomach cancer.

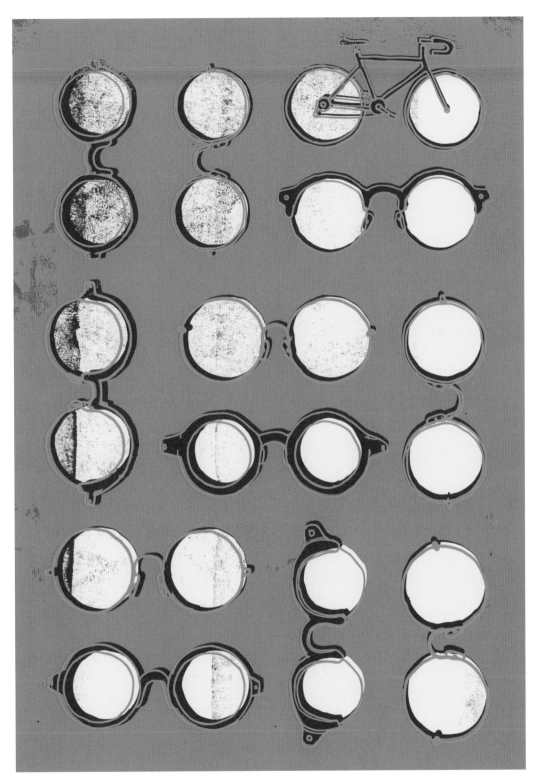

13 August

José Beyaert wins gold in London
(1948)

The 1948 Olympic Games road race comprised seventeen laps of a circuit around Windsor Great Park, for a total race distance of just over 120 miles. It was a flat course, ripe for strong, punchy riders. One such rider was José Beyaert.

Born in 1925, until 1948 Beyaert's best result had been third in the 1945 French amateur championships but he rode impressively in the run-up to the Games and made the final team, selected by Georges Speicher.

The race took place on the final day of the Games, which broke wet and windswept.

On a tight, technical circuit, in dangerous conditions, it made for a tense and nervous race. Breaks and escapes formed and were caught, their composition changing constantly, but, as the race entered its climax, Beyaert was in the lead group, with six other riders.

He attacked a mile or so out, catching his fellow escapees by surprise. His strength meant he was able to hold on and win by just over three seconds. He became the third French Olympic road race champion and he still remains the most recent French winner.

14 August

Coppi's faithful servant Andrea Carrea is born
(1924)

No occasion better typifies the mindset of the domestique than stage nine of the 1952 Tour de France. Fausto Coppi entered the race as the leader of the Bianchi team and riding with him was his team-mate Andrea 'Sandrino' Carrea.

To say Carrea was a faithful servant is an understatement. He was in awe of Coppi and knew the *Campionissimo*'s talents far outshone his own. He took pride in his role as Coppi's helper.

Stage nine took the riders to Lausanne. A group went away and Carrea, charged with protecting his leader's interests, got himself into the break. The gap grew. At the

finish they had over nine minutes on the peloton and Coppi. Unbeknown to him Carrea had inherited the race lead. He was more than five minutes ahead of his leader.

When Carrea found out he wept, not tears of joy but of sorrow. He had just earned the right to slip on the most revered jersey in cycling but felt he had no business wearing it. He sought Coppi out and excused himself. Coppi merely laughed and congratulated him.

Coppi would go on to win the Tour while Andrea Carrea would go down in history as the man who wore yellow without really wanting to.

15 August

Sara Carrigan takes Olympic gold
(2004)

The Athens 2004 Olympic Games road cycling events took place on a lumpy 13.2km circuit. On day two of the Games the women's road race was on the agenda – nine laps of the circuit making a total race distance of just shy of 119km.

The Australian team was strong: Olivia Gollan, Oenone Wood and Sara Carrigan took to the start line all hoping to medal. 'We were all keen to get on the podium and all of us were prepared for one to win the race,' Carrigan would later say.

With the riders cautious in the early part of the race, it wasn't until the halfway point that escapes started to form. But the Australians bided their time. At the bell Carrigan made her move. She bridged up to the leading group and then attacked. Only Germany's Judith Arndt could follow. Arndt then took over most of the pace-making with Carrigan content to sit on her wheel. In the closing straight Carrigan, the better sprinter, came around the German to record Australia's second women's road race Olympic gold.

16 August

Julien Absalon is born
(1980)

Probably the greatest mountain bike rider in history, Frenchman Julien Absalon was born in Remiremont, in the Vosges Mountains. In 1998 he became junior world champion, winning in Mont Sainte-Anne, Canada. Absalon has said that it was this win that convinced him that he had a future in the sport.

And what a future. In 2003 he won his first national title in Métabief, a title he has successfully defended every year since – his tally at the time of writing stands at twelve. But there was far more to come.

In the decade since that first national win, Absalon has won the world championships five times, the world cup six times and the European championship three times. He also claimed Olympic gold twice, in 2004 and then again in 2008.

Absalon shows no sign of fading. He has turned to Rio 2016 after having to abandon the London 2012 race early with a puncture and 2014 was his best non-Olympic year. With wins in the world championships, world cup, European championships and nationals, he claimed every major win available to him. '2014 was a dream season for me,' he said.

17 August

Filippo Simeoni is born

(1971)

Simeoni, a national champion and two-time Vuelta stage winner, is best known for the role he played in the Lance Armstrong story, long before the American admitted to his use of performance-enhancing drugs.

As part of a doping investigation, Simeoni had testified that in 1996 and 1997 he had asked his team that he be treated by Dr Michele Ferrari, who was already working with some of his team-mates and claimed that Ferrari had prescribed him doping products. Simeoni was banned for eight months and fined. Then Armstrong, who it was known had also worked with Ferrari, began to issue statements against Simeoni, accusing him of lying. Simeoni initiated proceedings against the American.

If all this courtroom action was rather unseemly for the sport of cycling, it was at least being played out in the offices of lawyers rather than on the road in front of the fans. Then, on stage eighteen of the 2004 Tour, all that changed. That was when it became downright ugly.

Two days from Paris, with Armstrong firmly in yellow, a break went. It was an innocuous enough escape. Simeoni, 114th overall and more than two hours behind, rode away from the peloton to bridge to the breakaway. He made it but one rider was on his wheel, a rider wearing a famous shade of yellow.

It was unheard of for the yellow jersey to leave the safety of the bunch to chase after someone who was no threat two days from glory. But Armstrong couldn't help himself. He publicly humiliated Simeoni, told him and his fellow breakaway riders that if the Italian remained in the break then he would stay there as well. That meant the peloton would chase the yellow jersey and the break would fail. Simeoni was sent back. Armstrong, back in the bunch, laughed and joked. He mimed the zipping of lips. Armstrong's point was all too clearly made.

Simeoni never rode the Tour again, and he remained something of a cycling outcast. In 2008 he became Italian national champion but, despite this, was denied a ride in the 2009 Giro while Armstrong was welcomed back following his return to the sport after his retirement in 2005. It was a huge snub and contributed to Simeoni's retirement in 2009.

18 August

Karel Kaers becomes youngest RR world champion
(1934)

The 1934 world championship road race took place in Leipzig, Germany, then in the grip of the National Socialist (Nazi) party. Cycling journalist Pierre Chany wrote of 70,000 spectators and military marches being played by bands from dawn till dusk.

Just twenty-six riders started the 225km race, and among the favourites were Learco Guerra, champion in 1931, and Antonin Magne, runner-up the year before. Certainly not among the fancied riders was Karel Kaers. The Belgian, large for a cyclist at just under two metres tall, was more of a track rider, with two national junior track titles his stand-out results. At only twenty years old, he was also very young.

Yet Kaers shocked the world. The final metres came down to a fourteen-rider sprint and the young Belgian won the dash to the line ahead of Guerra. The reaction was muted, with at least one writer highlighting the irony of having a road race champion who was much more regularly seen on the track than on the road.

But Kaers' win meant he became the youngest ever winner of the race, a record he still holds. He would go on to win the Tour of Flanders in 1939.

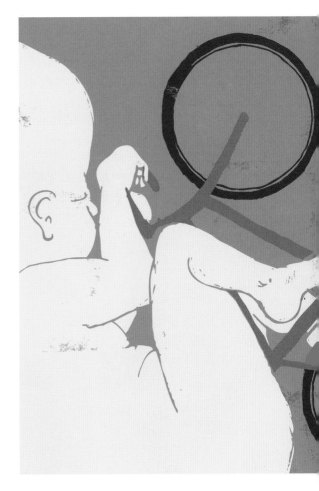

19 August

Pendleton wins first Olympic gold
(2008)

Britain's greatest female track sprinter, Victoria Pendleton, won her first Olympic gold in 2008 at the Beijing Games. Already a six-time world champion, having claimed the individual sprint rainbow jersey in 2005, 2007 and 2008, the team sprint in 2007 and 2008, and keirin in 2007, Pendleton entered the 2008 Games as the world's premier female speed machine.

Queen Vic was dominant throughout. She set an Olympic record in qualifying before sailing through the first round, quarter-finals and semis to set up a meeting with Australia's Anna Meares in the final.

Meares, whose own appearance in the final crowned a remarkable comeback from injury, having eight months earlier fractured two vertebrae, was no match for the Briton, who needed only two of three races to win gold.

Pendleton would go on to win further Olympic gold in 2012, this time in the keirin. She added silver in the sprint when Meares finally got her revenge, reversing the 2008 result. By then Pendleton had added another three world titles. She retired as Britain's most decorated female Olympian.

20 August

Hoy wins gold in 1km TT
(2004)

Sir Chris Hoy had a remarkable elite track cycling career that started in 1998 and ended thirteen years later in London.

Initially the 1km time trial was his main focus. Third place at the 1998 national championships in the discipline was followed by second place twelve months later. Then he went to the Sydney 2000 Olympic Games. There, along with Craig MacLean and Jason Queally, Hoy took silver in the men's team sprint while Queally took gold in the 1km time trial.

Four years later it was Hoy's turn to win gold. That August he defended Queally's gold for Britain, setting an Olympic record with his time of 1:00.711.

It was the start of a golden age for Hoy. He took three more golds in Beijing in 2008, becoming the first Briton to do so at a single Olympics since Henry Taylor in 1908, and added two more in 2012. His haul of seven Olympic medals places him alongside Bradley Wiggins as Britain's most decorated Olympian, although he has six golds to Wiggins' four.

Away from the Olympics, Hoy was equally successful, with eleven world titles. After taking time to consider his future following the 2012 Olympics, he announced his retirement in April 2013, bringing to an end the most glittering of cycling careers.

21 August

Odile Defraye, first Belgian to win Tour, dies
(1965)

Belgium's Odile Defraye rode in seven Tours throughout his ten-season career but only finished one. But what a finish that one was as, in 1912, Defraye entered Paris as the winner of the Tour de France.

Look at the list of Tour wins by nation and you'll see that Belgium, with eighteen victories, sits second only to France and their thirty-six victories. But it wasn't until the tenth edition of the race that Belgium took their first win. And it came courtesy of Defraye.

The 1912 Tour was the last one to be decided by a points system determined by a rider's finishing position on each stage, with the rider with the fewest points the winner, rather than elapsed time. Defraye won handsomely.

His forty-eight points placed him sixty ahead of Eugène Christophe, who finished in second place. Defraye also won three stages and it was the last of these, from Perpignan to Luchon, featuring climbs of the Port, Portet d'Aspet and Ares, in which he forged his unassailable lead.

After his win there was no stopping Belgium. While Defraye would never again finish the race nor even win a stage, Belgian riders won the next six editions in a row. For his part Defraye won just one more major race before his retirement in 1924 – the 1913 Milan–Sanremo.

22 August

Sarah Ulmer grabs New Zealand's first cycling gold
(2004)

Going into the 2004 Athens Olympic Games, New Zealand's Sarah Ulmer was the stand-out favourite for the 3km individual pursuit.

A junior world champion in the discipline in 1994 now, a decade on, she was looking to add the biggest title of them all to her 1998 and 2002 Commonwealth Games golds and her 2004 rainbow jersey, won two months earlier in Melbourne. She was also the world record holder.

Safe to say, then, that Ulmer was a marked woman, not least because of her pedigree. She came from a cycling family: her grandfather, Ron, had represented New Zealand on the track, and her father, Gary, was a national champion on both the road and the track. She more than lived up to her and her family's reputation. She set a world record in qualifying and then bettered it again in the final against Australia's Katie Mactier. Her time of 3:24.537 was more than three seconds faster than her opponent's. It was New Zealand's first cycling gold medal.

Ulmer switched to the road after Athens, picking up wins in New Zealand's national championships and at the Oceania Games. She won the Tour of New Zealand in 2006 before retiring the following year.

23 August

Audrey McElmury becomes first American world champ
(1969)

In 1969 Audrey McElmury, from San Diego, won the world championships road race, becoming the first American ever to take the title.

McElmury, who was riding her fourth worlds, had claimed fifth place in the 1968 race, held in Rome, but she wasn't considered one of the favourites going into the 1969 edition, with a 1966 national title her best previous result.

It was a tough course – five times around a 14km circuit in Brno, in what is now the former Czechoslovakia. Included on the route was a steep 4km-long climb and it was here that McElmury launched her bid for victory.

The American was used to tough climbing, for she'd trained in the hills of La Jolla, a community adjoining San Diego, California. Despite the World's course being hailed as the toughest the women's peloton had ever faced, afterwards McElmury told *Sports Illustrated* that La Jolla's hills had won her the title. 'Compared to them, the worlds was easy,' she said. She soloed to a win over Britain's Bernadette Swinnerton, the result surprising the organisers so much that the presentation had to be delayed while they sourced a recording of 'The Star-Spangled Banner'.

McElmury had made cycling history for the United States but her achievement was more recognised in Europe. Eventually, as the sport grew in popularity in the US, America came to see her as a true great. Upon her death in 2013, Joe Herget, executive director of the US Bicycling Hall of Fame, said that cycling had lost one of its greatest icons.

24 August

Roger De Vlaeminck is born
(1947)

Nicknamed both the Gypsy and Mr Paris–Roubaix, Belgian-born Roger De Vlaeminck was a one-day rider par excellence. Once described by Eddy Merckx as the only rider he ever feared, De Vlaeminck won a huge number of races. That he did this during an era when Merckx had a vice-like grip on the sport only adds to the impressiveness of his career.

Born in Eeklo to a family of travelling clothiers (hence his first nickname), De Vlaeminck was a world champion before he'd even joined the professional ranks, taking the 1968 amateur cyclo-cross worlds on the same day as brother Erik won the elite version.

When he did turn professional, with the Flandria team, at the start of the 1969 season, De Vlaeminck impressed immediately. He won his first race, Het Volk, came second in his first Monument, Milan–Sanremo, and won the Belgian national road championships. It was a startling first year as a pro, but he was only just beginning. The following year he claimed Kuurne–Brussels–Kuurne, Liège–Bastogne–Liège and then won a stage at the Tour.

His peak years came between 1972 and 1979, during which period he won Paris–Roubaix four times (see 17 April), Milan–Sanremo three times, the Tour of Lombardy twice and the Tour of Flanders once. That Flanders win remains controversial. Freddy Maertens virtually towed De Vlaeminck to the line, knowing that he was about to be disqualified for an illegal bike change on the Koppenberg. Maertens didn't contest the sprint. As a result De Vlaeminck didn't even celebrate as he crossed the line.

Despite the lack of celebration, that win completed his set of Monuments and he remains one of just three riders to have all five on his palmares, the others being Merckx and Rik Van Looy. Although he only rode the Tour three times and never made it to Paris, De Vlaeminck's record at the Giro was much better – he won twenty-two stages and took the points jersey three times.

De Vlaeminck was also good in short, week-long stage races. He won the Tour de Suisse in 1975 and Tirreno–Adriatico a record six times (see 16 March for more) and, while he never managed to win the world championship road race, he did take the cyclo-cross elite worlds in 1975.

25 August

Merckx completes first triple crown of cycling
(1974)

It's the final 300m of the 1974 world championship road race in Montreal. Two men are heading for a sprint to the line having caught and passed Bernard Thévenet who had been out front alone for 100km of the race but had now tired badly.

Eddy Merckx is on the wheel of Raymond Poulidor. Merckx tightens his toe straps and readies himself. Poulidor glances nervously about him. The sprint is on.

Poulidor leads but Merckx lifts his backside out of the saddle and draws level. He briefly sits, gazes across at his opponent, lifts his backside again and is gone. Poulidor is left to ride in second, with Merckx having more than enough time to take his hands off the handlebars in triumph. 'Merckx is Merckx,' says Poulidor later. 'I had no chance against him.'

It was Merckx's third rainbow jersey and a historical win. Not only did he join Alfredo Binda as the only rider then to have won the title three times, that year he had also taken home both the pink and yellow jerseys. Now he'd added the rainbow. It was the first time a rider had won all three in a single season. Merckx had won the first triple crown of cycling.

26 August

Tullio Campagnolo is born in Vicenza
(1901)

First the legend. Born in Vicenza, Tullio Campagnolo discovered cycling and raced as both an amateur and a professional but without much success. But it is a story from his racing days that has passed into cycling legend.

On 11 November 1927, Campagnolo was racing in the Gran Premio della Vittoria on a day of snow and freezing temperatures. On the climb of the Croce d'Aune, Campagnolo stopped to turn his wheel over for the descent. In those days, before derailleurs, bikes only had two gears, one fitted either side of the hub. To change gear you had to switch the wheel around. That meant first releasing the nuts holding the wheel in place. Numbed by the freezing weather, Campagnolo couldn't get his fingers to work the wing nuts free because his hands were so cold. Muttering that something had to change about the design, Campagnolo continued to struggle. Later, inspired by the events of that day, he invented the quick-release system and so was born perhaps the most iconic of cycling component producers, the eponymous Campagnolo of Vicenza.

It's a fantastic story, and one contained on the company's official website. But is it true?

In 2014 *Bicycle Quarterly* ran an extensive feature debunking the whole story as a myth, claiming that the 1927 race wasn't affected by snow, that Tullio Campagnolo's name doesn't appear in any race reports from the 1920s and that the patent supposedly issued in 1930 doesn't exist.

Whatever the truth of the company's origins, what is undeniable is that it changed cycling. With a reputation for quality, superior design and innovation, for decades Campagnolo were the dominant force in the sport. In 1962, the 50th edition of the Tour, Campagnolo riders won eighteen out of twenty-one stages and won the overall, mountains, points and team classifications.

Tullio Campagnolo died in 1983 at the age of eighty-one.

27 August

Maria Canins wins world TTT title
(1988)

When Maria Canins started cycling seriously she was thirty-two years old and a champion cross-country skier. Nicknamed the Flying Housewife, Canins, who in her ski career had amassed fifteen national titles, took her first national cycling championships in 1982. It was to be the first of six national road race wins.

Canins was a seriously talented rider. The stamina she had so successfully built up on snow served her well on the roads of Europe. In 1985 she won the Tour of Norway before heading to France and the Tour de France Féminine. She won five stages, all of them in the mountains, and won the overall by over twenty-two minutes. The next year she successfully defended both titles.

In 1988 she won the inaugural Giro Donne. It had been an incredible haul of wins in little more than five years as a cyclist, especially given how late she came to the sport. But one thing missing was a rainbow jersey. She had come close with two second places in the road races but the top spot had so far eluded her.

On 27 August 1988, Canins rectified that. In Renaix, Belgium, in a 54km-long team time trial, Canins and her three Italian team-mates took world championship gold. Now the national champion was a champion of the world. She retired from cycling competition in 1995, an incredible twenty-five years after she won her first Italian championship as a cross-country skier.

28 August

First Tour du Suisse starts
(1933)

Sometimes heralded as the most important stage race after the three Grand Tours, the Tour de Suisse was first held in 1933. Apart from missing three editions because of the outbreak of war in 1939, it has been held every year since the end of the conflict.

That first 1933 edition started in Zurich and was won by an Austrian, Max Bulla, who reportedly arrived in the Swiss city only an hour before the race started. Bulla had won three stages of the Tour in 1931 and worn yellow for a day. He was also a double national champion but the 1933 Tour de Suisse would be his crowning moment as he claimed two stage wins on his way to a nine-minute overall victory.

Initially five stages held on successive days, over time the race has grown both in length and prestige. Examine the list of former winners and a host of top-class riders leaps out – Gino Bartali, Eddy Merckx, Hugo Koblet and Ferdi Kübler among them (see 23 June for more on Koblet and Kübler's Tour de Suisse battles).

Italian Pasquale Fornara holds the record for victories, with four. In 2014 Portugal's Rui Costa became the first rider to win three in a row.

29 August

Félicia Ballanger sets her 6th world record in 500m TT
(1998)

On 13 June 1993 Canada's Tanya Dubnikoff set a world record for the 500m standing start time trial when, in Valencia, she stopped the clock in 36.705 seconds. Just three weeks later Félicia Ballanger destroyed that mark, taking nearly a second off the world's best time in Hyères, France.

For the next fourteen years Ballanger owned the record. She broke her own record for the first time later that same month, in Bordeaux. Then she did it again – twice in 1994 and once more in 1995. Her 1995 time stood for three years until, on 29 August 1998, she returned to Bordeaux.

On home boards, Ballanger blasted around the track in 34.010 seconds, seven-hundredths of a second faster than her previous best. It was the sixth time she had set a world record in the event in five years. It would stand until 2007, when it was finally bettered by Jiang Yonghua of China.

Ballanger's record-breaking exploits came at a time when the Frenchwoman dominated track sprinting. Born into a cycling family (she was named after Italian great Felice Gimondi), Ballanger won the world championships in both the sprint and the 500m time trial five years in a row, from 1995 until 1999.

Ballanger also won Olympic gold at both Atlanta and Sydney. She left the sport on a high, with the Sydney Games being her last international competition.

30 August

Elsy Jacobs wins inaugural women's road title
(1958)

There has been a men's road cycling world championships since 1927 but not until 1958 did the world's female peloton get the chance to compete on the road for a rainbow jersey.

After much lobbying of the UCI, and following promises from many countries to send strong teams, in 1957 the UCI agreed to stage a women's world championships the following year. Reims was the designated venue and a race over three laps of a lumpy 20km beckoned.

Twenty-eight riders from eight countries started. Among them was twenty-four-year-old Elsy Jacobs. Born in Luxembourg in 1933, her elder brothers Roger, Edmond and Raymond all rode professionally and Elsy, inspired by them, borrowed their bikes to train. Soon she was herself racing.

By the time of the inaugural women's world championships, Jacobs had been riding for five years and had become one of the most popular women in the peloton.

Jacobs got herself in the early and definitive breakaway. On the second lap she broke clear and pulled out a sizeable advantage over the closing half of the race. She crossed the line nearly three minutes ahead of Russian pair Tamara Novikova and Maria Lukshina. History was made: Jacobs was the first female road race world champion.

Elsy Jacobs never again reached the heights of that 1958 race, though she would win her country's national championships fifteen times. She died in 1998 and is remembered by the annual three-day race, the Festival Luxembourgeois du Cyclisme Féminin Elsy Jacobs.

31 August

Hinault wins his only Rainbow jersey
(1980)

Today, if the French anxiously await a successor to Bernard Hinault in the Tour (no Frenchman has won their national tour since Hinault's 1985 win), back in 1980 it wasn't a lack of success in the three-week jaunt around France that obsessed the country (thanks to Hinault and Bernard Thévenet they had won four of the last five editions) but the world championships.

By the time of the 1980 worlds, in the French Alpine town of Sallanches, it had been eighteen years since a Frenchman had last pulled on the rainbow jersey. Four riders had come close – Jaques Anquetil, Raymond Poulidor, Cyrille Guimard and Jean-René Bernaudeau all missing out in final sprints – but none had crossed the line first since Jean Stablinski's win in 1962.

The course was regarded as one of the hardest ever compiled for a world championships road race. At 268km, it might not have been as long as the two previous editions, but it was decidedly hilly and included twenty ascents of the short but sharp Côte de Domancy, which comes with a maximum gradient of 16 per cent.

The day was miserable: damp and cold, the Alps cloaked in leaden skies. The riders were in for a terrible day.

Of course, the harder the ride, the more it suited Hinault. Sure enough, as the race entered its second half, the Badger was at the front of the race in a five-man breakaway. Then he went to work.

Setting a ferocious pace, one by one his fellow escapees faltered until, on the last lap, there was just one left – Italy's Gianbattista Baronchelli. As the race hit the Domancy for the final time, Hinault launched himself.

'Et voilà! Now he attacks! Attack! Bernard Hinault!' yelled the TV commentator as Hinault pulled away. Baronchelli had no response. Soon Hinault was left alone to ride himself into history. 'Hinault! Hinault! Hinault!' the crowds cried as he sped to the finish.

Hinault finished in 7 hours, 32 minutes and 16 seconds, just over one minute ahead of Baronchelli. On a brutal day of bike racing there were only fifteen finishers out of 107 starters. But France didn't care. Its long wait for a French world champion was over.

SEPTEMBER

1 September

Ian Steel wins first Tour of Britain
(1951)

The first Tour of Britain took place in 1951, a time of dispute between British cycling's governing bodies.

The National Cycle Union (NCU) had banned road racing in the late 1800s but Percy Stallard, who had raced on the Continent in the 1930s, introduced mass-start road racing to Britain in the 1940s. The NCU banned Stallard and any rider riding his races, so he set up a rival organisation – the British League of Racing Cyclists (BLRC).

It was the BLRC who organised the first Tour of Britain (though Stallard was no longer involved with the organisation). Starting on 19 August, the fourteen-stage, 1,400-mile event started and finished in London, going via Plymouth in the south and Glasgow in the north. Forty-nine riders started, attracted by the prize purse of some £1,000 on offer from sponsors the *Daily Express*.

Scotland's Ian Steel won the race. He claimed three stages in total and took the race lead in his home town of Glasgow. He held the yellow jersey for the rest of the race, recording an overall winning margin of more than six minutes.

Steel would go on to win the Peace Race in 1952, the only rider from Britain to have done so (see 20 May for more).

2 September

Indurain is awarded the Prince of Asturias Sports award
(1992)

Oviedo, Spain: Miguel Indurain is awarded the Prince of Asturias Sports Award, pocketing nearly $125,000 in the process and taking home a Miró sculpture. The prize reflects the prestige of the award. The press release announcing Indurain as the winner said that the Spaniard's 'personality, temperament and character ... have always stood on par with his sporting ability'.

Despite the award, Indurain had barely started his winning streak: he was 'only' two Tour wins into a domination that would last for five years and had yet to win his world championship title (see 4 October) or his Olympic gold medal. He had, though, already won the Giro, completing the fabled Giro/Tour double in 1992, a feat he would repeat in 1993, becoming the only rider in history to do so two years in a row.

His achievements mean he should be revered, but Indurain is often maligned. He often triumphed by dominating time trials and then defending in the mountains. He won with control, never panache, and for that he suffered in the court of public opinion.

3 September

José Luis Laguía is born
(1959)

José Luis Laguía holds the record for the most victories in the mountains competition at the Vuelta a España.

Born in Pedro Muñoz, Laguía turned professional in 1980 after securing a podium spot at the 1979 Tour de l'Avenir. In 1981 he took the Vuelta's mountain prize for the first time. He'd finished third in the classification the year before as well as finishing second on the stage into Gijón, but

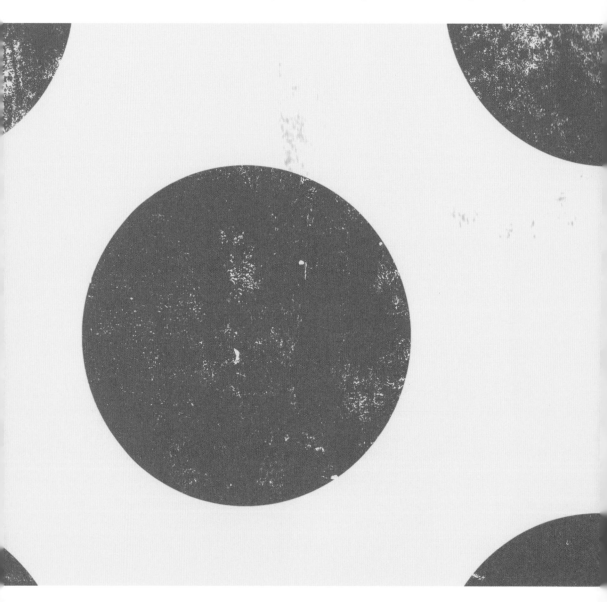

1981 was the year that he started to apply his stranglehold on the race's climber's jersey. He picked up 144 points, to win forty-six points ahead of Kelme's Vicente Belda. Laguía would win the competition for best climber again in 1982, 1983, 1985 and 1986. His five wins are a record, ahead of José María Jiménez and David Moncoutié, who have four jerseys each.

Laguía, who won four Vuelta stages over the course of his career and the 1982 national championship, never won outside Spain. He retired in 1992. He is currently a *directeur sportif* for the Movistar team.

4 September

Greg LeMond becomes first US men's world champion
(1983)

In 1982 Greg LeMond finished second in the world championship road race. It had been just three years since he had won the junior worlds (see 13 October) and, along with a stage win at Tirreno–Adriatico and three stages and the overall at the Tour de l'Avenir, it gave a hint of what LeMond was about to unleash on the world of professional cycling.

The 1983 worlds took place on a difficult 15km circuit in Switzerland. It was long and it was hilly, with two tricky climbs on the circuit. With 30km of the race to go LeMond was part of a three-man breakaway. With the American was Spain's Faustino Rupérez and Moreno Argentin of Italy. On the penultimate lap Argentin fell away. That left LeMond and Rupérez, 15km away from glory.

They matched each other until the final climb. Then LeMond upped his pace. A gap grew. One metre quickly became ten, twenty, fifty. All of sudden LeMond was alone with just a descent and a flat run between him and becoming the first American man to wear the rainbow jersey.

After more than seven hours of riding he crossed the line over one minute ahead of Adrie van der Poel of the Netherlands and Ireland's Stephen Roche. LeMond had made American cycling history. It wouldn't be the last time.

5 September

Eddy Merckx wins his first road world championships
(1964)

There's a photograph of Eddy Merckx, taken on this day in 1964. He is standing on the top step of the podium. Behind, a brooding mountain pierces the sky. Merckx has his arms raised wide above his head. In his right hand is a bouquet of flowers; around his neck a gold medal; on his back a white jersey with rainbow stripes. Eddy Merckx has just become the amateur world champion. He is nineteen years old.

The photograph was taken in Sallanches, France. Merckx nearly hadn't ridden at all. When subjected to medical tests prior to selection, he had been told that he had a problem with his heart and wouldn't be considered for a place on the team. His mother, Jenny, didn't believe it. She questioned the chief selector and then consulted the family doctor. He told her there was no problem with her son's heart.

Thanks to her intervention, Merckx got to ride and he repaid his mother in spades, soloing to a win twenty-seven seconds ahead of a bunch sprint led in by fellow Belgian Willy Planckaert.

Merckx turned professional the next year and cycling would never be the same again.

6 September

Stephen Roche wins cycling's triple crown
(1987)

If the first half of Stephen Roche's career had brought a number of good wins, including Paris–Nice, two Tour of Romandie titles and third overall and a Tour stage in 1985 (see 17 July), nothing that had come before can really be said to have paved the way for what he achieved in 1987.

Roche entered the 1987 Giro not as his Carrera team's leader, but as a team-mate of Italy's Roberto Visentini, the defending champion. Roche wore pink early on but lost it to Visentini after a mountain time trial. Visentini now had over two and half minutes on Roche, who was in second. They were on the same team; surely nothing could stop the Italian defending his title.

But Roche had other ideas. He had been told Visentini would work for him during the Tour, but had heard differently as the Giro progressed. So on stage fifteen, in the Dolomites, Roche got himself into a breakaway. The Carrera team ended up chasing their own man but to no avail. Roche finished nearly seven minutes ahead of Visentini and seized back pink.

His team was furious, as were the Italian tifosi. In 2012 Roche told the *Guardian* that rice and wine had been spat at him in the days that followed. But he held on and won the race; the first, and to date only, Irish rider to win the Giro.

A few weeks later Roche headed for France and went head-to-head with Spain's Pedro Delgado.

Roche had yellow entering the Alps but lost it to Delgado on l'Alpe d'Huez. The next day went over the Madeleine and up to La Plagne. Roche was only behind by twenty-five seconds, with a time trial still to come and he was far better against the clock than Delgado. All he had to do was mark the Spaniard to La Plagne and wait for the race of truth to take back yellow.

Instead, he went on the offensive. At the start of the Madeleine he was in a group that had over a minute on Delgado, but he had gone too early. As they came off the mountain the race came back together. Then, on La Plagne, Delgado sped off.

With 10km to go Roche was two minutes back. The Tour appeared to be slipping through his fingers. With TV coverage of Roche sporadic, no one knew exactly how far away he was when Delgado crossed the line, but everyone thought they'd be waiting minutes to see the Irishman arrive. They were wrong. In one of the great race-saving rides, Roche limited his loss to an incredible four seconds. He promptly collapsed on the finish line. Oxygen was given. Four days later he stood in yellow in Paris.

Roche had won the Giro/Tour double, but it was to get better still. On 7 September he took to the start line of the world championship road race in Villach, Austria. He found himself in the lead group in the final kilometres, ideally placed to launch his bid for victory.

Aware that, compared to the other riders, he was an inferior sprinter, Roche went early, attacking off the front. It worked. He caught the others unawares and won by a single second ahead of Italy's Moreno Argentin.

One season, three jerseys: pink, yellow and rainbow. Roche had become only the second rider to win the triple crown of cycling, putting himself alongside the incomparable Eddy Merckx.

7 September

Albéric 'Briek' Schotte is born
(1919)

A name synonymous with the Tour of Flanders, Belgium's Albéric 'Briek' Schotte was born in Kanegem, West Flanders. Part of a large farming family, the young Albéric was charged with taking his brothers to school every day, six miles away, on his bike.

Such 'training' in the end paid dividends. He turned professional in 1940, after winning the Tour de l'Ouest, a professional race that allowed *indépendants* (semi-professionals) to ride. Schotte was awarded the win as he led the classification when the race had to be suspended due to the outbreak of war.

He rode his first Tour of Flanders in 1940, the youngest rider in the peloton, coming third. Thereafter he started the race every year of his twenty-season career, winning twice and finishing on the podium a further five times. He later estimated that punctures and mechanicals cost him up to four more wins. When he rode the race for the last time in 1959 he was the oldest rider on the start line. Schotte and Flanders: from 1940 to 1959; from youngest to oldest.

Journalist Albert Baker d'Isy called Schotte the last of the Flandriens. Others knew him as the Iron Man. On top of his Flanders wins he took two world championships (1948, 1950), two Ghent–Wevelgems (1950, 1955) and finished second to Gino Bartali in the 1948 Tour.

8 September

Jean Aerts is born
(1907)

Born in Laeken, near Brussels, in 1907, Jean Aerts was the first rider to win both the amateur and professional world championship road races.

In 1927 Aerts rode in the world championships at Germany's Nürburgring. For the first time professionals joined amateurs on the start line of the race, with the UCI deciding to award two titles – one for the professionals in the bunch and a second for the amateurs. Two races in one.

While Italy's Alfredo Binda won the inaugural professional title, Belgium's Jean Aerts was fifth over the finish line, the best result of any amateur in the race. Aerts was therefore awarded the amateur title.

Aerts went to the 1928 Olympic Games and then turned professional. As a pro he won the overall at the Tour of Belgium as well as clocking up twelve stage wins at the Tour, including a brace of mountain stages in 1933 despite being hailed as a sprinter.

In 1935 he won the professional world title on the roads of his home country, when he soloed to the victory in Floreffe. He was the first rider to have won both the amateur and professional world championship road race, a feat repeated by Swiss Hans Knecht in 1946.

9 September

First Ghent–Wevelgem is held
(1934)

One of the most prestigious classics after the five Monuments, Ghent–Wevelgem has had a rich and varied history since its inception in September 1934.

Formed by businessmen Leon Baekelandt, Gerard Margodt and Georges Matthys, for its first two editions the race was for amateurs only. The first edition, 120km long, was won by Gustaaf Van Belle. In 1937 the race was opened to *indépendants* before, in 1945 it became fully a professional event.

Over the years the race course has changed. Ridden over the roads and cobbles of Flanders, despite its name the race no longer starts in Ghent, but, rather, in nearby Deinze. The modern route takes the riders to the North Sea coast, before turning south and then west to the finish via a number of short but steep cobbled climbs, including the famous Kemmelberg.

It is the quintessential Belgian race: leg-killing roads, lung-bursting climbs, bone-breaking cobbles. Often ridden in spirit-sapping weather. Four riders hold the record for most wins, with Robert Van Eenaeme, Eddy Merckx, Rik Van Looy, Mario Cipollini and Tom Boonen all, as of 2014, on three victories apiece.

10 September

Le Petit Journal confirms first winner of Paris–Brest–Paris
(1891)

'Has she aroused enough emotions, this epic struggle! Finally, the winner, Charles Terront, passed the finishing post yesterday … less than 72 hours after leaving Paris.'

So began the story of the first Paris–Brest–Paris, told on the front page of the 10 September 1891 edition of *Le Petit Journal*.

Pierre Gifford, who ran the paper, had organised the race as a means of demonstrating the usefulness of the bicycle. It was a staggering 1,200km long and *Le Petit Journal* included daily dispatches of the riders' progress over the course of the race. Race rules dictated that riders had to use the same machine for the entire race. Rather than discouraging entrants, however, the huge distance seemed to attract those seeking a challenge. More than 200 riders started in Paris.

Charles Terront, riding for Michelin, won in seventy-one hours and twenty-two minutes, reportedly having not slept the whole race. Second was Pierre Jiel-Laval, over eight hours behind. Incredibly, 100 riders completed the race, some arriving days later.

Such was the mammoth undertaking, not only for the riders but also for the organisers, that it was decided the race would be held just once a decade. Maurice Garin, future Tour winner, would win the second edition in 1901.

The last Paris–Brest–Paris run as a race for professionals was in 1951. The event continues to this day for amateurs, but as a *randonné* rather than a race.

11 September

Lucien Buysse is born
(1892)

Belgium's Lucien Buysse turned professional in 1914 after winning the amateur 1913 Tour of Belgium. His professional career interrupted in its infancy by the war, he returned to the sport in 1919 and set about forging a name for himself.

Good performances in some one-day classics, and fourth in the 1921 Giro, led to some great rides in the Tour, where he sealed his reputation as a tough, gritty rider. Eighth in 1923 became third in 1924 became second in 1925. Then came the 1926 race.

The 1926 edition of the Tour remains the longest in history: 5,745km over seventeen stages. It was on stage ten that Buysse took yellow. It was a day that would go down in Tour legend.

At 323km, the stage was by no means the longest that year, but going over the Aubisque, Tourmalet, Aspin and Peyresourde it was certainly the toughest. And to make things worse the day brought horrendous weather: with a cutting wind, torrential rain and ice forming on the mountain tops, the dirt roads became nothing more than trails of mud. In his book *Le Tour de France et les Pyrénées*, Dominique Kérébel described the stage as 'Dantesque'.

Thunder roared and lightning danced around the peaks of the Pyrénées as Buysse made his move. He had long marked this stage as the crucial one. And he had already suffered far worse. Early in the race his daughter had died but his family had urged him to continue. Bad weather wasn't about to stall his march.

Buysse attacked early and led over the Aubisque. He was in the lead group over the Tourmalet but then struck out alone. He rose over the Aspin and Peyresourde in glorious isolation and rolled into Luchon more than twenty-five minutes ahead of the next rider. He had been riding for over seventeen hours.

Behind Buysse it was carnage. Only fifty-four riders made it to Luchon. *L'Auto* described it as a day of innumerable suffering. Riders had abandoned or taken shelter in bars, unable to carry on. At midnight search parties were sent out to round up the missing riders.

Buysse, though, was in yellow. And he'd keep it until Paris to record the best result of his career.

12 September

Alto del Angliru makes its Vuelta entrance
(1999)

Stage eight of the 1999 Vuelta a España was 175km. It started in Léon and finished at the top of a new climb. While never tackled by the Vuelta before, it was about to become perhaps its most feared climb. Its name? Alto del Angliru.

Then known only as La Gamonal, its inclusion came at the suggestion of Miguel Prieto, the communications director for the charity ONCE, which sponsored a cycling team in the 1990s. He had discovered the climb in 1996 and wrote to the Vuelta's then race director, Enrique Franco, recommending he check out the climb, saying it could become the Vuelta's Mortirolo (the legendary Giro climb).

Franco did just that and was sold on it. In 1998 the race announced that the next edition would feature a new summit finish, to be known as the Alto del Angliru.

It was a name that would soon strike fear into the hearts and legs of every Vuelta rider. Part of the Sierra del Aramo in Asturias, the start of the climb sits some 15km from Oviedo. Its sting is in its tail. The first six kilometres of its 12.5km length are fairly benign, averaging just over 6.5 per cent. But the climb's average is over 10 per cent. That tells you all you need to know about the second half of the ascent.

It is brutal. The final 6.5km average more than 13.5 per cent, with stretches over 23 per cent. The hardest section comes just three kilometres from the top, at Cueña les Cabres. It is here that the climb is at its steepest, and where, when the Vuelta visits, the crowds flock. Thousands block the road, a continuous wave of fans, parting only at the last second to leave a tiny corridor of noise through which the riders can grind. They roar on the poor souls battling this merciless mountain, a struggle against nature, desperate to keep going, ever forwards, ever upwards.

That first visit in 1999 was won by José María Jiménez. The race returned in 2000 but has since used the climb sparingly. In total there have been only six summit finishes on the Angliru. But due to its severity (it was once called an inhumane climb by the Spanish rider Oscar Sevilla), it has become one of cycling's most infamous mountains.

13 September

Diana Žiliūtė wins ladies Tour Beneden–Maas
(1998)

Lithuania's Diana Žiliūtė won the junior world championships in 1994 but really arrived on the scene in 1998 when she won the inaugural world cup, before going on to claim the world championship road race in Valkenburg, in the Netherlands.

The 1998 world cup was the first edition of a competition that continues to this day. Contested over a number of races throughout the season, the 2008 edition comprised six one-day races, from March through to September.

Round five was the Tour Beneden–Maas, a 120km race around the western Netherlands city of Spijkenisse. Having won race three in Ottowa and also registering two other top three placings, Žiliūtė was leading the overall standings going into the race.

It was a cold and grim day in the Netherlands but Žiliūtė was not to be beaten. Her team worked tirelessly for her, chasing down the day's breaks, and come the end she didn't let them down, winning the sprint and achieving her second world cup win. The result meant that she secured victory in the inaugural world cup with one race remaining. In the end her tally of 271 points was more than double that of second-place Alessandra Cappellotto.

Her season then got even better when she won the world championships in October. She would go on to win the Tour de France Féminine in 1999, the world cup again in 2000 and stages at the Giro d'Italia Femminile. She also took bronze in the road race at the Sydney 2000 Olympic Games.

14 September

Alfons Van Hecke wins 10th Kampioenschap van Vlaanderen
(1922)

In September 2015 the Kampioenschap van Vlaanderen staged its one hundredth edition, making it one of the longest-running races on the calendar. Classified as a 1.1 race on the UCI Europe Tour the race dates back to 1908 and has an impressive roll call of winners. Joining Alfons Van Hecke are such stellar names as Eddy Merckx, Rik Van Looy, Freddy Maertens and Johan Museeuw.

Van Hecke won the tenth edition of the race on 14 September 1922. The Belgian

had turned professional in 1919 and while he picked up decent placings in the Tour of Flanders, Liège–Bastogne–Liège, Paris–Roubaix and Paris–Brussels, his win represented his best result before his retirement from the pro ranks in 1926.

Except for interruptions by both world wars, the race has been held every year since 1908. Belgium's Niko Eeckhout holds the record for most wins with four victories.

15 September

Chris Horner wins Vuelta a España
(2013)

Until 2013 American Chris Horner's biggest victories had been stage wins at the Tours of Switzerland and Romandie, and a stage and the overall at the 2011 Tour of California. He was better known as a super-domestique, a rider capable of posting decent results in important races but one unlikely to be given his own team to lead in the very biggest races. In 2013 that changed.

Horner was nearly forty-two at the start of the 2013 Vuelta. His season had been interrupted by a knee injury at Tirreno–Adriatico, and although he finished that race he later aggravated it in Spain and had to sit out five months after having an operation to repair the damage.

After placing second at August's Tour of Utah, Horner headed back to Spain for the start of the Vuelta. It was a tough route, with eleven summit finishes, including the fearsome Angliru on the penultimate day.

And it was on the Angliru that Horner sealed the biggest win of his career. The American held the leader's red jersey ahead of the stage but he only had three seconds on Vincenzo Nibali. Nibali already had two Grand Tours to his name and was one of the world's premier climbers. Surely he would grab red back on the Angliru?

Horner shocked the Italian, though. Nibali attempted to shake him four times on the final climb, but Horner clawed his way back and then, with two kilometres to go, attacked himself. He took twenty-eight seconds out of Nibali in the final 2,000m.

Horner had won his first Grand Tour, becoming both the first American to win the Vuelta and the oldest Grand Tour winner in history.

16 September

Mariano Cañardo Lacasta wins Volta Ciclista a Catalunya
(1928)

Mariano Cañardo Lacasta may have won stages of the Vuelta and, in 1935, placed second in his country's national tour. He may have won a Tour stage, but during the course of his eighteen-year career the Spaniard became synonymous with just one race – the Volta Ciclista a Catalunya.

Lacasta turned professional in 1926, promptly coming third in that year's race around Catalonia. In 1927 he improved that to second. A period of Lacasta domination in Catalonia was just around the corner.

The Volta Ciclista a Catalunya had started in 1911 as a three-stage race of 363km. By 1928, its tenth edition, the race had grown to nine stages and over 1,300km. Lacasta won three stages and the overall by over five minutes. He was soon to become used to the taste of victory.

By the time he retired, Lacasta had won the race seven times – the last coming in 1939 – picking up fourteen stage wins in the process. He still holds the record for most race wins. Lacasta died in Barcelona, his adopted city, in 1987.

17 September

Eddy Merckx wins his last race
(1977)

It is unlikely that anybody lining the road in Ruien, Belgium, on 17 September 1977 was aware that they were about to witness cycling history. But witness it they did, for on that day those watching the Kluisbergen Criterium were the last people ever to watch the great Eddy Merckx cross the finishing line of a professional race in first place.

It was the final victory of a remarkable professional career that would last fourteen years, riding for seven different teams, and amassing a staggering tally of 525 race wins.

But it isn't just the sheer number of race wins that sets Merckx apart in the pantheon of cycling greats. It is the quality and prestige of the races that he won. He won a total of eleven Grand Tours, nineteen Monuments and three professional world championships. He is the only rider to have won every Grand Tour and every Monument. He is the only rider to have won both the Tour and the Giro five times. He is the only rider to have won every Monument more than once. He holds the record for Tour stage wins (34), days in yellow (96), and days in pink (78). He holds the record for most world championship wins, although he shares that one with Alfredo Binda, Rik Van Steenbergen and Óscar Freire.

No one had dominated cycling like it before; no one has dominated cycling since. There was a three-year period where Merckx won a third of all the races ,he entered. Not for him the tactical targeting of certain races. He wanted them all and he was ruthless about getting them. Pierre Chany once likened him to a matador 'thirsty for blood'.

The 1977 Kluisbergen Criterium would turn out to be his last win. He'd had a decent enough season by any other rider's standards – sixth in the Tour and more than twenty wins, but he knew his time at the top of the sport was coming to an end. He announced his retirement in the spring of 1978. The Cannibal had finally left the peloton.

18 September

First Grand Prix des Nations held
(1932)

For over sixty years the Grand Prix des Nations was considered the unofficial world championships of time trials. First held in 1932, the race was the idea of Albert Baker d'Isy and Gaston Bénac, journalist and editor respectively at the newspaper *Paris-Soir*.

By the early 1930s the idea of a newspaper organising a bike race as a means of boosting circulation was frankly less than original. But that didn't mean it wasn't still effective. It was also a matter of prestige. *Paris-Soir* was a well-regarded evening paper competing against *L'Auto*. It needed a bike race of its own.

Baker d'Isy and Bénac therefore decided to organise a race. It was to be a time trial with a distance of 142km, starting and finishing in Versailles.

The race, won by Maurice Archambaud, was a huge success. The French press lapped up the spectacle, and bike manufacturers quickly realised the commercial potential of a successful showing. Soon the event was being considered as a classic, alongside some of the biggest races in the calendar.

Although its importance faded in the 1990s, mainly because the UCI introduced an official time-trial world championships, the list of previous winners illustrated the prestige once afforded it. Coppi, Bobet, Anquetil, Merckx, Hinault – they all won this particular race of truth.

19 September

The last London six-day is held
(1980)

In 1967 Earl's Court had hosted London's first six-day meet for fifteen years. Still popular on the Continent, the format had fallen out of favour in Britain and it took the muscle of the cycling industry to get it reinstated.

Run alongside a bike show, the event attracted 40,000 spectators over the course of its six days.

Sponsored by lager makers Skol and with decent prize money on offer, the event also attracted a good field of international riders, including Peter Post, a rider who claimed more than sixty six-day wins over the course of his career.

The event, won by the Danish pair Palle Lykke and Freddy Eugen, was a huge success with near-record trading reported. 'Money, backing, riders, a hard-fought race devoid of corruption and doping scandals – the Skol Six had all these,' enthused the weekly magazine *Cycling*.

From that point on the Skol Six became a regular annual event. It moved from Earl's Court to Wembley in 1968, where it stayed until its final edition in 1980. Don Allen and Danny Clark stood on the top of the podium, the last of the London Skol Six champions.

20 September

Alejandro Valverde wins the Vuelta a España
(2009)

Once heralded as a rider able consistently to trouble those on the top step of the podium at the world's greatest races, Alejandro Valverde took his only Grand Tour win to date in 2009 when he won the Vuelta.

This had long been coming. Although Valverde abandoned his first Vuelta in 2002 during the stage to Angliru, he had returned the following year, finishing third overall and taking a couple of stage wins. He followed that with fourth in 2005, second in 2006 and fifth in 2008. Throw in a couple of top ten finishes at the Tour in 2007 and 2008 and you had a rider always on the brink of standing at the top of a Grand Tour podium, but never quite getting there. Valverde always seemed to have at least one bad day. And a bad day at a Grand Tour costs dear.

That changed in 2009. Valverde won the Critérium du Dauphiné but was prevented from riding the Tour after being banned by the Italian authorities following doping allegations. This not only stopped him from riding in Italy but, with the 2009 Tour briefly crossing Italy's border, it ruled him out of the race, too. With the Giro also off-limits he was free to concentrate all his efforts on the Vuelta.

It paid off. He took the leader's gold jersey (it has since changed to red) on the lumpy stage nine to Xorret del Catí and held it for the rest of the race. For a long time his lead was a slender one, just over thirty seconds on Robert Gesink. That was until stage nineteen when a bad day for Gesink ruled him out of the running and offered Valverde a little breathing space. His final winning margin was fifty-five seconds.

Since his 2009 win Valverde has returned to the Vuelta, picking up more podium spots but never repeating his visit to the top step. (See 25 April for more on Valverde's career.)

21 September

Émile Georget is born
(1881)

A rider of immense stamina, Emile Georget's best results came in severe tests of endurance. He won Bordeaux–Paris in 1910 and 1912 and Paris–Brest–Paris in 1911.

His best year at the Tour came in 1907. There he won five stages, held the race lead for seven days and finally finished third. He would probably have won the race had he not been penalised for an illegal bike change on stage nine to Bayonne. That year the race was decided on points based on stage placings, with the rider with the fewest points winning. Prior to the stage to Bayonne, Georget's (then) four stage wins meant he was leading the overall with a sixteen-point margin, but the Tour's organisers slapped a massive penalty on him for swapping bikes, ending his bid for the win. He continued nonetheless and picked up one more stage win on his way to Paris.

Georget is best known for what he achieved in 1911, the year the mighty Galibier was introduced to the Tour. On the stage from Chamonix to Grenoble, Georget escaped and led over the Galibier, in doing so writing himself into history as the first rider to scale the now legendary climb. He went on to win the stage in Grenoble by fifteen minutes. He would again finish third in Paris, his place in the story of the Tour established.

22 September

Giuseppe Saronni is born
(1957)

It's the closing 500m of the 1982 world championship road race. Out in front is the American Jonathan Boyer. Behind, the peloton is chasing hard, led, somewhat inexplicably, by Boyer's team-mate Greg LeMond.

Boyer rounds a corner and moves over to the left-hand barrier. To his right comes a sudden blur of blue. Boyer, head down, catches it out of the corner of his eye and looks over. Too late. The blur of blue is gone. After lighting the afterburners, Italian Giuseppe 'Beppe' Saronni has disappeared from sight to take the rainbow jersey.

Saronni turned professional in 1977, aged just nineteen. He recorded his first big wins the following year, claiming Tirreno–Adriatico and three stages at the Giro.

In 1979 he won his first Giro, again taking three stages in the process. It was the start of a very real rivalry with Francesco Moser. In his book *Maglia Rosa*, Herbie Sykes describes their relationship as 'Coppi and Bartali but with genuine spite'. Saronni won the Giro again in 1983.

Saronni could also mix it in one-day races, as that 1982 world championship ride proved. He won three classics in his career: La Flèche Wallonne (1980), Tour of Lombardy (1982) and Milan–Sanremo (1983). He retired from professional racing in 1990 with more than 190 wins to his name.

23 September

Roberto Laiseka records Euskaltel's first GT stage win
(1999)

On this day in 1999 Roberto Laiseka won stage eighteen of the Vuelta to record the first ever Grand Tour stage win for the tiny Euskaltel-Euskadi team, a team that would soon become one of the most loved in the peloton. Laiseka escaped on the final climb to Alto de Abantos to claim his win. It was fitting that it came in the mountains, for it was among the peaks of Europe's mountains that the team would soon be most prominent.

Established as a crucial pillar of a cycling foundation formed in 1993, with the aim of promoting and developing Basque cycling, the professional Euskadi team was comprised solely of riders who had either been born in the Basque Country or whose formative cycling years had taken place in the region.

Perhaps their best moment came in 2001, when Laiseka won the Tour stage to Luz Ardiden in front of thousands of fans wearing the distinctive orange of the team and waving the Basque flag. The tangerine dream had become a reality.

For the next twelve years the team continued to punch above its weight. At the end of the 2013 season, however, the team folded. 'We're leaving with the feeling of a job well done,' said sports director Alvaro González de Galdeano after the team's final race.

24 September

Italo Zilioli is born
(1941)

If Raymond Poulidor is the most famous of riders to have been beaten by Jacques Anquetil, acquiring the unfair moniker 'the eternal second' along the way, he can at least take solace in the fact that there is another hugely talented rider of the 1960s who, like him, never quite managed to win his national tour. Like Poulidor he was denied, on at least one occasion, by Anquetil.

Italo Zilioli was born in Turin. He enjoyed a successful fifteen-year professional career, picking up more than fifty wins, including a stage of the 1970 Tour (he also won the Tour's team time trial that year with his Faemino-Faema team-mates).

But it is for his performances at the Giro for which he is truly remembered. He rode the race eleven times, winning five stages and standing on the final podium on four occasions. He came second three years in a row – 1964, 1965 and 1966 – coming closest to winning the race in 1964 when he finished just one minute, twenty-two seconds behind Anquetil. He retired in 1976, having never quite been able to make it to the Giro's top step.

25 September

Identical twins Rasa and Jolanta Polikevičiūtė are born
(1970)

Born in Panevezys, Lithuania, Rasa and Jolanta Polikevičiūtė enjoyed, if not quite identical, then very similar cycling careers, riding for the same teams until 2009 when Rasa retired from professional cycling leaving her sister to ride for one more year with the USC Chirio Forno d'Asolo team.

During their careers, both women competed in three Olympic Games: Rasa in 1996, 2000 and 2004; and Jolanta in 1996, 2004 and 2008. Neither managed to win a medal, Jolanta recording the best-placed finish between them of fifth in the 1996 Olympic road race.

In the two biggest stage races, the Tour de France Féminine, and the Giro d'Italia Femminile, both have one stage in each to their name.

But while Jolanta has marginally more wins to her name overall, her sister Rasa took the biggest win of their collective careers when, in 2001, she won the 120km-long world championships road race in Lisbon. Rasa won ahead of compatriot Edita Pucinskaite and France's Jeannie Longo-Ciprelli in an exciting and hotly contested sprint to the line.

26 September

Erik Zabel announces his retirement
(2008)

'There are no gentlemen's agreements in the final kilometre ... The men are no longer riders, they are devils, all driven by the same goal: to win.' That was what German sprint powerhouse Erik Zabel once told *L'Equipe*, and he should know. Retiring in 1998, over the course of his sixteen-season career Zabel won more than 200 races, including eight classics and twenty Grand Tour stages.

Between 1996 and 2005, Zabel was arguably the world's premier sprinter. He was certainly the peloton's best when it came to Grand Tour points competitions – every year between 1996 and 2004 he went home at the end of the season with a points jersey in his luggage, winning the Tour's green jersey a record six times in a row before turning his attention to the Vuelta. His most memorable win came at the Tour in 2001 when, trailing by two points on the final day, his stage win on the Champs-Elysées gave him the win over Stuart O'Grady. His record of nine points competition wins at Grand Tours puts him at the top of that particular leader board, ahead of Sean Kelly, who has eight.

Zabel's classics haul includes a record three Paris–Tours wins (see 9 October) and four Milan–Sanremo victories. That should have been five but for a mistake in 2004 when, sure of the win, Zabel celebrated too early, allowing Oscar Freire to pip him at the line.

27 September

Anquetil destroys the field in the GP des Nations
(1953)

It was in 1953 that a young Jacques Anquetil burst on to the cycling scene: he was to remain there for quite some time.

By 1953 the Grand Prix des Nations, entering its third decade, had become one of cycling's most prestigious one-day events. Previous winners already included the likes of Coppi, Koblet and Bobet.

Anquetil was just nineteen years old. The month before he had pulverised the peloton during the Paris–Normandie race, winning by over nine minutes. Watching was Francis Pélissier.

Pélissier was the director of the La Perle team and he was looking for a rider who could challenge Louison Bobet, who had ridden into French hearts. He'd been monitoring Anquetil: good-looking, young, talented. Pélissier had his man.

And so, on 27 September 1953, Anquetil took to the start of the 140km-long GP des Nations a relative unknown in the jersey of La Perle, ready to rock the world of cycling. One minute up after just 20km the young Frenchman never tired, never fell away. As Anquetil smoothly caressed the pedals the margin kept growing all the way to Paris.

His final margin was over six and a half minutes. Anquetil had not just won, he'd annihilated the competition and he wasn't even a fully-fledged professional yet. The French press went into overdrive. 'Sensation! J. Anquetil, 19-year-old "Indé" dominates from start to finish,' shouted *L'Equipe*. Pélissier just smiled. 'You haven't seen anything yet, we haven't even started,' he said.

History would prove him right.

28 September

Emile Massons wins the GP Wolber
(1923)

A short-lived race, the GP Wolber ran as a one day race, from 1922 until 1931. The race, which was held towards the end of the season, was unique in that riders were selected to take part, with only those who had recorded top-three placings at that year's major one-day races in France, Belgium, Italy or Switzerland securing an invitation.

With such selection criteria the race quickly assumed great importance and was considered an unofficial world championship road race. When the UCI introduced a formal world championships in 1927 the race's standing fell away. After 1931 the format changed to a stage race.

The second edition of the race was held on 28 September 1923. It was 361km long and only twelve of the thirty-nine starters finished. It was won by Belgian Emile Masson Senior, who took over thirteen and a half hours. Alongside his GP Wolber win, two Tour stage wins and victory in the 1923 Bordeaux–Paris are his stand-out results.

In 1915 Masson Senior had a son – also christened Emile. Emile Junior would also enter professional cycling, mirroring his dad's achievements in winning Bordeaux–Paris (1946) and a Tour stage (1938); and then bettering them, taking wins in classics Paris–Roubaix (1939) and La Flèche Wallonne (1938).

29 September

Felice Gimondi is born
(1942)

One week before the 1965 Tour de France, Luciano Pezzi, director of the Salvarini team, invited a twenty-two-year-old Felice Gimondi to dinner. Gimondi was in his first season as a professional and rode for Pezzi's team. Just weeks earlier he had finished third in the Giro. Over dinner Pezzi told Gimondi he was going to the Tour. 'Open your eyes and ears wide,' he told his young charge. 'If an opportunity presents itself, grasp it.'

On stage three an opportunity did present itself and Gimondi, eyes open, took it. He won the sprint into Rouen and took yellow, holding it for five days. A stage win and five days in yellow: an excellent week's work for a Tour rookie.

But Gimondi was no ordinary Tour rookie. Just two days later he grabbed it back after a terrible day in the Pyrénées, over the Aubisque and Tourmalet, in fearsome heat. Eleven riders abandoned. Not Gimondi. He was back in yellow.

And there he stayed. He fought off an attack by Poulidor on Mont Ventoux and won time trials on Mont Revard and into Paris to secure the win. 'I won a Tour I hadn't even intended to ride,' he said later.

Although he would again win Tour stages, Gimondi never wore yellow again. He focused more on the Giro, where he won pink three times and finished in the top three on a further six occasions. He won the Vuelta in 1968, to put his name against all three Grand Tours. Gimondi was the complete rider and won three Monuments – Lombardy (twice), Milan–Sanremo, Paris–Roubaix – and a rainbow jersey before his career was out.

30 September

L'Equipe's 'worst Tour climber ever' is born
(1982)

At the 2009 Tour this writer was standing on the side of the Col du Petit Saint Bernard. I stood and cheered as the leaders passed. I applauded as the various groups of trailing riders followed, hauling themselves up the mountain. Then ... silence. I craned my neck down the road – no more cyclists to be seen. The crowd began to disperse, fans started cycling back down the mountain. But the broom wagon hadn't been through. There must be one more rider on the road.

There was. Kenny van Hummel.

Van Hummel had become accustomed to riding up mountains alone. Last into Saint-Girons, last into Tarbes, last into Verbier. Today he would be last into Bourg-St-Maurice. His combined deficit to the winners of those four stages? Over two and a half hours. The following day L'Equipe would run a story in which Jean-François Pécheux, a director on the Tour, described van Hummel as the worst climber in Tour history.

'I'll quit when I fall off my bike,' van Hummel said.

Unfortunately for van Hummel, and for cycling romantics everywhere, that was exactly what happened the next day. Dropped early on a mountain again, van Hummel was descending quickly, trying to regain time, when he crashed and was forced to abandon.

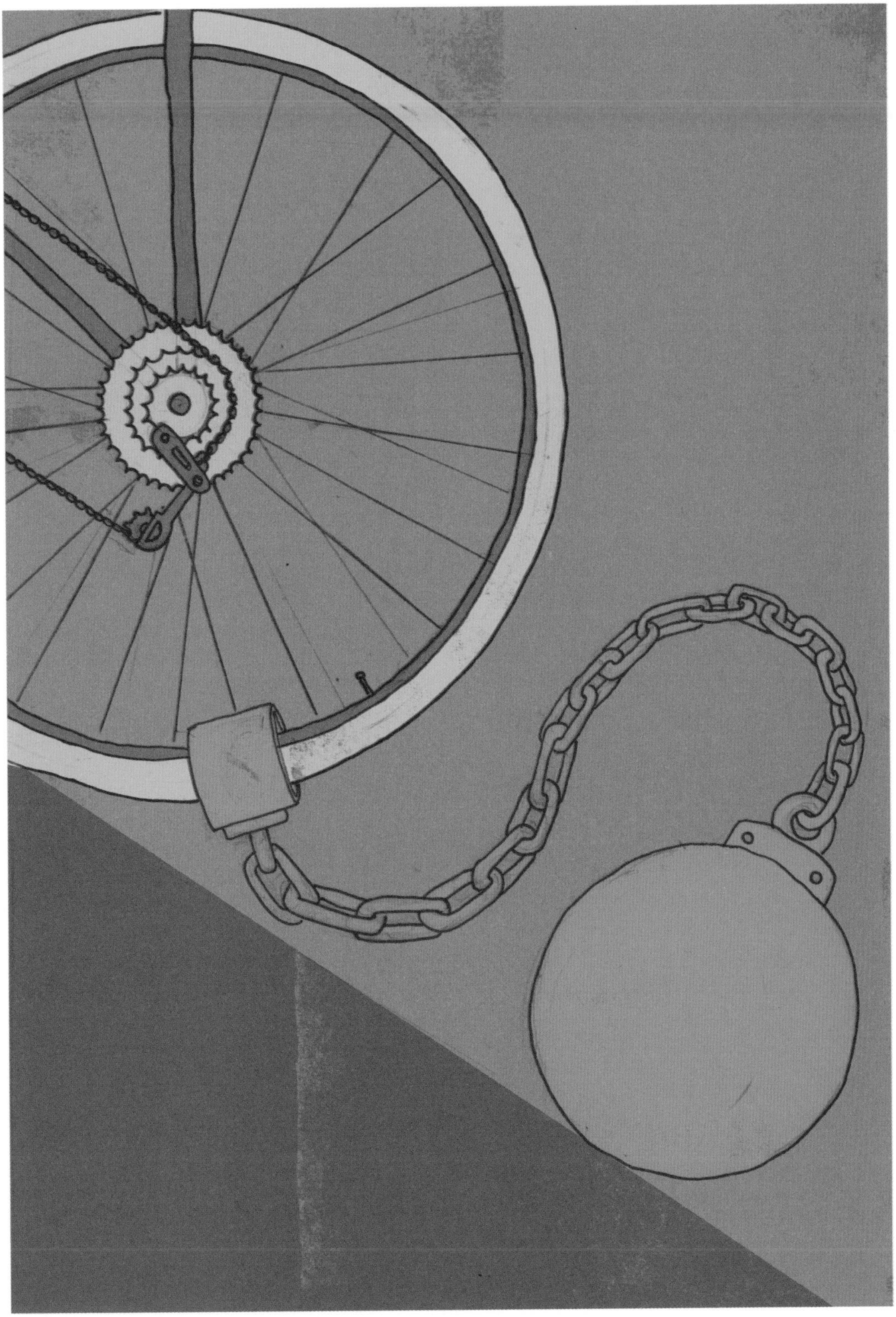

OCTOBER

1 October

Marianne Vos wins her first rainbow jersey
(2004)

At 9.30 on the morning of 1 October 2004, sixty-six riders lined up for the start of the women's junior world championship road race in Verona. Ahead of them were five laps of a 14.7km circuit, including five ascents of a tough three-kilometre climb known as the Torricelle. Among the starters was a seventeen-year-old Dutch girl named Marianne Vos.

Vos was born in 1987 in the southern Netherlands city of 's-Hertogenbosch. First attracted to cycling after watching her brother in action, she started riding a bike at the age of six. By eight she was racing and winning, and it was clear that the young Vos had a special talent for riding a bike. But back then no one could have imagined quite how special a talent it was.

At the 2004 junior worlds Vos showed her intentions within the opening kilometre. She attacked from the off but was quickly reeled back in – a little leg-warmer and teaser for what was about to come. Throughout the race attacks and escapes went and were brought back. No one had managed definitively to escape the clutches of the peloton. Then, on the final lap, everything changed.

Vos escaped on the climb of the Torricelle with 10km to go. Soon she had over twenty seconds. That was enough. Behind there was a desperate chase, but with three of her team-mates there to marshal things Vos powered to the win. She won by nearly thirty seconds. It was her first rainbow jersey and it would be by no means her last.

That seventeen-year-old Vos, loaded with potential then, is now widely regarded as the finest cyclist of her generation. The only rider who stands comparison with her is Eddy Merckx and she shares his nickname of the Cannibal. Vos has won everything worth winning. At the time of writing she has twelve elite world titles to her name across road, track and cyclo-cross and two Olympic gold medals. She has won the world cup overall a record five times; the prestigious Flèche Wallonne a record five times and the Giro three times. So far her wins number more than 300 and rising. Fast.

Marianne Vos: simply the best.

2 October

Millie Robinson wins the Tour de France Féminine
(1955)

Before Wiggins and before Froome. Before Cooke and before Pooley. When considering the British riders who have won the Tour de France you must add another name to the above. One that is today less heralded than the others, perhaps, but one who will for ever be known as the first Brit to win the Tour: Millie Robinson.

Jean Leulliot was a sports writer and organiser of bike races. In 1955, after the success of a three-day women's race called the Circuit Lyonnais-Auvergne, in which Robinson won all three stages and the overall, he decided to organise a five-day women's race in Normandy. He called it the Tour de France Féminine.

Britain sent a team of six and dominated the race. With a total distance of 373km, the race was split into six stages. Britain won three. June Thackeray took one and Robinson picked up two, including the decisive stage four during which she escaped, grabbed thirteen seconds on the bunch and took the race lead. She then increased her lead by winning the next day's time trial. Robinson and Thackeray finished first and second respectively, with two other British riders also making the top ten.

Robinson would go on to break the women's hour record in 1958. The Tour de France Féminine wouldn't be held again until 1984.

3 October

Oscar Freire wins third world title
(2004)

Four men share the record for most world championship road race wins: Alfredo Binda, Rik Van Steenbergen, Eddy Merckx and Spain's Oscar Freire.

Freire added his name to that select group of cyclists to have claimed the rainbow three times on 3 October 2004, in Verona, having already taken the rainbow jersey in 1999 and 2001.

The 265.5km race came down to a sprint of fifteen riders. Freire, his effort showing through his gritted teeth, powered to the win ahead of Germany's Erik Zabel after being given the perfect ride by his team.

Freire enjoyed a successful fifteen-year career in the sport as one of the premier sprinters in the peloton. Added to his three world titles are three wins in Milan–Sanremo and the classics Ghent–Wevelgem and Paris–Tours. He won four stages at the Tour, claimed the green jersey in 2008 and took seven stage wins in nine appearances at the Vuelta, wearing the leader's jersey twice but never completing the race.

4 October

Indurain wins world ITT title
(1995)

By October 1995, Spain's Miguel Indurain was one of the biggest stars in cycling. Earlier that year he had become just the fourth rider to win the Tour five times and the first to have done so in consecutive years. He was also a two-time winner of the Giro.

Indurain's wins had been forged in his rides against the clock. During his 1995 Tour success he won both the long time trials. He was the world's best time trialist, and so when the discipline was at last introduced to the road world championship programme, in 1994, it provided the perfect opportunity for 'Big Mig' to get his hands on a rainbow jersey.

He didn't ride the inaugural event, with the win claimed by Britain's Chris Boardman, but one year on Indurain travelled to Boyacá, Colombia, ready to stake a claim for a world championship title. Indurain was the main draw. His presence in Colombia attracted fevered attention.

The course was 43km, starting at 2,400m above sea level and finishing 300m higher. Indurain started last. At the first time check he trailed compatriot Abraham Olano by a single second. After 27km that had turned into a thirty-three-second advantage. At the finish it was forty-nine seconds. Indurain had added the rainbow jersey to his wardrobe.

Indurain only rode for one more season. He lost his Tour crown in 1996, then went to the Olympic Games and won time-trial gold, before retiring in January 1997. 'My family are waiting,' he said.

5 October

Henri Pélissier wins his first and only national title
(1919)

The name of Henri Pélissier loomed so large over French cycling during the course of his eighteen-year career, from 1911 until 1928 (see 22 January and 1 May for more) that it comes as a surprise to learn that during that time he only managed to win the French national championships once.

Henri was the first of the Pélissier brothers to get his name on France's national championship's roll of honour, winning the 1919 road race in Versailles ahead of Honoré Barthélémy. If it appeared to open the floodgates in terms of national titles, that wasn't to be the case.

The next year Henri came second to Jean Alavoine. He would come second again, in 1921 and 1924. On those occasions his younger brother, Francis, looked down at him from the top step of the podium.

Francis won the French national title three times in all – 1921, 1923 and 1924 – and came second on a further two occasions. Only Jean Stablinski has won the title more often. Another brother, Charles, also made the podium – in 1927 and 1930.

It was a remarkable period for the Pélissiers. From 1919 until 1931, there were only three years when the French national championships did not include a Pélissier on the podium.

6 October

Thor Hushovd wins Espoirs World ITT title
(1998)

In 2010 Thor Hushovd won the elite world championship road race. It wasn't the first time that the Norwegian had slipped on a rainbow jersey, however.

The God of Thunder had first come to prominence on the international stage some twelve years earlier. Already a double junior national champion in the time trial, and a winner of the Espoirs category in two classics – Paris–Roubaix and Paris–Tours – in October 1998 Hushovd travelled to Valkenburg in the Netherlands for the Under-23 time trial at the world championships.

While the Norwegian had picked up good wins earlier in the year, he had also suffered injury problems, to his knees in particular, that kept him out of racing for six months.

So Hushovd hadn't considered winning a possibility. A podium position perhaps, but not the top step, not the rainbow jersey. After nearly 33km riding against the clock in wind and rain, however, that was exactly where he found himself. The strength that would soon be obvious for all to see had taken him to the top of the pile in the dreadful conditions.

He was still only twenty years old and at the start of what would turn out to be a fantastic career (see 18 January for more).

7 October

Jeannie Longo-Ciprelli wins a fifth road race rainbow jersey
(1995)

When France's Jeannie Longo-Ciprelli took to the start line of the women's world championship on 7 October 1995 she was thirty-seven years old and looking to make history.

For six long years, Longo-Ciprelli had shared the record for most world championship road race wins. Along with Belgium's Yvonne Reynders, who took her wins in the 1950s and 1960s, Longo-Ciprelli had four wins. She wanted a fifth. She wanted to sit at the top of the tree alone.

The race didn't start well for her: she crashed on the second of five laps. In intense pain she continued (at the end of the race she would require stitches in an inch-wide gash in her leg). Finally she made it back to the leading group with two laps to go, broke away with team-mate Catherine Marsal and then, on the final climb, attacked and rode away and into the record books.

Fast-forward nearly twenty years and Longo-Ciprelli is still riding. She has had a career rare in both longevity and success. Her first national road title came in 1979, her most recent in 2011. That's a thirty-two year gap. In total she has claimed the national road race title twenty times, the national time-trial title eleven. As well as a five-time road race world champion, she is a four-time time-trial world champion. All those tallies are records. Add in track titles and Longo-Ciprelli has a staggering fifty-nine national and thirteen world titles to her name. And Olympic gold. And she won the Tour de France Feminine three times. That's a record as well although one she shares.

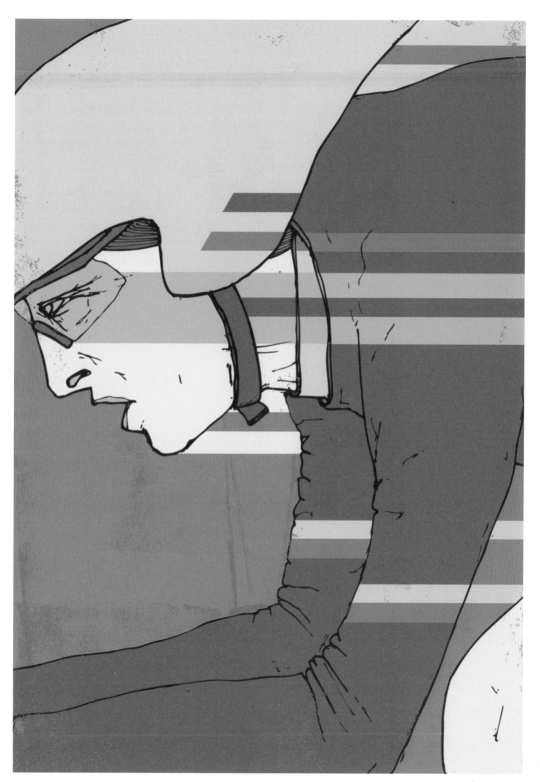

8 October

Philippe Thys is born
(1890)

Born in Anderlecht in 1890, Belgium's Philippe Thys was the first rider to claim three Tours. He first won the race in 1913, defended his title in 1914 and then added a third in 1920. It took thirty-five years for another rider to equal his record, when Louison Bobet won his third Tour in 1955, and another eight for Jacques Anquetil to beat it (in 1963). That fact alone means that Thys deserves to be regarded as one of the best riders in Tour history; factor in that his peak riding years were interrupted by the outbreak of war and you have a rider who perhaps could have won the race five or more times.

Because his successes came early in Tour history, with the race still in its infancy, Thys is sometimes overlooked when the great stories of the race are retold. In more than a hundred years of the Tour, only four riders have won the race more often, and yet the Tour tales of others are today far better known: Coppi, Bartali, Fignon – we talk of these men and the great Tours they won, but Thys won more Tours than any of them and yet we seldom mention him in the same breath. Sometimes we can be guilty of forgetting the first great Tour champion.

One of the first riders to focus his season on the Tour, Thys rarely won other races – the Tour of Lombardy and Paris–Tours are the only other races of real note on his palmares.

He is described by Belgian author Johan Van Win as a highly intelligent rider, a man who won races with his head as much as his legs and lungs. In an era of long-range attacks and solo escapades, Van Win says Thys was a rider who bided his time and attacked sparingly but definitively. He paints a picture of a rider ahead of his time, one who trained with specific aims rather than just getting the kilometres into the legs, and as an individual who was careful about what he ate. On the bike his low posture brought him the nickname the Basset Hound.

After his 1920 win Thys claimed another seven Tour stages over the next five years, but he would never again lead the race. He retired in 1927 with a total of thirteen stage wins and those three overall wins to his name.

9 October

Erik Zabel wins Paris–Tours for the third time
(2005)

Four men have won Paris–Tours, the sprinter's classic, three times. The most recent is Erik Zabel, who sprinted to his third title on 9 October 2005 (see 17 May for the others).

Zabel had first won the annual dash into Tours in 1994. He won it again in 2003 when he beat Italy's Alessandro Petacchi and Australia's Stuart O'Grady to the line.

Zabel's third win came in his final season with the German T-Mobile team. He had been with the squad, in its various incarnations, since 1993 and the race into Tours was his final appearance in their colours. It very nearly went wrong. With a little over 25km of the 252km race to go, and with an earlier breakaway that at one point had a lead of over nine minutes

caught, a couple of riders chanced their luck and escaped, desperate to avoid a sprint finish. The two who went, Philippe Gilbert and Stijn Devolder, would both go on to win classics in future years, with Gilbert becoming one the world's best one-day riders, but in 2005 they were still in the infancy of their careers.

With Gilbert and Devolder engaged in a tactical battle, the peloton burst on to the Avenue de Grammont, the race's now traditional, long, straight finish. In the closing metres they swept past the Belgian pair. Zabel timed his sprint to perfection to claim the win by half a wheel. It was his final major one-day race win.

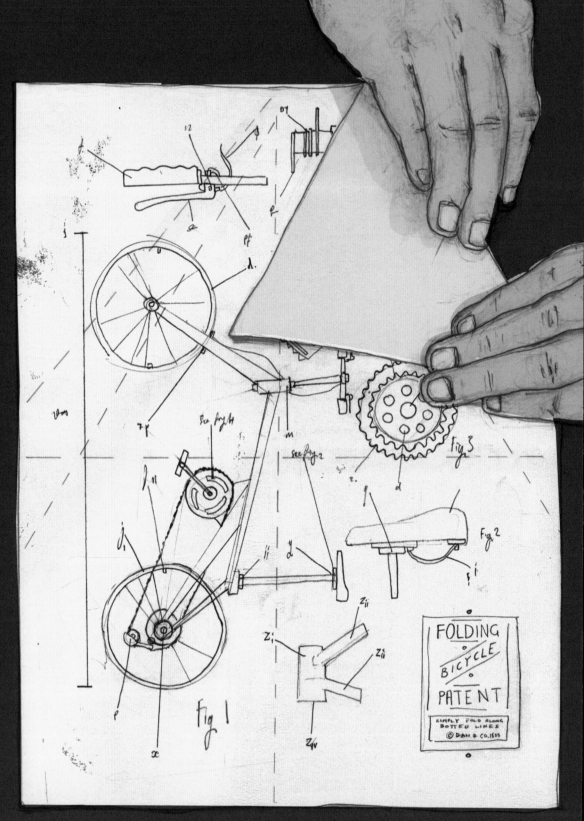

12

λ

See fig H

See fig 2

Fig 3

Fig 2

Fig 1

Zii

Zi

Ziii

Ziv

FOLDING
BICYCLE
PATENT

SIMPLY FOLD ALONG
DOTTED LINES
© DAN & CO. 1855

10 October

A collapsible bicycle frame is patented by Isaac R. Johnson
(1899)

For those commuters and travellers who take their folding bicycles on to trains, buses and planes the world over, a debt is owed to an American inventor who, in the final year of the nineteenth century, was granted a patent for the world's first folding bicycle frame.

Isaac R. Johnson, from Manhattan, New York, filed his patent application in April 1899. In it he described his invention as a frame that could separated to enable it to be 'compactly stored as, for example, in trunks or compartments or other small places, or conveniently carried, or the like'. This was made possible by the use of sheaths and sleeves, hinges and catches, slots and studs. The complicated assembly arrangements, painstakingly described and illustrated in Johnson's patent application, meant that the frame could be fully dismantled as desired. The patent was duly granted on 10 October 1899.

Technically speaking, while today's folding bikes bear little resemblance to Johnson's invention, those common links of convenience and practicality remain. Today there are numerous folding bike races, the largest of which is the Brompton World Championships. Organised by the folding bike manufacturer of the same name, the race involves competitors running to the folded bike, assembling it and then racing for just over 15km. All dressed in business attire. In 2014 the race attracted 800 competitors.

11 October

First women's Chrono des Herbiers is held
(1987)

The first women's Chrono des Herbiers was won by Jeannie Longo (now Longo-Ciprelli). It was the sixth time that the event had been held but the first time that a women's race had been included on the race programme.

Held in France's La Vendée department, the event first took place in 1982 as a race for amateurs before opening to both amateurs and professionals five years later. It changed again in 1995 when it became a solely professional race. For the past ten years it has featured on the UCI international race calendar, bringing the curtain down on its Europe Tour.

After that first edition, Italy's Maria Canins won the next two editions. Longo-Ciprelli wasn't finished, though, and came back to win the event again in 1992, 1995, 2000, 2009 and 2010. Her six wins mean she holds the record for most victories. In the men's edition that honour belongs to Pascal Lance with four wins (1987, 1988, 1994 and 1995).

The race's name changed in 2006 to the Chrono des Nations-Les Herbiers-Vendée.

12 October

Iranian cyclist Mehdi Sohrabi is born
(1981)

Iran's Mehdi Sohrabi hit the headlines in Europe's cycling press when he signed with the Belgian WorldTour team Lotto-Belisol for the 2012 season.

Why did his signing create headlines? Because of the convoluted way that UCI WorldTour licences are allocated. A finite number of WorldTour licences are granted to teams every year and they guarantee entrance to the world's biggest races. If more teams are chasing licences than are available, the combined UCI ranking points accumulated by the teams' riders in the previous season are used to help decide which teams get in and which teams are left out and have to rely on wildcard entries to races such as the Tour.

In 2011 Sohrabi had been plying his trade very successfully in Asia, winning the UCI Asia Tour title. He had accumulated a considerable number of UCI points. Whoever signed him for 2012 would get the benefit of those points, and with a number of teams battling for licences suddenly Sohrabi was hot property.

He signed for Lotto, duly helping them secure their spot. He lasted only one season with them, failing to win a single race, but his work was really done the day he signed. In 2013 he returned to Asia and to winning ways.

13 October

LeMond wins junior world championship
(1979)

When, as a teenager, Greg LeMond decided he wanted to be a professional road-racing cyclist he famously wrote on a yellow notepad a list of things to achieve. Number one on that list was to place well in the 1978 edition of the junior world championship road race. Number two was to win it twelve months later.

By the time of the 1979 junior world championships, LeMond had developed into a very promising rider, with two junior national titles to his name (1977 and 1979) and a placing in the top ten in the 1978 worlds. Now he travelled to Buenos Aires for the 1979 race focused on ticking off number two on his list.

At the close of the 120km race LeMond found himself in a two-man sprint with Belgium's Kenny De Maerteleire. In the sprint De Maerteleire came off his line repeatedly, forcing LeMond into the tyres that flanked the race circuit. The Belgian crossed the line first. LeMond, lucky still to be upright, came in second. But the commissaires didn't like what they had seen and relegated De Maerteleire. LeMond had his first rainbow jersey. It was the first time an American had taken the title. He followed the junior win with the elite title in 1983, adding a second in 1989, and remains the only man to have won both the junior and elite world road race titles.

14 October

Floyd Landis is born
(1975)

Born in Lancaster County, Pennsylvania, into a family of Mennonites, Floyd Landis came to international prominence in 2006 when he won his first Tour and then, shortly after, became the first rider to be stripped of it.

Landis first began competing as a mountain-biker, something he initially kept from his family, knowing that they wouldn't approve. He became national junior mountain bike champion in 1993 but by 1999 he had switched full time to road racing, turning professional with the Mercury team.

After serving as a domestique in Lance Armstrong's US Postal and Discovery teams, he moved to Phonak in 2005, into a team-leader role. Ninth in the Tour that year became first in 2006, despite intense pain in his hip from osteonecrosis, a disorder caused by lack of blood supply. With such a condition it was remarkable even to see him ride a bike, let alone win the world's toughest race. But he was stripped of the title after a positive dope test following a legendary stage in the Alps (see 20 July).

Then came the usual denials, court cases, funding drives and book. A long and expensive attempt to clear his name finally came to an end in 2010 when Landis admitted on the TV channel ESPN that he had doped during his career, saying the hardest phone call he had had to make was to tell his mother the truth.

15 October

Kelly wins his first classic
(1983)

By October 1983 Ireland's Sean Kelly was twenty-seven years old. He'd been a professional bike racer for seven seasons. He'd won stages at the Tour and at the Vuelta. He'd won the Tour of Switzerland and Paris–Nice. He'd won the points jersey at the Tour and at the Vuelta. He was a very successful cyclist – a leader of his team. But he hadn't yet won a major classic.

It was a puzzle that was hard to understand. Kelly clearly had the talent to dominate the classics but it wasn't working out. Some thought that perhaps he lacked the killer instinct needed in one-day races. It took until the 1983 edition of the traditional monument-season-closing Tour of Lombardy for Kelly finally and definitively to put any such thoughts to bed.

With three kilometres of the 255km race to go all the main favourites were together. Among them was Kelly. On his wheel was Greg LeMond. The sprint was on.

And what a sprint it was. Eighteen riders are credited in the results books with the same time but at the head of that select bunch were four riders: Kelly, LeMond, Adrie Van der Poel and Hennie Kuiper. At the finish line all four were spread across the road. Kelly nicked it from LeMond. Van der Poel was third. There were inches in it but Kelly had taken his first major one-day win.

The dam had been breached. Kelly would finish his career with nine Monuments to his name as well as a host of other one-day classics.

16 October

Samuel Sánchez wins his second Montjuïc hill climb
(2005)

Once one of the most famous hill-climb races in the cycling world, the 2005 edition of the Escalada a Montjuïc was held on 16 October with Spaniard Samuel Sánchez claiming the title for a second time, beating future Tour winner Carlos Sastre into second place.

But the race's future would prove to be bleak. In September 2008, just two editions after Sánchez's win, the race organisers were forced to pull the event, blaming lack of funding and sponsorship as most of Europe fell into deep economic recession. European cycling had lost another of its famous races.

It was a cruel blow. The Escalada a Montjuïc, held on the hill that overlooks Barcelona, had been run annually from 1965. It was a one-day event with two stages – a mass start ascent followed by a shorter individual time trial. The riders' times for both stages were added up, with the quickest overall time deciding the winner.

Among those winners were some of the best cyclists ever to take to the saddle: Bahamontes, Poulidor, Merckx, Thévenet, Zoetemelk, all won on Montjuïc, Merckx no fewer than six times.

The last winner was Daniel Moreno when he became the eleventh Spanish rider to add the race to his palmares.

17 October

Philippe Gilbert wins first monument
(2009)

Born into a family of cyclists, Belgian classics specialist Philippe Gilbert turned professional in 2003 with the Française des Jeux team after impressing in Belgium as both a junior and an Espoir.

In the six full seasons that he was with the team, Gilbert picked up a number of decent wins, including the Omloop Het Volk and Paris–Tours one-day races. In 2009 came a move back to Belgium with the Silence-Lotto team, and it was now that Gilbert's career really took off. A stage in the spring at the Giro was trumped by a fantastic run of form in the autumn as Gilbert racked up four wins in succession in October: Coppa Sabatini, Paris–Tours, Giro del Piemonte and then the Tour of Lombardy.

Gilbert's win in Lombardy came after he broke away on the climb of the San Fermo della Battaglia with six kilometres to go. He was joined by Spain's Samuel Sánchez but Gilbert outsprinted Sánchez to take the win. It was his first Monument and the first time a Belgian had won the race since Alfons De Wolf in 1980.

Today Gilbert has a number of classics to his name, including a second Lombardy title. In 2011 he became the first Belgian to win the three Ardennes classics (Amstel Gold, La Flèche Wallonne and Liège–Bastogne–Liège) in a single season. He has also won stages at all three Grand Tours and became world champion in 2012.

18 October

Tony Doyle wins his first six-day event in Berlin
(1983)

Britain's best six-day rider, Tony Doyle, rode his first six-day event in 1980 at the London Skol Six but it wasn't until 1983 that he would take his first win.

Doyle had finished fourth in the pursuit at that year's worlds and fifth in the points race. If he was disappointed with his performance, he had impressed a number of promoters, including the head of the Berlin and Dortmund six-day events, Otto Ziegler. Doyle was put in touch with Australian Danny Clark, a hugely successful six-day racer who was looking for a new partner. They rode their first event together in Berlin and won. Then they won again in Dortmund. It was the start of a fruitful partnership. Together Doyle and Clark would win nineteen six-day races over the course of the next eight years.

In 1989 Doyle's career, indeed his life, was nearly cut tragically short when he had a terrible accident during the Munich six-day race, which left him in a coma for ten days. So seriously was he injured that the Last Rites were read. Once he recovered, it took him months to learn to walk again, but to the astonishment of many, a year after the crash he returned to Munich, where he presented race tickets to the hospital staff who had saved his life. Those who attended watched their former patient win.

When Doyle retired from racing in 1991 he had twenty-three six-day wins, and two world championships to his name.

19 October

André Mahé dies
(2010)

Born in Paris in November 1919, for ten years from the mid-1940s André Mahé was a professional cyclist. Something of a journeyman, he rode for seven different teams throughout his career (eleven if you include regional teams assembled for the Tour), picking up just a handful of wins. But it is for one of those wins that he is remembered today.

It is 17 April 1949. Late afternoon. The velodrome in Roubaix is packed with expectant fans waiting to see the finale of the forty-seventh edition of the Paris–Roubaix classic. Three riders are approaching the velodrome: Mahé, Jesus-Jacques Moujica and Frans Leenen. They have minutes on everyone else. The three get to the track but a race official sends them the wrong way. Instead of sprinting to the line they are now cycling around outside, trying to get in. The race is slipping away. Moujica falls. Mahé and Leenen leave him. In confusion and desperation they try a door. It opens! They shoulder their bikes, go through the door and find themselves in the press tribune. The crowds, all peering expectantly at the usual entrance, are treated to the sight of professional bike racers climbing over seats, trying to get down to the track. There they remount and sprint to the line. Mahé takes the sprint and is awarded a bizarre race win.

The next arrivals are led in by Serse Coppi, Fausto's brother. They enter the velodrome the usual way and Coppi wins the sprint. Due to Mahé's diversion, Coppi then claims he is the first rider to have actually completed the race route. And so starts months of wrangling.

In November 1949 a compromise was finally reached: both Coppi and Mahé would be awarded the win. When you look at the history of Paris–Roubaix winners, that is why you see the names of both André Mahé and Serse Coppi listed in 1949.

Mahé died on 19 October 2010 at the age of ninety.

20 October

Christophe Bassons is suspended
(2012)

It was a twist in cycling's tale of doping woe that defied belief and one that briefly shook the sport on its already unsteady foundations. In October 2012 Christophe Bassons received a one-year ban for missing a doping test after the French mountain bike marathon championships.

Bassons had risen to prominence over a decade earlier when he was the only member of the Festina team not implicated in the 1998 doping affair that rocked the sport. During the investigation Bassons was considered a rider beyond reproach. In 1999 he rode his first Tour and in a daily column for *Le Parisien* wrote of the shock and surprise within the peloton at Lance Armstrong's performances.

In doing so, Bassons had committed the ultimate sin. He had implied that all was not as it appeared. He had spat in the soup and for that he was ostracised by his fellow riders. Armstrong told him he should leave the race, leave cycling. His team-mates refused to support him. He abandoned on stage twelve, never to ride the Tour again. Two years later he was out of the sport altogether. Bassons became the face of the fallen ones: the riders who refused to cheat during cycling's dirtiest era and forfeited their careers as a result.

But now he was banned, too? Bassons, exhausted, had quit the championship race, notified the organisers and gone home. On his way home he received a call telling him to attend a doping test within thirty minutes. By now too far away to get there in time, he missed the test. Suspension was inevitable.

There was no suggestion of anything untoward. Bassons was furious and appealed. The ban was reduced to one month but Bassons refused to accept it. He was furious with the French Ministry of Sport and the French anti-doping authorities. He appealed again and in May 2013 was finally acquitted.

21 October

Alfred de Bruyne is born
(1930)

Born in Berlare, a Belgian town in the region of Flanders, Alfred de Bruyne had a nine-year professional career that ran from 1953. De Bruyne's best years came between 1956 and 1959. In that four-year period he won three stages at the Tour (to add to three he had won in 1954), Paris–Nice twice, the Challenge Desgrange–Colombo three times (the precursor to the UCI rankings prize) and seven major classics.

His first classics win came in 1956 at Milan–Sanremo. Part of a group that caught an earlier breakaway and then snuffed out a volley of attacks and counter-attacks, De Bruyne escaped with around 30km to go and, in terrible conditions, rode alone into Sanremo. Quite a way to win your first classic. Seven weeks later he added Liège–Bastogne–Liège.

In 1957 he won the Flanders/Roubaix double and Paris–Tours before adding two more Liège wins in 1958 and 1959, becoming only the third man at that time to have won the race three times (Léon Houa and Alfons Schepers were the others). Both Eddy Merckx and Moreno Argentin would later beat that mark with five and four wins respectively.

After retiring De Bruyne stayed in the sport, working variously for television, cycling teams and writing a handful of books, including his memoirs. He died in 1994 at the age of sixty-three.

22 October

Wilfried Peeters retires
(2001)

Belgian rider Wilfried Peeters retired in the autumn of 2001 after a sixteen-year professional career. He was known as one of the peloton's premier domestiques.

His best results came in the spring classics. In 1994 he won Ghent–Wevelgem, taking the two-man sprint ahead of Franco Ballerini, and he landed on the Paris–Roubaix podium twice, finishing third in 1998 and then going one place better in 1999, when he was runner-up to Italy's Andrea Tafi. Peeters was riding for Mapei at the time, as was Tafi. Their team-mate Tom Steels finished third, making it the third time in five years that the team had recorded a 1-2-3 finish.

In 2001, Peeters' final season, he was again involved in a Paris–Roubaix 1-2-3, although this time he didn't make the podium himself. Now riding for the French team Domo-Farm Frites, Peeters escaped and with 25km to go had a lead of over one minute. That forced other favourites to chase and allowed three of his team-mates to sit in the chasing bunch and not work.

After two hours alone, Peeters was finally caught with less than 15km to go. But the team's tactics had played out perfectly. His three team-mates completed a clean sweep of the podium places. Peeters finished fifth.

After retiring Peeters became a *directeur sportif*, and at the time of writing works for the Etixx-Quick Step team.

23 October

Alex Zanardi is born
(1966)

In 2001 Italian racing driver Alessandro Zanardi suffered a huge crash during a CART series race at Lausitz, Germany. Returning to the track after a pit stop, Zanardi spun into the path of oncoming cars travelling at full race speed. He was struck by Alex Tagliani, the impact demolishing the front of his car. Zanardi's heart stopped seven times. He was given the Last Rites, but he survived, though he lost both legs.

He returned to motorsport, racing in the World Touring Car Championships for six years. In 2009 he took up handcycling, initially competing in marathons. His first major medal came in 2011 when he took silver in the T4 time trial at the world championships.

Zanardi made the Italian team for the London 2012 Paralympic Games, where he won two golds, claiming the H4 individual time trial and the H4 road race. He celebrated by holding his wheelchair aloft. 'I've had a magical adventure and this is a fantastic conclusion,' he said.

But the tale wasn't over. More world titles followed in 2013 and 2014 but perhaps his greatest achievement came in September 2014 when he completed the Ironman world championships in Hawaii alongside able-bodied athletes. Zanardi finished inside the top 300 of more than 2,000 competitors in this incredibly tough event, adding another chapter to an already extraordinary story.

24 October

UCI introduces the biological passport
(2007)

On 24 October 2007 the UCI announced the latest weapon in its battle with drug cheats – the biological passport. Heralded by cycling's governing body as a 'new stage in the fight against doping', the biological passport enables the sports' authorities to build up a picture of a rider's biological parameters in order to better identify unusual patterns emerging over time, the causes of which could then be investigated.

Introduced for the start of the 2008 season, the nature of the passport required that results be collated over a period of time so that individuals' performances could be assessed accordingly. The UCI was the first governing body to adopt the passport and the first to sanction riders based solely on biological passport evidence.

Since 2009 the passports have provided evidence of a number of suspected violations. In Britain one of the highest profile cases involved Jonathan Tiernan-Locke, who signed for Team Sky following a stunning 2012 season with Endura. In 2013 he came under investigation when his biological passport indicated abnormalities caused by blood doping from the 2012 season. In 2014 Sky terminated his contract. Given a two-year ban, Tiernan-Locke still maintains he is the victim of a flawed system.

25 October

Merckx sets hour record
(1972)

At 9.56 a.m. on 25 October 1972 a gun is fired into the air at the Agustín Melgar Velodrome in Mexico City. It signifies the end of Eddy Merckx's one and only attempt at the hour record. Merckx continues to cycle around the track, steadily slowing down. The crowd, numbering a few thousand, chant 'Eddy, Eddy' as he does so. Merckx comes to a halt and, head thrown back in exhaustion, lungs gasping desperately in the thin Mexico City air, is supported by his crew. On the scoreboard appear the words everyone has been waiting for: 'Eddy Merckx, New Record'.

For the previous hour Merckx had been the picture of concentration. Despite being warned about preserving his strength by no less a judge than Jacques Anquetil, Merckx had planned to start fast and he did just that.

By 20km he was already eleven seconds up on the record. Thereafter he never wavered. UCI records state that Merckx rode 49.432km, beating the previous mark set by Ole Ritter by 778m. Merckx's mark stood until 1984 although changes in bike technology and design meant that the UCI later had to recategorise some records (see 11 May for more on the evolution of the hour record).

26 October

Sarah Storey is born
(1977)

Dame Sarah Storey (née Bailey) is one of Britain's greatest athletes. Born without a properly formed left hand as a result of her arm being caught in the umbilical cord in the womb, Storey has dominated the para-sport scene across three decades and two sports. And she is still going strong.

Storey's first sport was swimming and she excelled at it. Determined one day to represent her country after watching the Los Angeles Olympic Games as a six-year-old, she not only trained relentlessly but repeatedly and doggedly pressed the authorities for invitations to trials. Her talent, focus and determination ensured she would not be overlooked. Storey took part in her first Paralympic Games at Barcelona in 1992 at the age of fourteen and won five medals, two of them gold. She followed that with more golds at Atlanta and silvers at Sydney and Athens. In all she won sixteen Paralympic medals in the pool across four Games as well as a host of world championship titles.

In 2005, still competing in the pool, Storey suffered a severe ear infection, which kept her out of the water for months. In order to maintain her fitness she took to the bike. It was to transform her career. By the end of the year Storey had claimed the para-cycling world record for the 3000m individual pursuit. A future on wheels beckoned.

Her first major competition on the bike was the 2005 European championships and she returned with a case full of medals – three golds and a silver. Soon everyone in para-cycling knew her name.

Since her switch to cycling Storey has ridden at two more Paralympic Games, claiming another six medals, all gold. Four of those came at the London 2012 Games, where her performances elevated her profile still further and after which she was awarded a DBE in 2013.

The number of Storey's wins is startling, and not all have come in para-sport. Such is her talent that she often competes and wins in able-bodied competitions. In 2010 she represented England in the Commonwealth Games and she has also won gold medals in world cup team pursuit races as well as claiming a number of national titles on the track. At the time of writing Storey has amassed 22 Paralympic medals, of which 11 are gold; 24 world championship titles; 21 European titles; 7 world cup titles, including two able-bodied; and over 140 national titles, five of them able-bodied.

'Knowing that all the hard work has come together and worked out is a special feeling,' she told me. 'The time you stand on the rostrum is the first time you get to be quiet and realise what you have done. It is a time like no other you get in sport.' It is a feeling that she knows better than any other British Olympic or Paralympic athlete.

27 October

Greg Hill is born
(1963)

One of the most successful BMX riders in history, US professional Greg Hill was taken to a BMX race by a friend when just ten years old. The young Hill was instantly smitten with the sport. Over the coming decades racing BMX bikes would come to dominate his life.

He turned professional at thirteen in 1977, and over the course of a career that would last until 1998 won numerous titles. He was one of the stand-out riders of the 1980s when BMX was still finding its place in cycle sport. He claimed five world championships (this before BMX was integrated into the UCI), as well as winning International BMX Federation (IBMXF) and ABA/NBL worlds races.

In 1983 Hill took the ESPN Series Pro Champion's title. The series was run over seven races and Hill won the final two races to claim the title. In an interview with website bmxultra, he said the win was one of his most prized.

Nicknamed the Businessman, Hill played a significant part in developing the sport internationally, not just by winning new fans for the sport with his performances but also in developing new technology and products. In 1983 he founded Greg Hill Products (GHP) and in 2005 he was inducted into the US Bicycling Hall of Fame.

28 October

Ina-Yoko Teutenberg is born
(1974)

A junior world champion on the track and on the road at the age of sixteen, and national champion at elite level on the track just three years later, Ina-Yoko Teutenberg turned professional in 2001 with the Saturn team. Wins soon came her way, including stages at the Tour de l'Aude Cycliste Féminine, a race in which she enjoyed success throughout her career and one where her final tally of twenty-one stage wins is a record.

It was after her move to the T-Mobile team in 2005 that her career really took off. Riding with the German team under the leadership of Bob Stapleton, Teutenberg flourished. She won stages at the Route de France Féminine and the Giro d'Italia Femminile, the most important women's stage race on the calendar. In 2009 she won the Tour of Flanders, securing her biggest one-day race victory, and in 2012 was part of the Germany team that secured the team time trial at the world championships.

Teutenberg was forced to retire in 2013 after a heavy crash during the Acht van Dwingeloo race ended her season early. Four months later, she announced she would not be returning in 2014. She retired with more than 200 wins to her name.

29 October

Jens Voigt wins Commonwealth Bank Classic
(1994)

Much-loved professional rider Jens Voigt rode professionally from 1997 until 2014, winning a number of high-profile races and endearing himself to his fellow professionals, the cycling media and the sport's fans because of his huge heart and personality.

His 1994 win at Australia's Commonwealth Bank Classic was his first outside Europe. After his win Voigt said he hadn't expected the race to be so tough: 'Before I came to Australia I thought, "Oh, Australia. Down Under, a little bit racing, little bit holiday. An easy race",' he told the *Canberra Times*. 'But now [I know] it is a really hard race.' It was the first of many entertaining post-race interviews that was to give Voigt a reputation as one of the more interesting voices in the peloton.

Voigt was a tough rider, known for driving hard at the front of the peloton and long-range escapes. During one Tour, when he had been at the front of the bunch and in breakaways for days on end, he was asked by Danish television how he did it. 'I say "shut up, legs",' he replied. That was soon to become his catchphrase.

His biggest wins came at the Tour (two stage wins), the Critérium International (where he shares the record for most wins – five) and his home Tour of Germany, which he won twice.

In 2014 he broke the hour record and then promptly retired. In his blog for *Bicycling* magazine he wrote: 'So my friends, don't cry because it's over. Smile because it happened!'

30 October

Apo Lazaridès dies
(1998)

Nicknamed by the French public *l'enfant Grec*, because his family hailed from Athens, Jean-Apôtre 'Apo' Lazaridès rode from 1946 until 1955. A talented climber, he was taken under the wing of René Vietto after the war.

And it was just after the war had ended that Lazaridès would take his most notable victory. With *L'Auto* closed, a number of interested parties were vying for the rights to organise the Tour de France. In 1946 two rival races were used as showcases to win the rights to relaunch the Tour.

The newspaper *Ce Soir* organised the Ronde de France, while nine days later *Le Parisien Libéré* joined with *L'Equipe* (the successor to *L'Auto*) to organise the Course du Tour de France. It was a five-stage race, starting in Monaco and ending more than 1,300km later in Paris.

Despite not winning a stage, Lazaridès beat his mentor Vietto to the overall win by nearly forty minutes. Lazaridès was awarded a yellow jersey in Paris and *L'Equipe* was awarded the rights to relaunch the Tour for the following year.

Lazaridès would ride in the Tour proper on seven occasions and, although he never won a stage or threatened the podium, he finished in the top ten twice. His elder brother Lucien also rode in the Tour, finishing third in 1951 and picking up stage wins in 1954 and 1955.

31 October

Binda wins Lombardy by 30 minutes
(1926)

By 1926 Alfredo Binda was the dominant Italian rider in the peloton. He had an armful of Giro stages and one overall title in the bag. He had the Tour of Lombardy to his name. And he was still only twenty-four, about to enter his prime.

Binda had won the 1925 edition of the Tour of Lombardy by over eight minutes from Battista Giuntelli. If that was an impressive margin it was nothing compared to what he would do twelve months later.

Sixty-nine riders started the 1926 race. The flag was dropped by the great Costante Girardengo, who had been kept out of the race by an injured wrist. In pouring rain Binda, at the head of the bunch, gradually saw his companions fall away as the day progressed.

On the first ascent of the Ghisallo, Binda found himself alone with nearly 160km to go. Rain falling, wind blowing. Stick or twist? Drop back to safety or go for broke? Binda knew what he had to do.

One hundred and sixty kilometres later Binda rode into Milan alone. The second-placed rider was Antonio Negrini. He turned up twenty-nine minutes and forty seconds later. The last of the twenty-four riders to finish came in more than two and a quarter hours after Binda. The Italian had decimated the field. No Lombardy winner since has come even close to recording a similar margin of victory. It was, in the words of La Stampa, a revelation.

1 November

Anquetil and Poulidor ride Trofeo Baracchi

(1963)

One of the most famous rivalries in cycling history was that between Frenchmen Jacques Anquetil and Raymond Poulidor. Though their cycling careers did not run at entirely the same time, as the 1960s progressed their careers became inextricably linked and it was impossible to talk of one without reference to the other.

Like their personalities, their careers were very different. Anquetil won many races but was considered a cold individual and never captured the imagination of the French public; Poulidor on the other, thanks to his warmth, won a lot of fans despite not winning nearly as many important races. It was a something that gnawed away at Anquetil.

In 1963 they came together to ride the Trofeo Baracchi, a two-up time trial in Bergamo, Italy, that had been held since 1949. Magni, Coppi and Baldini had all won the race in the past. So, in fact, had Anquetil. He'd first ridden it in 1953 but had to wait until 1962 to record a win, a long time considering he was the best time trialist in the business. Even more surprising was the manner of that win. Sprinter Rudi Altig had to carry the Frenchman, doing huge turns on the front and even pushing his partner along. Anquetil was so exhausted that when he entered the finale at the Vigorelli Velodrome he promptly crashed into a post. Despite Anquetil's travails the pair still won. The after-race photos show an Anquetil bruised, bloodied and looking a little humiliated, anything but victorious.

One year later, now paired with Poulidor, Anquetil was set on making amends.

It didn't quite go to plan. Over the course of the 113km race there were only ever two teams in the hunt for the win: Anquetil and Poulidor and their compatriots Joseph Velly and Joseph Novales. At the 35km mark Velly and Novales led by two seconds over Anquetil and Poulidor. Thirty kilometres later that had grown to eighteen. Over the second half of the race Anquetil and Poulidor gradually whittled away at the lead but Velly and Novales held on, their ultimate winning margin being nine seconds.

Anquetil would go on to win the race on another two occasions. Poulidor never did.

2 November

First Vuelta a Bolivia starts
(2008)

The first Vuelta a Bolivia took place in 2008, its roots in the Doble Copacabana de Ciclismo race that had been run by Fides Ciclismo since 1994. That was a two-day affair that took the riders from La Paz to the Copacabana Sanctuary on Lake Titicaca, where there is a shrine to the Virgen de Copacabana, the patron saint of Bolivia, before returning to La Paz.

The race gradually grew in length and importance. In 2000 it was granted UCI status and by 2007 it totalled over 950km and six days. It was now one of the most important sporting events in Bolivia.

In 2008 it changed. Now called the Vuelta a Bolivia, the new race came with a mission to integrate the country through cycling. 'We want much of Bolivia to vibrate with this party,' the organisers said.

Incredibly tough, with a route that for the most part was over 3,000m with a highpoint of nearly 4,500m, the race was the highest on the UCI calendar. The first edition ran for eight days and 1,277km and was won by Fernando Camargo.

Unfortunately the race would last only six editions, folding after the 2013 edition failed to secure financial backing. Perhaps the 'party' will return one day.

3 November

Brian Robinson, first Brit to finish the Tour, is born
(1930)

Until 1955 Brian Robinson's most notable result had been second in the Tour of Britain. Robinson, born in Yorkshire, had turned professional in 1955. In July of that year he headed to the Tour as part of a ten-man Great Britain team.

The team was unprepared for what lay ahead. None of them had taken part in a race of such scale and importance. With just ten stages of the twenty-two-stage race gone, they were down to two riders – Robinson and Tony Hoar. Both held on to finish the race, Hoar finishing sixty-ninth, dead last, over six hours back. Robinson was twenty-ninth, a result that meant he became the first Brit to finish the Tour.

Of Britain's class of '55, Robinson was the only one to return to the race. In all he rode seven Tours, his best placing fourteenth in 1956. In 1958 he recorded another first when he won stage seven, from Saint-Brieuc to Brest. Robinson was part of a three-man escape and actually crossed the line second but was awarded the win by the commissaires. It was the first time a British rider had won a stage in the race. He won a second the year after, soloing into Chalon-sur-Saône.

Away from the Tour his biggest win came at the 1961 Critérium du Dauphiné, where he won a stage and then the overall by over six minutes.

4 November

Éric Barone, holder of bike world speed record, is born
(1960)

Nicknamed le Baron Rouge, Frenchman Eric Barone holds the world record for the fastest speed ever recorded on a bicycle.

Barone holds two records for speeds set on a prototype bike on both snow and gravel. Markus Stöckl holds the records for speeds on both surfaces set using a serial production bike.

Barone, a former stuntman, set his first speed record in 1994 when he recorded 151.57kmh at the Alpine ski resort of Les Arcs. One year later he went an incredible 42kmh faster and twelve months on again he reached 200kmh.

By now his equipment was far more sophisticated. In less than four years he had gone from essentially being a man in a ski-suit on a mountain bike to resembling a superhero perched on a machine with looks more in common with a F1 car than the humble bike.

In 2000 Barone returned to Les Arcs. There he set the record that still stands today: 222.22kmh. He set the record for speed on gravel eighteen months later on the Cerro Negro volcano in Nicaragua, where he reached 172.661 kmh.

Aged fifty-four at the time of writing, Barone is still going strong and trying to beat his own records.

5 November

Thomas (Tommy) Godwin is born
(1920)

In 1948 Tommy Godwin won two bronze medals in the cycling events at the London Olympic Games, riding the team pursuit and, with just two days' notice, the one-kilometre time trial.

Godwin had been born in Connecticut, USA, in 1920 to British parents, the family returning to Britain in the 1930s. Godwin's interest in cycling was inspired by the stories of the Olympic Games. His father once asked him as a child if he would run for him in the Olympics. Instead, he ended up riding for him.

After his competing days were over Godwin remained in the sport. He opened a bike shop in 1950 and started coaching, a move that would ultimately lead to him becoming Britain's first paid national coach. He organised the first training camp to Majorca and took his team to the 1964 Olympics in Tokyo.

Godwin remained active until his final days. He was instrumental in the successful bid to renovate the Herne Hill Velodrome in south London, the scene of his Olympic medal winning performances, and in 2012 carried the Olympic torch through his home town of Solihull.

Godwin passed away in November 2012. Brian Cookson, then the president of British Cycling, paid tribute to him, saying: 'Our sport is privileged to have been associated with him.'

6 November

Cofidis trial begins in Paris
(2006)

An investigation into doping that had started in 2004 at the French Cofidis team finally reached its conclusion in a criminal trial that began in Paris on 6 November 2006.

Ten people associated with the team were facing charges. A technician, pharmacist and soigneur were charged with supplying drugs while seven cyclists were accused of acquiring and possessing banned substances.

Among the cyclists was Britain's David Millar. Millar had already confessed to using the banned drug EPO after his apartment was raided in 2004. By the time of the trial he had already served a two-year ban from the sport and had returned to the peloton with the Spanish team Saunier-Duval a committed anti-doping campaigner.

Millar testified to the culture at the team, describing it as one of 'get results and do what you have to do' to win. Two months after the end of the five-day trial the sentences were announced. Millar was acquitted, the other cyclists received suspended sentences.

Millar went on to ride for a further eight seasons, becoming a rider for, and part-owner of, the Garmin team. He remained vociferous about driving doping from the sport and retired in 2014 as one of the most intelligent and respected voices in the peloton.

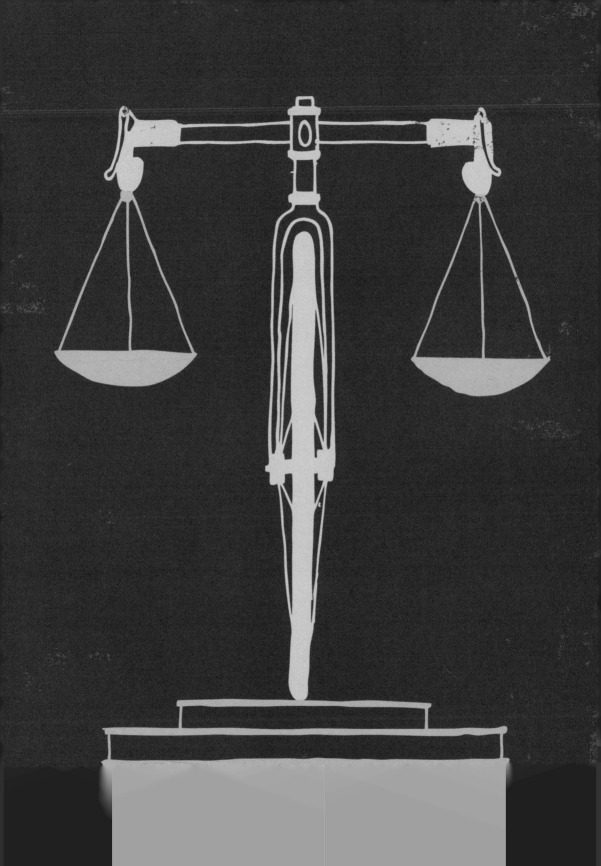

7 November

First long-distance road race is held – Paris–Rouen
(1869)

Bicycle racing first took place in France in the late 1860s. A plaque in Paris states that the first races were held in May 1868 in the Parc de Saint-Cloud, although there is evidence of earlier races. What is certain is that the Saint-Cloud races were a great success. They took place over 1,000m (apart from one which challenged riders to go as far and as slowly as they could without falling) and attracted a great deal of interest. Soon races were being held all over the country.

The courses were always fairly short and some felt that the fledgling machines, known as *vélocipèdes*, were incapable of covering longer distances. The owners of one of the principal manufacturers, the Michaux Company, had organised the Saint-Cloud races. Buoyed by their success, and keen to prove the robustness of their machines, they organised a longer race.

With assistance from the fortnightly newspaper *Le Vélocipède Illustré*, on 7 November 1869 came Paris–Rouen, the first long-distance bicycle race. The route was 123km and hundreds took part. James Moore, born in Britain but then living in Paris, won in a time of ten hours, forty-five minutes to claim the prize of 1,000 francs. Thirty-four riders made it to Rouen, including the mysteriously named 'Miss America'.

8 November

Léon Houa is born
(1867)

Born in Liège, Léon Houa won the first three editions of the one-day classic Liège–Bastogne–Liège.

Known as *la Doyenne*, the Old Lady, Liège–Bastogne–Liège is the oldest major classic still raced today and one of the five most important one-day races of the season. The first edition took place in 1892, organized by the Liège Cyclists Union. It was for amateurs only and thirty-three riders started out from Liège shortly before 5.40 on the morning of 29 May for the 250km race.

Léon Lhoest, who had won the amateur national championships two years earlier, was the favourite. Soon there were three riders at the head of the race: Lhoest, Houa and Louis Rasquinet. When Lhoest punctured, Houa told his coach, who was following, to pass him his bike. It was an act of huge generosity. But then Lhoest punctured again. They had not yet ridden halfway.

Houa rode alone for the rest of the race. He crashed 10km from the finish, breaking a pedal and so was forced to finish the race pedalling with just one leg. Lhoest finished second, twenty-two minutes down.

Houa returned to win again in 1893. In 1894 he turned professional. That year *la Doyenne* was opened to professional riders for the first time. Houa again entered and again won. Later that year he won Belgium's first professional national championships.

He retired from professional riding just two years later.

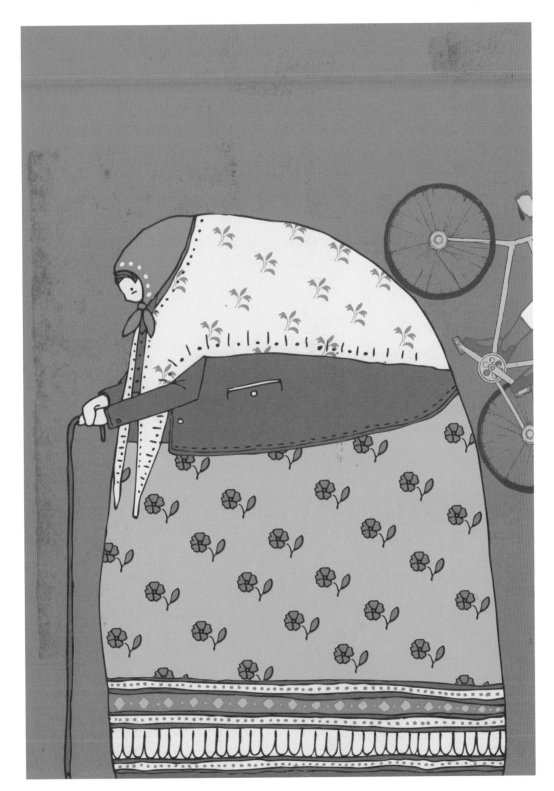

9 November

Corriere dello Sport Discobolo award given to Castelli
(1979)

Awarded the Discobolo by the Italian newspaper *Corriere dello Sport* for revolutionising cycling apparel on 9 November 1979, the story of the Italian sports clothing manufacturer Castelli starts over a century earlier.

In 1876 a tailor named Vittore Gianni opened a shop in Milan. He provided clothing for a wide range of sportsmen and women but it wasn't until nearly thirty-five years later that he started working with cyclists, including a young Alfredo Binda.

Working for Gianni was one Armando Castelli, who would eventually take over the shop. His son, Maurizio, later joined the family firm, working for his father.

It was Maurizio who started the Castelli brand in 1974. It soon became known for its design-led innovation: Lycra shorts … thermal winter clothing … aerodynamic skinsuits … they all came from Castelli. The company invented a dye process that enabled the names of sponsors to be integrated into Lycra clothing and were also responsible for inflicting the first coloured cycling shorts on an unsuspecting cycling world during the 1981 Giro.

Maurizio died in 1995 at the young age of forty-seven, suffering a heart attack while out cycling. His name, though, lives on through one of cycling's most well-known and respected brands.

10 November

Kristina Vogel is born
(1990)

Kristina Vogel is a German track sprinter who has won multiple world championships and took gold at the London Olympic Games in the team sprint, the first time the event had been included in the women's Olympic programme.

Vogel was born in Leninskoje, Kyrgyzstan, and moved to Germany with her parents before her first birthday. By the time she was seventeen, she was a junior national, European and world champion.

Two years later she was involved in an accident while out training. She was placed in a medically induced coma for two days having suffered multiple fractures. Remarkably, the following year she was

back racing on the track, claiming three national titles (her first at elite level) and winning the sprint at the Cali World Cup meet.

A first elite world title came in 2012 in the team sprint, riding with Miriam Welte. The pair then went on to win gold in London, beating Great Britain in the semi-finals and China in the finals (both wins coming after the opposition teams were relegated for rule infringements).

Vogel continues to rule the sprint events on the track, winning five more world titles and ending the 2013/14 season top of the UCI rankings for the team sprint, match sprint and keirin disciplines.

11 November

Tour Director Christian Prudhomme is born
(1960)

Throughout its ongoing 112-year history, the Tour de France has had only eight men at its helm.

Henri Desgrange, the father of the Tour, held the reins until ill health forced him to pass the baton on to the head of *L'Auto*, Jacques Goddet, in 1936. Goddet retained the post when the race returned following the Second World War and held it until 1962, when he was joined by Félix Lévitan. Lévitan was then the head of the newspaper *Le Parisien Libéré* and that paper's owner, Emilien Amaury, had agreed to sponsor the race but with his own man at the top. Together Goddet and Lévitan ran the race for another twenty-five years and are credited with making it the commercial success it is today. In all, Goddet was in charge of the race for fifty years. Today a memorial to him stands at the top of the Col du Tourmalet.

The race's current director is Christian Prudhomme. Born on 11 November 1960, Prudhomme took over the Tour in 2007. A former sports reporter for radio and television, he has proved to be something of an innovator. With his background comes an awareness of what makes great viewing on TV. Shorter mountain stages to encourage more aggressive riding, fewer time-trial kilometres and stages full of short but sharp climbs have become his trademark as he continuously looks for new directions in which to take his race.

12 November

The Red Devil wins Lombardia
(1905)

Nicknamed the Red Devil for his favoured scarlet jersey Giovanni Gerbi had a rather cunning approach to winning races. In 1905 he won the inaugural Tour of Lombardy, 230km starting and finishing in Milan. There were fifty-four starters on a day of terrible cold and dense fog and Gerbi had done his homework. He knew the route intimately. He knew the roads were in a bad way and that his route knowledge could gain him a huge advantage if he used it well.

Accounts vary as to the precise details of what followed, but in his book, *La Fabuleuse Histoire des Grandes Classiques et des Championnats du Monde* (1979), Pierre Chany tells us that Gerbi discovered a section early in the race where the road narrowed to a point through which only one rider at a time could squeeze. Aware that it was a key strategic point in the race, the Red Devil hatched a plan. He would fake abandoning shortly before the road narrowed, leaving the bunch to ride headlong into the impassable section.

A pile-up was all but guaranteed, leaving the wily Gerbi to pick his way through the carnage and ride alone to victory while everyone else sorted themselves out.

And so Gerbi came to ride the final 199km of the inaugural Tour of Lombardy alone. He had twenty minutes' advantage at Lecce and wasn't yet halfway. While his initial break may have had much to do with his cunning, the rest was down to his legs. By the time he powered into Milan his lead had grown to over forty minutes. The Red Devil was the first winner of Lombardy.

In 1907 Gerbi would again cross the finish line of Lombardy in first place. Again he had employed a little cunning, this time involving locked level-crossing gates, tacks and nails, and pacing from training buddies. But the organisers had grown tired of Gerbi's 'tactics' and he was disqualified.

Gerbi rode until 1932 (see 14 May) but that 1905 Lombardy win would remain his biggest victory, establishing his place in history as the first winner of the Race of the Falling Leaves.

13 November

James 'Choppy' Warburton is born
(1845)

Recognised as one of cycling's first coaches, James 'Choppy' Warburton was born in Lancashire in 1845. He grew into a man of great athletic ability, becoming a national amateur athletics champion and travelling to the USA to race.

He gained a reputation of selling his performances to the highest bidder and was accused of running for gangs and bookmakers and only winning when he was told to by his associates, many of whom were of ill repute.

Warburton's running days ended in 1892, whereupon he turned his focus on to the cycling world. He trained a number of cyclists, including the Welshman Jimmy Michael, who became a world champion on the track in 1895.

However, Warburton's reputation for dark dealings followed him into cycling. With great show he would produce a black bottle at races and administer its contents to his riders, often with startling effect. Curiosity grew as to the bottle's contents and Warburton became known as a coach who doped his riders. In 1896 Michael himself accused Warburton of poisoning him during a race when he cycled off in the wrong direction after sipping the contents of Warburton's bottle. Warburton filed for libel against Michael but the case never made it to court.

Although nothing was ever categorically proven, and despite the fact that at the time there were no anti-doping regulations, Warburton was eventually banned from attending races by the National Cycling Union. He died in 1897, aged fifty-two.

14 November

British League of Racing Cyclists is formed
(1942)

With the relatively new invention of the bicycle being viewed with suspicion by the upper classes in Britain, in 1890 the National Cycling Union (NCU) banned road racing on bicycles. It meant that while in mainland Europe the sport went from strength to strength, developing quickly and capturing popular imagination, in Britain official races were restricted to the track. It would be more than sixty years before officially sanctioned road races were re-established.

An underground movement emerged. Time trials were organised discreetly by the Road Racing Council (today known as the CTT) and run under the cover of near darkness, with riders wearing black and no race numbers. Eventually the NCU came to accept there was little it could do to prevent time trials on open roads. Officially sanctioned events soon followed.

Mass-start road races remained banned, however, but the NCU was continuously lobbied by Percy Stallard, a road-racing enthusiast who had competed in the amateur world championships (see 1 September).

With the NCU standing firm, Stallard took matters into his own hands and organised races himself. On 14 November 1942 he formed the British League of Racing Cyclists (BLRC). It was hugely successful and set in motion the chain of events that would lead both to the first British team going to the Tour de France and the first Tour of Britain.

In 1959 the NCU and the BLRC finally merged to become the British Cycling Federation.

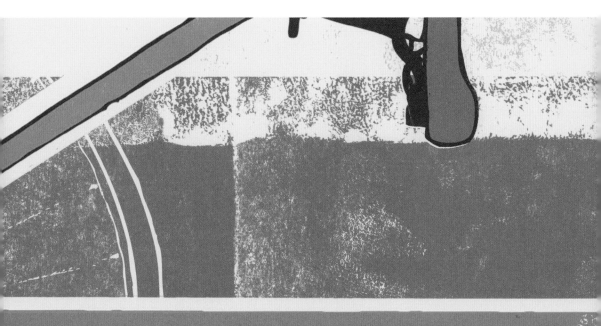

15 November

Urs Freuler wins European sprint title
(1981)

Urs Freuler was a professional rider from 1980 until 1995. Born in Bilten, Switzerland, he rode on the road and on the track, finding success on both.

Having won his first European title the previous year in the omnium, in 1981 Freuler won two more European championship titles. First he successfully defended his omnium title, before two days later winning the sprint title in front of 7,000 fans in Dortmund.

Freuler would only win one more European title (the 1987 omnium) but that was because he had moved on to bigger things. Over the course of his career he claimed ten rainbow jerseys on the boards, including eight points race world titles, seven of them in a row. His eight wins are a record in that event, double the number of anyone else.

Famous for his trademark moustache, on the road Freuler won multiple stages at the two biggest races in his homeland – the Tour de Romandie and Tour de Suisse. He tackled one Tour, abandoning (as planned) before the mountains, but managing to pick up a stage win before leaving. He rode the Giro more often, winning fifteen stages and, in 1984, taking the points jersey.

16 November

The Tour of Rwanda goes international
(2009)

Born in 1988 as a race for cyclists from Rwanda and neighbouring countries only, in 2009 the Tour of Rwanda became an international event as part of the UCI Africa Tour. This was the dream of Aimable Bayingana, the head of the Rwanda Cycling Federation. He wanted to give something to the people of a country that had experienced unimaginable horrors, when an estimated 800,000 were murdered during the 1994 genocide. As with most cycle races, his overall aim was to showcase the country to the world by having professional cyclists race on its roads.

So, on 16 November 2009, for the first time there were riders from France, Germany, Portugal and the Netherlands among the sixty-three-strong peloton that started the eight-stage, 1,069km Tour of Rwanda. Nine days later Morocco's Adil Jelloul, a multiple national champion, was crowned as the race winner with a three-minute advantage over compatriot Abdelatif Saadoune. Making up the podium places was home rider and 2008 winner Adrien Niyonshuti, a man who had lost six brothers and sisters in the genocide.

17 November

Lucien Michard is born
(1903)

Born in Epinay-sur-Seine, France, Lucien Michard was one of the world's finest track sprinters in the late 1920s and early 1930s. As an amateur he won multiple national and world titles before winning gold in the Paris 1924 Olympic Games. He turned professional in 1925. Multiple national and world titles would follow over the next ten years.

Michard won four sprint world championships in a row, from 1927 until 1930, but his most famous world championship ride came in 1931, when he was awarded second place despite having crossed the line first.

The 1931 track world championships were held in Copenhagen. The sprint title came down to Michard and a Danish rider, Willy 'Falk' Hansen. Michard, four-time reigning champion and recent winner of the GP de Paris, was the overwhelming favourite. However, Hansen had home advantage. In the first race the crowd roared him to victory. No matter: Michard still had another two races available.

In the second, coming into the last corner, Hansen was on the inside, leading. When he left a small gap between himself and the track edge, Michard didn't need a second invitation. He darted into the gap and sprinted to the win on the inside of Hansen.

But then, in the words of Pierre Chany, the event descended into pantomime. The commissaire, having seen the riders coming round the last bend and not realising Michard had later taken the inside line, announced the winner as the rider he thought was on the inside – Hansen. Protests immediately followed but the regulations did not allow the commissaire to reverse his decision.

Hansen was awarded the title of world champion. *L'Auto*, which recognised Michard as the moral victor, awarded the Frenchman a white jersey with world globes printed on front and back. Michard would again try to win the title in later years but his efforts were in vain, coming second in 1932 and 1933.

18 November

Henri Pépin is born
(1864)

Henri Pépin was a wealthy man who was obsessed with the bicycle. History has portrayed him as a Count or Baron with the title Baron Pépin de Gontaud, but in reality he was no nobleman, at least not in a formal context. Pépin was, rather, a man with enough money to allow him to spend his time pursuing his interests. And that meant taking part in the world's toughest bike race.

Pépin was no mug. He had stamina. He rode his first Tour in 1905 and lasted until stage seven. That represents over 1,800km of riding a heavy bike on poor roads – no light undertaking.

In 1907 he returned. This time he paid two men who had also ridden the race before to ride with him. There was no attempt to disguise his intention of treating the event as a pleasure ride. At the start of the race he is described as holding court with the ladies of Paris as the other riders disappeared into the distance. He finally arrived in Roubaix more than four hours after the stage winner.

Pépin made it until stage five before paying off his companions and heading home. Instead of the daily race allowances he was entitled to, he wrote to Henri Desgrange asking for a medal. He rode the race again in 1914, but abandoned during the first stage. He died later that same year at the age of fifty.

19 November

BMX makes its debut at the Asian Games
(2010)

After the Olympic Games, the world's biggest multi-sport event is the Asian Games, organised by the Olympic Council of Asia. Held every four years, the event dates back to 1951, when it was first hosted in New Delhi.

There were just four cycling events at the first Games – a men's road race and a men's sprint, time trial and team pursuit on the track. All were won by Japan.

By the time Guangzhou, China, hosted the twenty-sixth Games in 2010, the cycling programme had grown hugely. Women's races had been introduced in 1986 and in 1998 the first mountain bike events were held.

The Guangzhou Games introduced BMX to the Asian Games programme for the first time. Held over a single day on a specially constructed course on the same site as the Guangzhou velodrome, the men's race was won by Hong Kong's Steven Wong with Ma Liyun of China taking the women's title. Amazingly, only four riders entered the women's race. BMX remained on the programme for the 2014 Games, attracting double the number of female entrants.

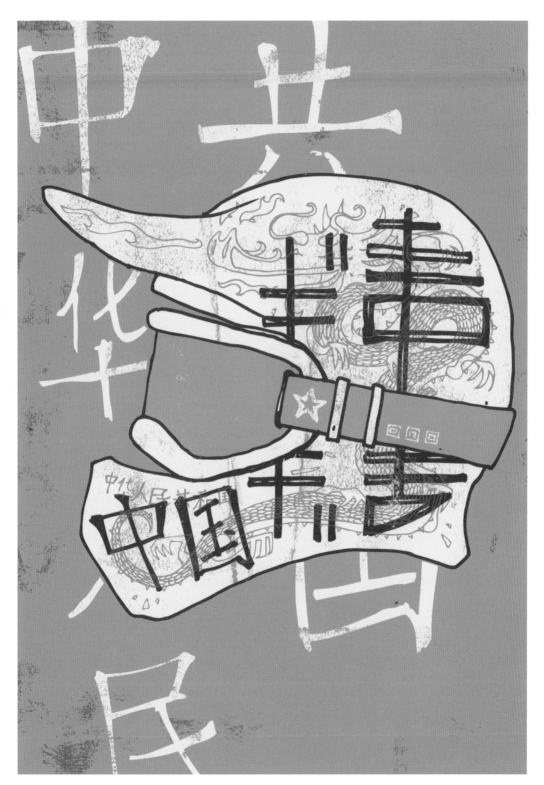

20 November

The rotary crank bicycle is patented by Pierre Lallement
(1866)

Born in France, Pierre Lallement is credited by some as the inventor of the modern bicycle. It's a difficult claim to substantiate. Back in the 1800s inventions that in time were to morph into what today we know as the modern bike were moving at pace and developing rapidly. Many are the claims and counter-claims as to who invented what and when, and who stole what from whom.

What is certain is that by the mid-1860s Lallement had moved from France to the USA. On 4 April 1866 he rode his new invention, a two-wheeled machine with pedals, cranks and handlebars, twelve miles from the town of Ansonia into New Haven, Connecticut. He later filed a patent application for his invention, stating that with a little practice his 'velocipede' could be driven at 'incredible velocity, with the greatest of ease'.

On 20 November 1866, patent number 59,915 was granted to Lallement. He returned to France two years later, having been unable to exploit his invention commercially. What's more, he faced claims that he had stolen the idea from Pierre Michaux, for whom he had worked before travelling to America.

He returned to the United States, where he died in 1891, by now widely discredited. Later, research carried out in America supported his claims as the inventor of the first pedal-propelled bicycle. In 2005 he was inducted into the US Bicycle Hall of Fame.

21 November

Welsh cyclist Jimmy Michael dies at the age of twenty-seven
(1904)

A former charge of 'Choppy' Warburton (see 13 November), Jimmy Michael was born in Aberaman, South Wales. Tiny, standing at just over 5 feet, 1 inch, Michael took the cycling world by storm in the 1890s.

He won the Surrey Hundred in 1894, stunning a crowd that had at first laughed at him because of his slight stature compared to the other riders. They stopped laughing when he destroyed the field. Michael's life was about to change.

In 1895 he turned professional and won the Stayers world championship title. He became one of the biggest names in cycling, attracting tens of thousands to his races. He was a superstar. William Spears Simpson commissioned Henri de Toulouse-Lautrec to design a poster showing Michael riding a bike fitted with Simpson's new lever chain. He began to ride in America, attracted by the massive sums of money on offer there.

In 1903 he suffered a huge crash in Berlin and cracked his skull. He started to complain of constant headaches and steadily turned to drink. In November 1904 he boarded the liner *Savoi* to travel to America to take part in some six-day races. He died in his cabin en route. His death certificate stated cause of death as congestion of the brain.

22 November

Fabio Parra, Colombian cyclist, is born
(1959)

In 1988, Fabio Parra became the first South American to stand on the podium at the Tour de France, when he finished third in Paris.

Parra was born in Sogamoso, Colombia, in 1959. Colombians had been riding in the Tour since 1975 with Luis 'Lucho' Herrera becoming its first stage winner in 1984, when he won on l'Alpe d'Huez. Not a bad place to record your country's first stage win.

In 1985 Parra entered the fray in what was a terrific year for the Colombians. Riding for the Café de Colombia team, both Herrera and Parra lit up the Tour. First Herrera took a stage win at Avoriaz, beating Bernard Hinault in a two-man escape. Then the pair rode into Lans-en-Vercours together at the head of the race, this time Parra taking the win. Two days later, Herrera won again. In Paris, he wore the polka-dot jersey of the king of the mountains and Parra was crowned the race's best-placed young rider.

Parra rode again in 1986 but was forced to abandon on stage four. The following year he finished sixth but it was in 1988, now riding for Kelme, that he made history.

He won the stage into Morzine, escaping alone with 20km to go, but it was the next day that saw him rise into the top three. It was a long day in the saddle, 227km over the Madeleine, Glandon and up to l'Alpe d'Huez. Parra finished fourth, just twenty-three seconds down on stage winner Steven Rooks; it was enough to take him into third.

He slipped to fourth briefly but rose again in the Pyrénées and by Paris he was firmly ensconced in third place, becoming the first Colombian to stand on the Tour's final podium. It remained the best performance by any South American until Nairo Quintana finished second in 2013 (see 4 February for more on Quintana).

Parra also rode in the Vuelta a España seven times, winning two stages, finishing fifth on four occasions and, in 1989, coming second, just thirty-five seconds behind winner Pedro Delgado. He retired in 1992. In 2010 he made an unsuccessful bid for election to the Colombian Senate.

23 November

Katie Compton wins Koksijde Cyclo-cross
(2013)

The 2013/14 UCI Cyclo-cross World Cup competition took place over seven separate races, from 20 October 2013 through to 26 January 2014.

Round three was the prestigious Koksijde meeting. With a men's edition having been held every year since 1969, the first Koksidje race for women wasn't until 2003, with a further three-year gap before the race returned in 2007.

The women's record for most wins at Koksijde is held by American Katie Compton. An eleven-time national champion at the time of writing, Compton won her fourth Koksijde title in 2013 when she finished the five-lap, 15km race more than one minute ahead of Belgian Sanne Cant. Compton took the lead on the opening lap and never looked back as she tamed the sandy Koksijde course.

Compton had won the previous round in Tábor and she would go on to win the next three races as she dominated the world cup. She won the overall competition by a final margin of sixty-six points, repeating her win of 2012/13.

24 November

First six days of Amsterdam
(1932)

Held in the RAI exhibition centre, the first Amsterdam six-day meet reached its conclusion on 24 November 1932. It was won by the Dutch pair Jan Pijnenburg and Piet Van Kempen, who beat Germany's Viktor Rausch and Gottfried Huertgen. Pijnenburg went on to a second title the year after, this time with Cor Wals.

Remarkably, it took until 2002, some seventy years after that first meet, for the Amsterdam Six to record its tenth edition. Interrupted by economic downturns and then the Second World War, its fourth edition, held in 1936, was its last for some thirty years.

In 1966 it returned, thanks mainly to the hard work of the businessman Kurt Vyth. A track was built in the new RAI centre and the race remained on the calendar for a further four years. It disappeared again after the 1969 edition.

The third coming of the Amsterdam Six was in 2001. This time it was to stay for longer than four years. In 2012 it celebrated its twentieth edition and at the time of writing it is still going strong. The record for most wins was held by Danny Stam, who won four titles between 2003 and 2008.

25 November

Six days of New York finishes
(1939)

Six-day racing was first held at Madison Square Garden, New York, in 1891 when it was the very first event held in the now legendary arena. At first riders raced alone, with the only limit to the amount of time they could ride being stamina and their ability to go without sleep. That first race was won by William Martin, a professional who had earned the nickname Plugger because of his consistent and durable style.

By 1899 the format of the race had changed. With organisers concerned for the wellbeing of riders who, only too aware of the financial rewards on offer, were now pushing themselves beyond all reasonable levels of endurance, a rule was introduced stating that no individual could ride for more than twelve hours a day. (In 1898 the winner, Charles Miller, had spent 126½ hours out of a possible 142 on the track – half an hour of that downtime spent getting married.) The ruling led to teams of two being formed and in 1899 the Garden hosted New York's first two-man six-day race.

Into the 1900s and the event grew in popularity. Soon six-day races were springing up in other American cities. Six-day riders were among the most famous and best-paid athletes in the States. Demand grew so much so that from 1920 New York hosted more than one race a year, attracting the celebrities of the day to the Garden to watch the action.

The last six-day meet in New York prior to the Second World War took place in 1939. Started by baseball star Joe DiMaggio, the race finished on 25 November with Cesare Moretti and Cecil Yates winning. Six-day

racing returned to New York in 1948, but not at the Garden. It wouldn't be until 1961 that the event, dubbed by at least one writer the 'Mad Whirl', returned to its spiritual home. At the time it was hoped that it would be the first of many but any such optimism soon faded and the 1961 edition proved to be the last of the New York Sixes.

26 November

Marshall 'Major' Taylor, the Black Cyclone, is born
(1878)

Heralded by Lance Armstrong as the greatest American cyclist in history, Marshall Taylor was an African-American who blazed a trail around the world, winning countless bike races while fighting racial prejudice. At his peak he was considered the fastest cyclist in the world, earning him the moniker the Black Cyclone.

Born in 1878, Taylor was just two generations from slavery, his grandfather having been a slave in Kentucky. He was befriended by a wealthy white family, who employed his father, and it was they who gave him his first bicycle, which he used to deliver papers and learn tricks. A local shop saw him and employed him, setting him to work performing tricks outside the shop dressed in military uniform. Thereafter, life would never be the same for 'Major' Taylor.

By his teenage years he was winning races and setting records. Before he was twenty he had turned professional and is today recognised as the first African-American athlete to have received commercial sponsorship. In 1899 he became world champion.

For years he dominated track racing but he suffered appalling racial abuse, having to fight prejudice virtually everywhere he went – and this at a time when the League of American Wheelmen had also voted to bar black members. At one race a white rider was so incensed at being beaten by Taylor that he throttled him so badly it took Taylor fifteen minutes to regain consciousness.

Deeply religious, Taylor refused to ride on Sundays. For a while this prevented him travelling to Europe, where the majority of track races took place on a Sunday. By the early 1900s, however, such was his reputation that races were rescheduled to enable him to ride. He found equal success on the tracks of Europe as he had in the US.

Taylor retired in 1910. Bad investments meant that he lost his fortune and was reduced to selling his self-penned, self-published autobiography door-to-door. He died in 1932, broke and anonymous, and was buried in a pauper's grave. In 1948, when his fate became known, his body was reburied and a memorial service held in his honour.

27 November

Julien Moineau is born
(1903)

Sometimes it takes a little bit of cunning to win a bike race, something that Julien Moineau, born on this day in 1903, understood better than most.

Moineau had won stages of the Tour in 1928 and 1929, as well as Paris–Tours in 1932. By 1935, however, he was approaching the end of his career and searching for his last big win. That came on stage seventeen of that year's Tour, one ridden in insufferable heat. So bad was it that half the starters didn't make Paris, including a sizeable proportion of the pre-race favourites.

Wednesday 24 July, the day of stage seventeen, was one of the hottest. On the road from Pau to Bordeaux the peloton passed a stall that had been set up offering cold beer. A cold beer on a hot day? Even the cyclists of the Tour couldn't resist that. So they all stopped for refreshment. All apart from one – Monsieur Moineau.

Moineau stamped on the pedals and was gone, leaving the rest of the race far behind him. He won the stage by over fifteen minutes. The whole thing had been a set-up: the fans handing out the beers were in fact his friends and supporters, charged with holding up the race while Moineau rode on alone. At the finish he toasted his fellow riders as they arrived. With a beer.

28 November

Patrick Sercu wins his first six-days race
(1965)

The greatest six-day racer of them all, Belgium's Patrick Sercu won his first six-day title in November 1965, when he won the Ghent Six, partnering Eddy Merckx.

Sercu was already an Olympic and amateur world champion on the track by the time of this win, so he was hardly an unknown. Riding with his friend, the soon-to-be all-conquering Merckx, the pair were unstoppable. An eighteen-year professional career followed, during which time Sercu rode 233 six-day races, winning eighty-eight of them and claiming the records for most six-day wins at Ghent, Frankfurt, Dortmund and London.

Sercu was the major attraction at the winter Sixes for well over a decade but he was far from just a track racer. In the spring and summer he competed on the road and won there as well. In fact, he would rightly be considered to have had a very successful racing career even if he had never turned a pedal on the track, such is the scale of his achievements on the road: six stage wins and the points jersey at the Tour; thirteen stage wins at the Giro; stage wins at Romandie, Paris–Nice and the Criterium du Dauphiné; wins at Kuurne–Brussels–Kuurne and Kampioenschap van Vlaanderen; and an armful of top-ten finishes in a number of Classics.

Sercu retired in 1983. In 2014 he was awarded the Order of Merit by the Belgian Olympic Committee.

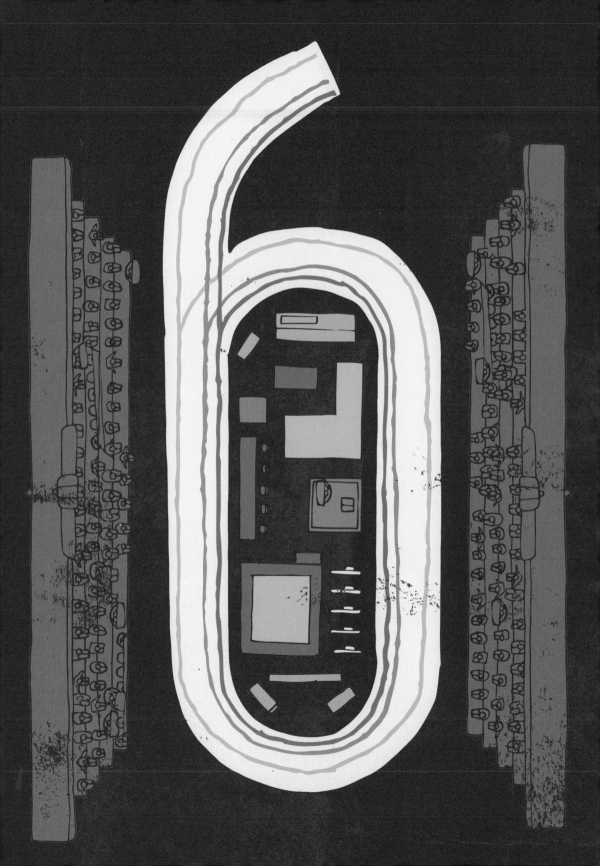

29 November

Alphonse Steinès is promoted to France's Gloire du Sport
(2010)

The man responsible for inflicting the high mountains of France on a hitherto unsuspecting peloton was not the father of the Tour, Henri Desgrange, but his assistant at *L'Auto*, Alphonse Steinès.

The Tour had tackled mountains before, most notably the Ballon d'Alsace, first climbed in 1905, but Steinès suggested to Desgrange that his race needed to go higher. He proposed they head into the Pyrénées.

Desgrange liked his riders to suffer (see 31 January) but even he thought the idea mad. Steinès set out to prove him wrong. He went south and set out to drive over the Col du Tourmalet. Starting from Sainte-Marie-de-Campan, four kilometres from the top he found the road was blocked by snow. The car could go no further.

So, with darkness falling, Steinès did something only he would do. He left his driver to tackle the climb on foot. His driver, justly concerned, alerted *L'Auto*'s local correspondent, who set out with a search party.

Eventually they found Steinès on the brink of hypothermia. Once he had recovered, he sent a telegram to Desgrange that read simply: 'Crossed Tourmalet. Stop. Very Good Road. Stop. Perfectly Passable. Stop'. Later that year the Pyrénées entered the Tour (see 21 July).

30 November

Mavic is sold by the Gormand family
(1990)

One of the most iconic brands in cycling, Mavic's foundations were laid in 1889 when a company was formed to make bicycle components by Charles Idoux and Lucien Chanel. In the 1920s the firm was bought by its then president, Henry Gormand, who also owned a nickel-plating business. He combined both companies and formed Mavic – Manufacture d'Articles Vélocipediques Idoux et Chanel.

The company began to thrive. Focusing principally on wheel technology, under the stewardship of Gormand and then his son Bruno, it gained a reputation for pushing the boundaries. Aluminium rims in the 1920s; clincher rims in the 1970s; disc wheels in the 1980s; tri-spoke wheels in the 1990s – Mavic was at the forefront of them all, and many more besides.

For all their innovative products, however, Mavic is perhaps best known for its neutral service support at races. An idea born in 1972, when Bruno Gormand picked up a team director after his team's car had broken down, Mavic have been providing neutral race assistance for more than thirty years. Their distinctive yellow and black cars and motorbikes now follow races laden with wheels. To say it revolutionised racing isn't hyperbole – it meant the end of riders standing helplessly at the roadside with a broken bike waiting for their team to arrive.

The firm finally passed out of the Gormand family's control in November 1990 when a management buyout was agreed. It is today owned by Finnish company Amer Sports.

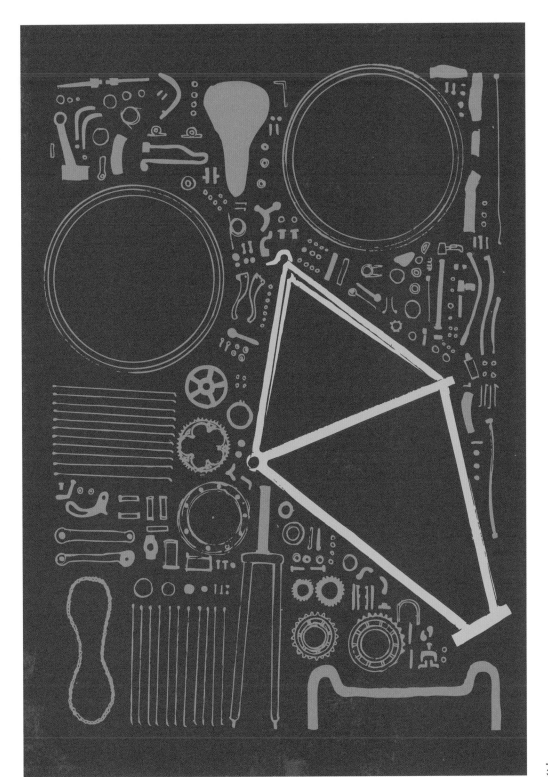

DECEMBER

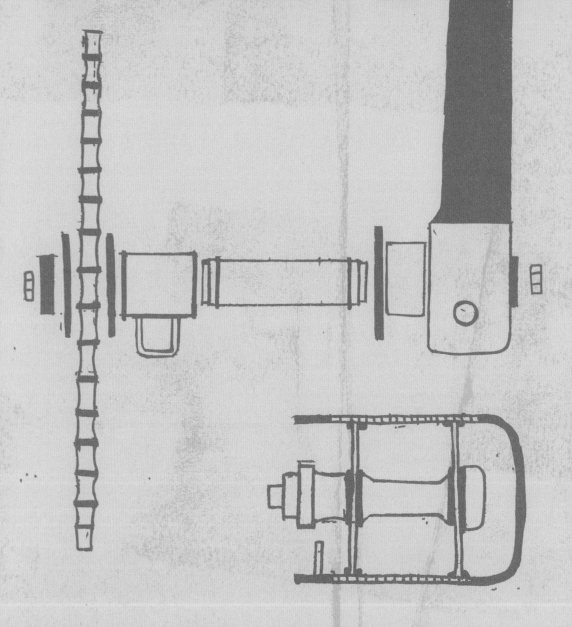

1 December

Luigi Ganna is born
(1883)

A bricklayer who honed his cycling legs riding 100km a day to and from work, Luigi Ganna turned to professional cycling after an impressive third place in the first Tour of Lombardy convinced him, and his family, that he could earn far more money by riding a bike for a living than he could building houses.

A strong, powerful rider and particularly good in bad weather, he was known as the King of Mud. His best season came in 1909. Riding for the Atala-Dunlop team, Ganna won his first major race, claiming Milan–Sanremo by over three minutes ahead of Emile Georget.

Even better was to come. Just over one month after his Sanremo win Ganna took to the start line of the very first Giro d'Italia. Seventeen days later he returned to Milan crowned as the first winner of what would become Italy's greatest race (see 13 May for more).

Ganna retired in 1915, entering the world of bike manufacturing. His company went on to sponsor a professional team for more than twenty years with Fiorenzo Magni winning the second of his three Giro titles while riding for the team.

2 December

Cornet wins the Tour four months after it ended
(1904)

If the first Tour in 1903 had captured France's imagination in a way no one in the offices of *L'Auto* had dared hope, the 1904 Tour was nothing short of a disaster.

With huge rewards on offer, cheating was rife. Riders drafted behind cars, took the train or accepted lifts. They traded places at stage finishes. Partisan supporters blockaded roads, allowing only their favoured riders through and then threatening others with sticks and rocks, the organisers even brandishing revolvers in order to rescue their racers.

After three weeks of mayhem Maurice Garin was the winner. But Henri Desgrange was deeply embarrassed by what had happened and the Union Vélocipédique de France (UVF) was none too happy either.

Desgrange announced that the second Tour would be the last – it had been 'killed by its own success,' he said. For their part the UVF stated Garin's win was only provisional until it was able to unravel what had gone on.

It took the UVF more than four months to do that unravelling. On 30 November 1904 they announced that Garin, along with twenty-eight others, including the rest of the top four riders, had been disqualified. Two days later, the revised results of the race were officially issued, with Henri Cornet, who had finished fifth in Paris, being declared the winner. Cornet was just twenty at the time of the decision and remains the youngest winner of the race. Despite the words of Desgrange the race of course returned the following year.

3 December

Joop Zoetemelk is born
(1946)

Born in The Hague, Joop Zoetemelk grew up in Rijpwetering and at the time of writing is one of only two Dutch riders to have won the Tour.

Zoetemelk first entered the race in 1970, the year he turned professional. He came second behind Merckx. Over the course of the next seventeen years he would ride every Tour bar one, finishing second on six occasions, behind some of the greatest riders in history – Merckx; Van Impe; Hinault.

He finally won the Tour at the tenth attempt, beating his compatriot Hennie Kuiper by just under seven minutes, a win forged by two devastating time-trial rides.

The very epitome of consistency, Zoetemelk won his fair share of other races as well: the Vuelta, a world championship, Paris–Nice, the Tour of Romandie, La Flèche Wallonne, Amstel Gold, Paris–Tours, as well as claiming ten Tour stage wins, among them wins on top of the legendary climbs l'Alpe d'Huez and Puy du Dôme.

Despite all that winning Zoetemelk never really captured the imagination of the sport's fans. He was accused of being a follower rather than an attacker. 'Why is Zoetemelk so pale?' ran a famous, if unfair, joke. 'Because he rides in the shadow of Merckx.'

4 December

Christa Rothenburger-Luding is born
(1959)

Germany's Christa Rothenburger-Luding made history in 1988 when she added silver in the match sprint at the Olympic Games in Seoul to the speed skating gold and silver medals she had won seven months earlier at the Calgary Olympic Winter Games. It was the first time any athlete had won medals at both the winter and summer Olympic Games in the same year.

Rothenburger-Luding was a supremely talented speed-skater, who claimed world records as well as multiple Olympic medals in the sport. She had only started cycling as a way of keeping fit during skating's off-season.

Realising she was a more than capable track sprinter, she entered the 1986 world championships in Colorado Springs, USA. She made it to the final of the sprint, where she won the rainbow jersey ahead of Estonian Erika Salumäe, who was riding for the Soviet Union.

Two years later in Seoul the positions were reversed: Salumäe took gold, Rothenburger-Luding silver. But it was the East German who had made history. History that, after the Winter Games were moved so that they no longer fell in the same year as the Summer Games, can now no longer be repeated.

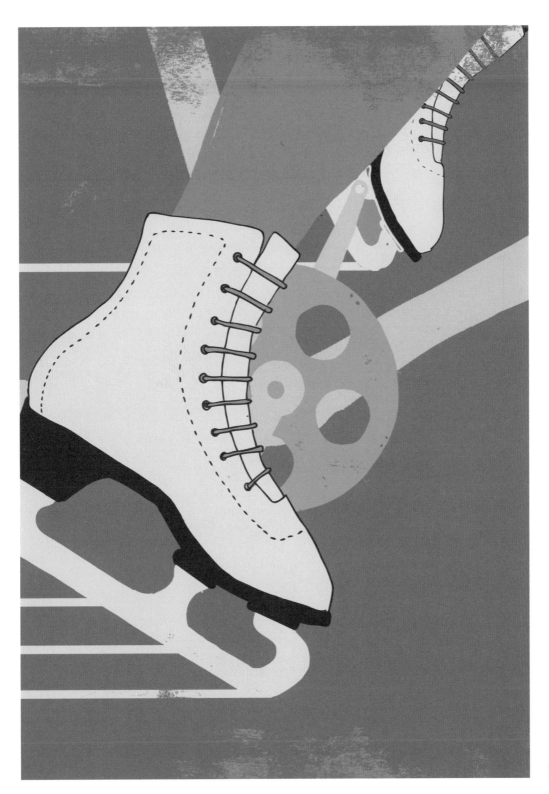

5 December

Team GB set 4km women's team pursuit world record
(2013)

Since the addition of the women's team pursuit to the track cycling world championships programme in 2008, Great Britain has dominated the event. Of the eight world championship events that at the time of writing have been held, Britain has won six of them. Britain's women pursuit riders have proved themselves to be as close to a sure thing as it is possible to get in sport.

In 2012 they entered the London Olympics as the hot favourites and didn't disappoint: Laura Trott, Dani King and Joanna Rowsell ruled the boards, crushing the opposition. They set a world record in each of the three rounds of the Olympic competition, bettering their own record each time, on their way to gold. Over three kilometres GB's team of three were simply unbeatable.

So when, in 2013, the UCI changed the format to a team of four riding four kilometres, the world of track cycling was keen to see how this would affect Britain's stranglehold on the discipline. They didn't have to wait long. In October 2013 Britain set the world record at the European Track Championships. Two weeks later they broke it. Then, on 5 December, they travelled to Mexico and smashed it again.

In a little over six weeks they had set the inaugural record and then broken it twice, taking a barely believable ten seconds off their initial mark. In 2014 they won the world championships before Australia raised the bar, winning the 2015 worlds and breaking Britain's world record.

6 December

Alberto Contador is born
(1982)

Possibly the finest Grand Tour rider of his generation, the Spaniard Alberto Contador is one of only six riders to have won all three Grand Tours. At the time of writing he has two Tours, three Vueltas and one Giro to his name.

Although his career has been blighted by his 2010 positive test for clenbuterol and the subsequent appeals and counter-appeals (see 25 January for more), and while he has never threatened the top placings at a major classic or a world championships, over the past eight years or so Contador has been one of the few consistently able to make sustained challenges in three-week races.

He claimed his first Tour in 2007 in just his second start. He lit up the race in the Pyrénées, inherited the yellow jersey when Michael Rasmussen was thrown off the race (see 1 June) and kept it until Paris.

Good against the clock, Contador is devastating when the road tips skywards. He has a rare turn of pace on a climb, repeatedly able to accelerate for short bursts, enabling him to drop any riders desperately hanging on. It is this ability to suddenly sprint away, and then to do it again and again if need be, that sets him apart from most other Grand Tour contenders.

It would be a major surprise if he were not to add to that already impressive Grand Tour tally before his career is over.

7 December

Fiorenzo Magni is born
(1920)

All cyclists are born tough. They have to be in order to ride hundreds of kilometres day after day, in whatever weather Mother Nature throws at them. They scale precipitous mountains and battle the wind for hour after torturous hour. If cyclists are born tough, some are born tougher than others. Like Fiorenzo Magni, for example.

Born in Tuscany, Magni loved bad weather. Intense heat or freezing cold, scorching sun or blinding snow, he wasn't bothered. When others packed their bags, Magni shot to the top of the classification. He won the Giro, the Tour of Flanders and Italy's national championships three times each. While he shares the record for most Flanders wins with five other riders, he is the only one to have claimed all his titles in succession.

Nicknamed the Colossus of Monza, if his first Giro win in 1948 came with a hefty dollop of controversy, having been given a time penalty for receiving some 'helpful' pushes from fans in the mountains (prompting Fausto Coppi to withdraw in protest when he felt the penalty not harsh enough), Magni's performance in his final Giro showed just how tough he really was.

He had already announced that he was retiring from the sport when he took to the start line of the 1956 Giro. Halfway through the race he crashed. He climbed back on the bike and finished the stage but afterwards a visit to hospital revealed a broken collarbone. Doctors advised he abandon. Magni quit a race he'd won three times? Not a chance.

Stage thirteen was a short uphill time trial. Magni found it too painful to pull on the handlebars and so his inventive mechanic fitted a piece of rubber tubing to the top bar. Magni rode with hands placed only gently on the top bar, the tubing gripped hard between his teeth so that he used his mouth to pull on the bars. His face showed his agony.

As the race progressed he crashed again. This time an ambulance carted him away. That is until Magni yelled at them to turn around and take him back. He'd broken his humerus. Still he rode on.

It gets better: 1956 was the year of the Bondone snowstorm – a day when sixty riders abandoned during a stage in the Dolomites when nature unleashed the very worst of winter on a frozen peloton. Was Magni one of the sixty? Of course not.

In the end, despite two broken bones, Fiorenzo Magni made it to Milan. He finished second.

Some are just born tougher.

Magni changed the future of cycling. In 1954, with his team struggling to fund another season, he was the first to successfully seek sponsorship from outside the sport, something that would soon become commonplace. Who was the sponsor the hardest man in cycling found? Nivea.

Magni died in October 2012 at the age of ninety-one.

8 December

The first recorded mass start bicycle race
(1867)

At 10 a.m. on 8 December 1867, more than a hundred people gathered in front of the Panorama National on the Champs-Elysées. They had all brought their velocipedes and together they rode to Versailles.

Whether it was a race in the truest sense of the word is perhaps debatable, but it is known that times were recorded and that the first of the participants took just under one hour to cover the 17km route. The journals of Paris recorded the occasion, taking great pains to explain how this newly introduced machine, the velocipede, worked:

'We know that the velocipede is a vehicle with two wheels, that the rider, sitting on a small seat, moves by alternately pressing his feet on two paddles that communicate with the wheels,' said the report in *Le Petit Journal*.

'The velocipede is one of the most beautiful gifts you can give,' gushed *Le Courrier de la Drôme*, having witnessed the race.

The age of the bike was about to arrive.

9 December

Ryder Hesjedal is born
(1980)

Born in Victoria, British Columbia, Ryder Hesjedal became the first Canadian to win a Grand Tour when he took the Giro in 2012.

Hesjedal turned professional in 2004. Riding principally for others in his early career, he saw modest results but a stage win at the Vuelta in 2009 was the start of a turnaround in fortunes. Top ten placings in a couple of Ardennes Classics were followed by fifth at the Tour in 2010 when his initial sixth place was bumped up thanks to Alberto Contador's disqualification. It was the best placing by a Canadian for over twenty years and only the third time that a rider from Canada had broken into the top ten.

If that 2010 performance at the Tour hinted at Hesjedal's Grand Tour potential, the 2012 Giro confirmed it. Over the course of the race he fought with Spain's Joaquin Rodríguez for the pink jersey. With Rodríguez, a very accomplished climber, in pink heading into the final mountainous few days, the Spaniard seemed to be in pole position. But Hesjedal stuck with him, limiting his losses.

Going into the final 28km individual time trial, the Canadian was only thirty-one seconds behind. The tables had turned. With Hesjedal the superior rider against the clock he now became the favourite. And he lived up to the billing. That night he wore pink in Milan, the first Canadian ever to do so.

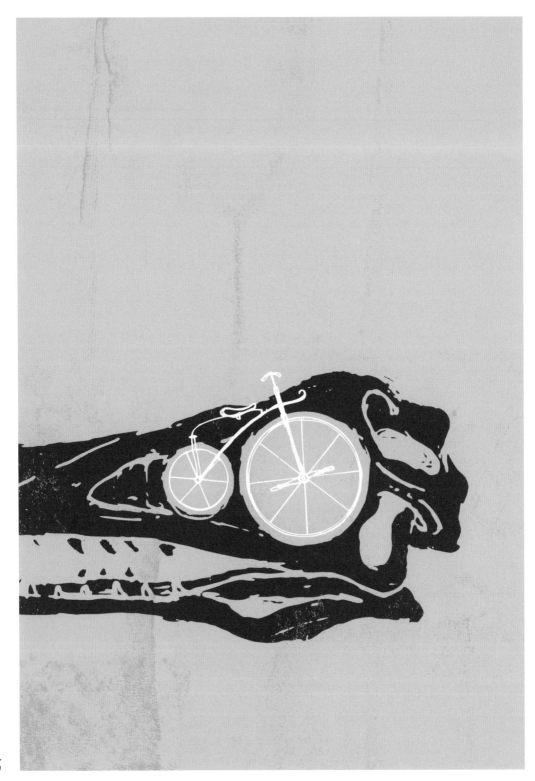

10 December

Baron Karl von Drais de Sauerbrun dies
(1851)

The evolution of cycle sport can be traced back to the invention that led to the bicycle itself: the *Laufmaschine* – or running machine. The Laufmaschine was invented by Baron Karl von Drais de Sauerbrun. Born into an aristocratic family in Germany, Drais studied maths, physics and architecture before working for the state forestry service.

He was a prolific inventor, creating contraptions as diverse as a typewriter and a meat grinder. But he is most famous for his running machine.

With two wheels placed one behind the other, a frame, a steering mechanism and a seat, it was the first machine to resemble the modern bicycle. The rider would place his feet on the ground and push off, propelling himself along. It became known variously as the Draisine, velocipede or hobby-horse.

After much initial interest, however, it fell out of fashion. With poor roads, riders were forced on to pathways and eventually the machine was banned in many countries because of the threat it posed to ordinary pedestrians.

Although he was awarded an annual pension for his invention, Drais was never able to fully profit from his running machine. Despite his aristocratic background he was a strong supporter of democracy and became known simply as Karl Drais. He supported the doomed revolution of 1848 after which he was ostracised by the ruling classes and his financial means cut off. He died in 1851, destitute.

11 December

Czech cyclo-cross sensation Zdeněk Štybar is born
(1985)

It is the final lap of the 2010 cyclo-cross world championship race in Tabor, a city 90km south of Prague in the Czech Republic. The ground is covered in deep-lying snow. Thousands of fans are crowding the tight, technical course. Czech flags are waving.

At the front of the race is Zdeněk Štybar, born just 175km away. Approaching the finish line he looks behind him. There's no one there and there hasn't been for quite some time. Štybar shakes his head, raises his hands to his head and punches the air. Amid the snows of Tabor the Czech people will have their first cyclo-cross world champion since 1991.

Štybar's win had been on the cards for some time. By the time of the 2010 race the two-time Under-23 world champion had been second in the elite race twice in succession. It was therefore just a matter of time.

Starting as a BMX racer, claiming wins at world, European and national level, Štybar took his first cyclo-cross title in 2002, winning the junior Czech national title. At the time of writing his cyclo-cross wins at elite level include three world championship titles, seven national titles and one overall world cup title.

For the past few seasons Štybar's main focus has been road racing. He has claimed several noteworthy results, including a stage win in the Vuelta, an overall win at the Eneco Tour and top-ten finishes in one-day classics.

12 December

Tsujiura wins 9th national 'cross title
(2010)

Not known for its cyclo-cross scene, Japan's national championships was dominated by Keiichi Tsujira for little under a decade.

Born in the Kansai region of Japan in 1980, Tsujiura started winning his national cyclo-cross championships in 2003. By 2008 he had amassed seven straight titles and was starting to bemoan the lack of competition in Japan. 'I regret the fact that no one could stop it [his seventh title]. I hope more riders participate to raise the national level,' he said after his 2008 win.

In fact, it would take three more years for someone to stop him. He won again in 2009 and then, on 12 December 2010, claimed his ninth title, extending his record further still.

Tsujiura was finally defeated in 2011 when Yu Takenouchi pushed him into second place. The two raced head-to-head until the final lap when Takenouchi edged away to win by thirty-six seconds.

If Takenouchi's 2011 win at last ended an era of dominance it would start another. The new challenger has won every edition of Japan's national championships since with, at the time of writing, four titles to his name.

13 December

First Tour of Argentina is won by Rik Van Steenbergen
(1952)

Known more for his one-day classic wins (see 2 April), in late November 1952 Belgium's Rik Van Steenbergen travelled to South America for the inaugural Tour of Argentina.

It was a fourteen-stage affair, run over eighteen days, starting and finishing in Buenos Aires and calling in at Santa Fe (de la Vera Cruz), Mendoza and Córdoba along the way. It was dominated by Europeans with riders from Belgium, Italy, France and the Netherlands winning thirteen of the stages. Only one stage was claimed by an Argentine, Saul Crispin taking stage six.

The overall race was won by Van Steenbergen. He claimed four stages and the General Classification by over twelve minutes from his compatriot Stan Ockers. It was one of only three GC wins for Van Steenbergen over the course of his twenty-three-year professional career (although his most impressive performance at a stage race would be the 1951 Giro, in which he finished second).

The Tour of Argentina was short-lived to say the least. The 1952 edition was the first but also the last for nearly forty years. It returned for one edition in 1991 and then again in 1999. It has not been held since 2000.

14 December

Rochelle Gilmore is born
(1981)

Australian professional Rochelle Gilmore won Commonwealth Games medals and World Cup races on both track and road before establishing the professional women's road racing team Wiggle-Honda.

Gilmore started racing at the tender age of three. Initially, she raced BMX but then, with eyes on riding at the Olympic Games, switched to the track and road (BMX didn't enter the Olympic programme until 2008). In 2001 she won a stage at the Giro d'Italia Femminile, repeating the feat in 2003. Her first road world cup win came in 2005 in Geelong, Australia, a win that Gilmore later identified as a highlight of her career.

She announced plans to set up a women's team in 2012. Sponsored by Wiggle-Honda,

Gilmore's team signed a number of high-profile riders in time for the 2013 season, including British Olympic gold medal winners Joanna Rowsell, Laura Trott and Dani King, and Italy's two-time world champion Giorgia Bronzini.

By August they were creating history. At the Route de France, Bronzini won six stages in a row, a record. Her team-mate Linda Villumsen won the final seventh stage to claim the overall title. The only stage the team didn't win was the race opening prologue.

Gilmore continued racing until the 2014 season before quitting to concentrate on running her team.

15 December

Charles Holland dies
(1989)

In 1937 Charles Holland travelled to France, taking his place in a three-man British Empire team, cobbled together to ride the Tour.

Alongside Bill Burl and Canadian Pierre Gachon, Holland rolled out of Paris bound for Lille with ninety-eight other riders. Gachon didn't last long and withdrew en route to Lille. Burl followed the next day. Two stages in and Holland was alone.

Holland turned professional only a few months before. He'd ridden in two Olympic Games, winning a bronze on the track in 1932 and finishing fifth in the road race in 1936, narrowly missing out on a medal in a fifteen-man sprint. He'd also just missed the podium at the 1934 amateur world championships. But with mass-start road

racing banned in Britain, taking on the Tour was a whole new proposition.

Given his lack of experience, and his lack of backing, Holland fared remarkably well. He lasted eighteen days and finished six stages in the first fifteen places. He finally retired in the Pyrénées. He punctured three times on the stage to Luchon. His pump was broken and he eventually ran out of spare tyres. He had no option but to call it a day. He never rode the race again.

Before the Second World War halted his career, Holland claimed a number of long-distance records, including Land's End to London. Later he would win time-trial championships as a veteran. He died in 1989 at the age of eighty-one.

16 December

Charly Mottet is born
(1962)

Known as *Petit Charly*, Charly Mottet was a talented climber who won a number of high-profile races without ever really hitting the heights of cycling. Born in Valence, south-eastern France, Mottet rode in the era of Hinault and Fignon and was destined to remain in the shadow of those two French giants of the road.

Still, Mottet won races, and won them well. From 1985 to 1994 he started ten consecutive editions of the Tour, finished eight of them, won three stages, wore yellow for six days and finished fourth overall twice. In 1990 he won Queen Stage of that year's Giro, over five mountains and up to a summit finish on the Pordoi. That win elevated him to second overall, a position he held until Milan, bringing him his best Grand Tour result. It also meant that, when added to his two stage wins at the 1986 Vuelta, Mottet won stages at all three Grand Tours.

Away from three-week racing he shares the record for most wins at the Critérium du Dauphiné, his three wins placing him alongside Hinault, Nello Lauredi and Luis Ocaña. He also won the Tour of Lombardy in 1988, escaping on the final descent and soloing to the win.

He retired in 1994 but stayed in the sport, taking up various posts with race organisers, the French cycling federation and the UCI.

17 December

Moreno Argentin is born
(1960)

In April 1987, Italy's Moreno Argentin started Liège–Bastogne–Liège looking for his third straight win. Only two men had tamed *la Doyenne* three years in a row before. The first ever winner, Léon Houa, was one, Eddy Merckx the other. Argentin was keeping good company.

But as the race entered Liège it all looked to have gone wrong for Argentin. Belgium's Claude Criquielion had ridden the Italian off his wheel on the Côte du Sart-Tilman, taking Ireland's Stephen Roche with him. The two were still together with a seemingly unassailable lead as they entered the final kilometre.

Argentin had all but given up hope, resigning himself to trying to get on the bottom step of the podium, but, as Criquielion and Roche slowed, playing a fatal two-man sprint game of cat and mouse, the Italian, wearing the rainbow jersey and riding with Robert Millar and Marc Madiot, powered into Liège. They began to gain on the leaders. And to gain fast.

In a flash it was over. Before Criquielion or Roche could comprehend what was happening, Argentin and co. were on them. Argentin sprinted for the line straight away, blasting past the Belgian and the Irishman without so much as a sideways glance.

Stunned, Roche and Criquielion responded but it was too little too late. Argentin had stolen one of his most famous victories.

Born in San Donà di Piave in 1960, Argentin was a junior champion on the track who became one of Italy's finest classics riders. In total he won four Liège titles, the Tours of Lombardy and Flanders, as well as La Flèche Wallonne three times, a shared record. He won the world championship road race in 1986, thirteen stages at the Giro and two at the Tour.

Nicknamed *Il Capo*, Argentin was a proud man. He famously had a run-in with a young Lance Armstrong in 1993 when he mistook the Texan for one of his team-mates. Armstrong responded in kind, deliberately addressing Argentin by the name of one of the Italian's own compatriots – Chiapucci. Argentin, winner of Monuments, Grand Tour stages and a former world champion, was furious at the slur. A few days later, the two were about to contest the sprint at the Trofeo Laigueglia. Just before the finish line Argentin slammed on the brakes and let riders pass through, so determined was he not to share a podium with the Texan. Armstrong later called it a curiously elegant insult.

18 December

Michael Barry, cyclist and writer, is born
(1975)

Canadian Michael Barry rode in the professional peloton for fourteen years. He was a domestique, his job being to ride in the service of others. As a result his palmares are wafer-thin. He has just ten wins to his name and four of them are in team-time-trials. But such is the life of a domestique and Barry knew it. He was a student of the sport before he entered the peloton and later said that it was exactly that notion of self-sacrifice, that unique blend of a team riding itself into the ground for hours on end so that the main man could later take flight and fight for glory, that attracted him to cycling in the first place.

Barry has perhaps become better known than some other domestiques for his off-bike pursuits. During his cycling career he wrote a number of insightful articles for the *New York Times* and the *Toronto Star*, among others. He has also written four books, including *Inside the Postal Bus* (2005) and *Le Métier* (2010). In 2014 he wrote *Shadows on the Road*, in which he addressed the issue of his doping, having been banned in 2012 as part of the investigation into the US Postal team by USADA

19 December

Zoulfia Zabirova is born
(1973)

Zoulfia Zabirova became the first athlete from Uzbekistan to win a gold medal at the summer Olympic Games when, in 1996, she won the individual time trial in Atlanta.

Born in Tashkent, the capital of Uzbekistan, Zabirova chose to ride for Russia after the break-up of the Soviet Union. Introduced to the bike by her grandfather, she has since spoken about the hardships and difficulties she faced as a woman in Uzbekistan wishing to pursue a cycling career (in certain parts of the country she couldn't ride for fear of being stoned). She moved to Russia before her Olympic win, meaning the history books credit her gold medal to her country of adoption.

In 2002 she added a rainbow jersey to her wardrobe, winning the individual time trial ahead of the Swiss pair Nicole Braendli and Karin Thuerig.

Talented against the clock, Zabirova won four Chrono des Herbiers (now known as the Chrono des Nations) titles between 1997 and 2002. At the time of writing she is the only woman to have won the title three years in a row. She also picked a number of other important wins, including stages at Giro d'Italia Femminile and the Tour de France Féminine, as well as the Tour of Flanders and the Primavera Rosa.

In 2005 Zabirova switched nationalities once again, this time taking up residence in Kazakhstan, where she claimed multiple national titles until her retirement in 2009, making her a former national champion of both Russia and Kazakhstan.

20 December

Rik Van Looy is born
(1933)

A rider once described by the legendary Jacques Anquetil as his real rival in the Grand Tours, Belgium's Rik Van Looy was a winning machine who won nearly every classic during an exceptional eighteen-year career.

Dubbed the Emperor of Herentals (after the small Belgian town where he lived), in 1961 Van Looy became the first rider to grab a full suite of Monument wins when he claimed a three-man sprint into Liège. Only Eddy Merckx and Roger De Vlaeminck have since matched Van Looy's achievement.

He opened his classics account three years after he turned professional when he won in Ghent–Wevelgem in 1956. He won Milan–Sanremo two years later and for the next few years he dominated the important one-day races. In all Van Looy claimed fourteen major one-day classic wins.

He also won two straight world championship road races, in 1960 and 1961, controversially missing out on a third title in 1963 when he was the designated team leader. To his surprise when he opened up his sprint he found he was riding against his team-mate Benoni Beheyt, who took a narrow win. Van Looy had been denied the chance to take his third rainbow jersey and join the greats Binda and Van Steenbergen. His supporters claimed he had been betrayed.

Away from one-day races, Van Looy won thirty-seven stages at the Tour, Giro and Vuelta. He also won jerseys at all three, claiming the points jersey at the Tour and Vuelta and the mountains jersey at the Giro, courtesy of a long solo ride through the Alps.

He retired in 1970, going on to manage a bike-racing school.

21 December

The Melbourne Cup on Wheels Carnival is held
(2013)

An annual fixture on the Australian track calendar, and now in its eightieth year, the Melbourne Cup on Wheels is a handicap race, run over 2000m.

Today hosted in the Darebin International Sports Centre, the eight-lap race starts with riders positioned at different points around the track – from scratch (the start line) through to 250m (a one-lap head start) depending on the handicap awarded to them. As the race unwinds the faster riders, having started further back, gain ground. With booming commentary whipping up the atmosphere, the race builds into an exciting climactic sprint. Over recent years the race has steadily become more international with Josiah Ng of Malaysia becoming the first non-Australian to win the event in 2008.

The Cup on Wheels Finals are the highlight of a carnival of racing in which numerous races are held. The 2013 meet was the first time the sprint and keirin races were awarded UCI Category 1 status, a move that helped boost an already prestigious event and attracted world-class riders to Melbourne. World champions Matthew Glaetzer and Anna Meares both rode and picked up wins.

22 December

Oscar Aaronson dies
(1900)

Going into the 1900 Six Days of New York, Oscar Aaronson, teamed with Oscar Babcock, was among the favourites. Newspapers recorded that Aaronson had been 'riding like a fiend', and that he and Babcock were considered likely winners by 'many wise men in the sport'.

And with good reason. For three days they were at the front of the race but tragedy struck when Aaronson was involved in a huge crash. Thrown from his bike, he cracked his head on the track. Riders smashed into him, bikes colliding with his motionless and battered body.

Aaronson was taken to hospital, his life in the balance. The sport held its breath; six-day racing had been under intense scrutiny for the strains it placed on its participants. The death of a rider could prove to be the final blow.

Aaronson held on for six days, the strength and stamina that he had shown on the track manifest in the hospital ward, but on 22 December he finally succumbed to his injuries, the cause of death being reported as pneumonia brought on by exhaustion. Aaronson had been due to marry his long-term partner just three days later. He had planned on setting up their home with the prize money from the very race that ultimately cost him his life. He was twenty-five years old.

23 December

Wim Vansevenant is born
(1971)

On the last day of the 2008 Tour, while the world of cycling toasted the yellow jersey of Carlos Sastre, Belgium's Wim Vansevenant was celebrating his own bit of cycling history.

He hadn't claimed a stage. Nor had he won a jersey as a classification leader. Far from it. Out of the 145 riders who had made it to Paris, Vansevenant was 145th. He had finished dead last, the same as the previous year. And the year before that.

It was the first time the same rider had finished the Tour last on three occasions. Vansevenant was the Tour's first three-time *lanterne rouge*, an expression that derives from the red lamp that would be hung on the last carriage on a train. Over the years, however, it has come to symbolise the spirit of the Tour, a statement of grit and determination, of refusing to yield to the challenge the race throws at you.

Often the Tour's *lanterne rouge* would become better known and earn better post-Tour contracts than riders who placed far higher. That led to curious incidents in which riders actively tried to come last: deliberately riding slowly, taking longer than normal natural breaks or even hiding.

Rules were introduced in the late 1970s to stamp out such behaviour but the cult of the *lanterne rouge* persists to this day. Websites are dedicated to the subject and books written on its peculiar history. A history of which Wim Vansevenant is now a notable part.

24 December

The back pedal brake is patented
(1889)

Towards the end of the nineteenth century bicycle design was evolving fast with inventors all over the world rapidly filing for patents as they sought to improve the ease and efficiency with which the bicycle could be operated.

Daniel Stover owned the eponymous Stover Experimental Works, founded in the 1860s to manufacture machinery, including windmills. In 1888 he founded the Stover Bicycle Works to produce bicycle accessories. In August 1889, along with William Hance, he filed a patent application for a back-pedal brake.

With the patent taken out on 24 December, the invention became known as the safety brake and a common feature on bikes of the era. Stover's bicycle company moved into the manufacture of bicycles themselves in 1891 and filed several other patent applications relating to bicycles, including tubing manufacturing methods and designs of saddles and cranks.

The company manufactured bikes under the iconic Phoenix brand from 1892 until 1898 when it folded.

25 December

Guido Reybrouck is born
(1941)

Possessed of a devastating turn of speed, Guido Reybrouck was a Belgian sprinter who claimed multiple classics wins and Grand Tour stages. His happiest hunting ground was Paris–Tours, where he won three times. Success there ran in the family – his three wins matching the record for most victories held by his uncle Gustave Danneels (and also Paul Maye and Erik Zabel). His third victory came in 1968 after being set up for the sprint by his Faema team-mate Eddy Merckx, who was being too closely marked to be able to go for the win himself.

Reybrouck also won Kuurne–Brussels–Kuurne in 1965, Belgium's national championships in 1966 and the 1969 edition of the Amstel Gold race, beating Jos Huysmans in a two-man sprint.

He rode the Tour for the first time in 1965, picking up two stage wins, including one in the Pyrénées, and would ride the race six times over the course of his nine-year career, claiming six stages. He also won stages at the Giro and Vuelta, winning the points competition in the latter by just two points in 1970.

26 December

Sven Nys wins Hofstade cyclo-cross
(2003)

From 2001 until 2007, Boxing Day in Belgium for elite cyclo-cross riders meant one thing – the Kersttrofee at Hofstade. Held on a 2.6km-long course taking the riders through woods and over sand, mud and gravel, the first winner of the 'Christmas Trophy' was Mario De Clercq, a rider who would finish his career with three world championship titles. The first women's race was won by Daphny Van Den Brand.

Over the course of its first three editions the race grew in popularity and prestige. From 2004 until 2007 it was part of the UCI's world cup programme, eventually folding when the Boxing Day world cup race was moved to Zolder.

Over the course of its short history the men's race was dominated by one man, Sven Nys. Of the seven races held, Nys won four and finished second on two other occasions. The only year he didn't finish on the podium was in 2006 when he came fifth. The record for wins in the women's race is shared by Daphny Van Den Brand and Hanka Kupfernagel, each of whom claimed three wins.

27 December

Muenzer confirmed as Female Athlete of the Year
(2004)

In the prologue to her autobiography, *One Gear, No Brakes*, Lori-Ann Muenzer describes sitting alone on a bus, thoughts spinning in her head. The bus is taking her to a training session at the Olympic Velodrome in Athens, four days before her event, the match sprint, is scheduled to start. Muenzer writes despairingly of her feelings of loneliness, of being written off and of being jettisoned by her team. Doubts are creeping into her mind. What is she even doing here?

She was thirty-eight years old. Why did she think she could mix it with younger, better-supported riders? Not even her team believed in her. They'd disappeared. She didn't even have anyone to time her during training. But then Lori-Ann Muenzer did what she had done for years. She got off the bus and went riding.

Four days later she stood in Athens as her national anthem was played, wearing gold around her neck. Muenzer had become Canada's first, and to date only, cycling gold medallist.

Suddenly people noticed her. In December the same year Muenzer became the winner of the Bobbie Rosenfeld Female Athlete of the Year award, a prestigious prize that has been awarded to Canada's athletes since 1933. Muenzer was only the second cyclist to have won the award.

28 December

Marianne Vos wins Azencross
(2011)

Marianne Vos is the most dominant rider of her generation. Of any generation, in fact. When not ruling the roads in summer, she is mastering the mud of winter.

Want proof of her dominance? Look no further than the 2011/12 cyclo-cross season. In her first race she came second in the Koksijde world cup race. The next day she went to Gieten and opened her 2011/12 'cross account. There would be many more deposits to come over the next four months.

By the time Vos won the Azencross race on 28 December she had extended her winning streak to eight. Vos had left her fellow riders wallowing as she skipped over the mud and filth that constitutes a cyclo-cross course. 'Boring? Yeah, a bit,' she said afterwards. 'But you have to maintain focus.'

Vos maintained that focus right through into the New Year. By the time of the world championships she had won another six races. She was the overwhelming favourite to claim her fifth rainbow jersey and she did so with something to spare, winning by thirty-seven seconds.

She won her last cross race of the year at Valkenburg on 18 February 2012. Three weeks later she rode her first world cup road race of the year. She won, of course.

29 December

Juan Carlos Rojas Villegas wins his third Vuelta a Costa Rica
(2013)

Held every year since 1965, the Vuelta a Costa Rica is a multi-stage race that takes place every December. With a route that features climbs of over 3,000m, before plunging back down to sea level, calling in on coastal towns, the race takes the peloton through a rich and dramatic landscape throughout its two-week duration.

The 2013 race featured twelve stages, including three in the mountains and a couple of time trials. It was won by Juan Carlos Rojas Villegas, a Costa Rican who had also won the race in 2005 and 2010. His 2013 win set a record for the most victories.

Villegas repeated his win in 2014, taking his tally to four wins. It was the crowning of a great season for the thirty-three-year-old, one in which he became national champion for the first time and finished top of the UCI America Tour rankings.

30 December

Lars Boom is born
(1985)

Now principally a road rider, Dutchman Lars Boom first burst on to the international cycling scene in 2003 when he won the junior world cyclo-cross championship in Monopoli, Puglia, southern Italy. It was a stellar cast that year, with Zdeněk Štybar and Niels Albert also riding, but Boom won easily. It was the start of things to come.

Over the next few years Boom won national and European titles until, in 2007, he added the Espoirs world title. Again Štybar and Albert were in the field. Boom was looking for revenge – Štybar had won the title in 2005 and 2006 when he'd outsprinted the Dutchman. This time it was different. This time Boom was too powerful. He rode alone to take the win by well over a minute.

Twelve months later and he had another rainbow jersey in the bag. This time it was at elite level. Junior, Espoirs, Elite: Boom had a complete set of 'cross world championships.

He switched his focus to the road after that, although he still returns to cyclo-cross occasionally. His biggest win to date on the road came at the 2014 Tour when he won a memorable stage run over the treacherous cobblestones normally reserved for Paris–Roubaix, in conditions more associated with Boom's first love, cyclo-cross, than the Tour.

'When I saw the weather this morning, I smiled,' he said. 'This is my most beautiful win.'

Boom's career continues. He currently rides for the Astana team.

31 December

Tommy Godwin sets Year Record of 75,065 miles
(1939)

Before dawn on 1 January 1939, Tommy Godwin, a twenty-six-year-old cyclist who had been born in Stoke-on-Trent in 1912, got on his bike and started riding. For the next twelve months he would barely stop.

Godwin had been riding bikes since taking a job as a delivery boy at fourteen. He soon started racing – and winning – and grew into one of the country's top time-trial riders, racking up numerous wins across the country. By 1938 he had switched his focus to an altogether different type of challenge, one barely believable in terms of scale: the Year Record.

The challenge had been established as far back as 1911 when *Cycling* magazine started a competition to see how many 100-mile rides a cyclist could complete in a year. The competition soon morphed into the number of miles ridden in a year. Marcel Planes was the first holder with 34,666 miles. His record stood for over twenty years but throughout the 1930s it fell again and again. By the time Godwin started his attempt the mark to beat was an incredible 62,657 miles, held by Ossie Nicholson. That's nearly eight times the diameter of the world as measured at the equator.

Three Brits actually started 1939 separately focused on breaking the record. Along with Godwin there were attempts made by Edward Swann and Bernard Bennett. Swann suffered a bad crash early in his attempt and had to stop but Bennett continued and for a while was beating Godwin.

As the year proceeded Godwin started to post some truly staggering miles. His distances for May, June, July and August read 6,557, 7,661, 8,583 and 7,367 miles respectively. On 21 June, the longest day of the year, he rode 361 miles – his greatest single-day distance.

Such mileage meant his equipment had to be the best that he could get. Initially sponsored by his employer, Ley Cycles, by May the cost of maintaining his custom-built bike was beginning to hurt and so a new sponsor was sought. Raleigh stepped in and gave him a four-speed, steel-framed machine.

On 26 October 1939 Godwin rode into London's Trafalgar Square, the new record holder. But still he kept going. By midnight on 31 December he had 75,065 miles under his wheels. He had smashed the previous record, averaging 205 miles a day. He took only one day off from riding the entire year.

But it wasn't enough. Now he reset his sights and targeted the record for 100,000 miles. Onwards Godwin cycled. On 14 May 1940 he finally stopped, having reached his target. It had been 500 days since he started early that New Year's morning, and he had beaten the previous record for 100,000 miles by over a month. A few weeks later Godwin signed up with the RAF and went to war.

Godwin's Year Record still stands. It has long been considered unbreakable, although at the time of writing there are at least two separate challenges to his seventy-five-year-and-counting record underway.

GLOSSARY OF TERMS

Abandon – the quitting of a rider during the race, either through injury, mechanical problems or exhaustion.

Arrivee – the finish line of a road race.

Bidon – a plastic water bottle that is clipped to the frame. They used to be made of tin and carried in cages that were fixed to the handlebars.

BLRC – the British League of Racing Cyclists, founded in 1942 to promote mass-start road racing in Britain, at the time banned by the National Cycling Union.

Bmx racing – a mass-start sprint race held on a custom-built, off-road course featuring jumps and banked turns. Up to eight riders compete in the same race.

Boards – a colloquial term for the track in a velodrome. Tracks are oval in shape and feature high, banked corners. UCI regulations state they must be between 133m and 500m in length, however Olympic and World Championship races must be held on a 250m-long track.

Break / breakaway – a rider, or group of riders, that breaks free from the front of the main bunch. Often teams will assess the riders in the break to see if they should try to prevent the break getting away or whether they can let them go as they pose no threat to their own leaders (also see Teamwork).

Broom wagon – the vehicle that follows a road race to collect any riders that abandon the race. Voiture-balai in French.

Classics – a collective term for the most prestigious one-day road races. Most

have been included on the cycling calendar for decades. Also see Monuments.

Clenbuterol – a drug that is used to treat asthma but also promotes muscle growth and burns fat. Its use is prohibited by WADA.

Criterium – a multiple-lap race held on a short circuit, normally in a town or city centre. Historically held in northern Europe. Successful professional riders would negotiate large contracts to appear in criterium races, boosting attendance for organisers. It remains a popular form of racing.

Cyclo-cross – a form of bike racing that takes place over multiple laps of an off-road course featuring sharp climbs over a variety of terrain including mud and sand. Successful cyclo-cross racers need strong running skills as well as great bike handling as they are forced to carry bikes on their shoulders and run when riding becomes impossible. Races are most commonly held in the winter.

Depart – the start line of a road race or stage.

Derny – a small motorbike used for pacing cyclists.

Director sportif – the head coach of a cycling team.

Domestique – French for servant, these are the real heroes of road racing. They spend their days looking after the leaders on their team, fetching water, ferrying food and chasing breaks. This is the reality of life as a professional road cyclist for the majority of riders. Also see Teamwork.

EPO – Erythropoietin, or EPO is a hormone produced naturally in the body that controls red blood cell production. Red blood cells

deliver oxygen to the muscles and the more red blood cells, the more oxygen delivered, resulting in increased stamina. EPO can be produced artificially and injected in order to boost red blood cell production and therefore enhance athletic performance.

Espoir – French for hope, in cycling terminology an Espoir is an under-23 rider, specifically one aged nineteen-twenty-two years old.

Festina affair – the doping investigation sparked by the discovery of a large amount of performance-enhancing drugs in a car allocated to the Festina team prior to the 1998 Tour de France. The discovery exposed the extent of doping in cycling, particularly the use of EPO, and threw the race into chaos.

Flamme rouge – the red flag that hangs at the start of the final kilometre of a road race, advising riders there remains only 1000m left to the finish.

General Classification (GC) – the overall standings in a stage race. The leader of the GC at any one time wears the leader's jersey. The rider at the top of the GC after the final stage wins the overall race.

Grand depart – the overall start of a stage race.

Grand tours – a collective term for the three most prestigious stage races: the Tour de France, Giro d'Italia and Vuelta a España. They are the only stage races that run for three weeks.

Grimpeur – a rider who specialises in riding uphill.

Indépendant - a category of rider no longer in use. An indépendant was a semi-professional rider who could ride against both

professionals and amateurs. While they had not signed professional terms, unlike amateurs they were able to accept payments from sponsors and race for money.

Jerseys – special jerseys are awarded to classification leaders in a stage race. The classifications featured can vary race to race but will always include the GC leader and normally also include a sprinters and a climbers classification. Jersey colours also vary race to race, famous examples include the leader of the Tour de France, who wears a yellow jersey, and the leader of the Giro d'Italia, who wears pink. World champions win a white jersey with rainbow-coloured stripes printed on it. They wear the rainbow jersey throughout the season in races where they are the world champion in that discipline.

Keirin – a paced track race. Normally around 2km in distance, riders follow a derny which gradually increases the pace before peeling away with around a third of the race to go, leaving the riders to sprint for the win. Its origins lie in Japan.

Kermesse – a multiple-lap race held in Belgium on a closed-road circuit. Similar to a Criterium but often smaller and held as part of a wider celebration – a village fair, for example.

Madison – a team track event, usually ridden in pairs. Only one rider races at a time, the other switches in only when their partner touches them, normally by way of a hand-sling. There is no limit to how long each rider spends racing. The winning team is the one which gains the most laps. Points are also awarded in intermediate sprints and are used in the result of a tie.

Monuments – the collective term for the five most important and most prestigious one-day Classics. They are: Milan-Sanremo, Tour of Flanders, Paris-Roubaix, Liège–Bastogne–Liège and the Tour of Lombardy.

Mountain bike racing – held off-road on courses that can feature testing climbs, descents and obstacles, mountain bike races are split into various types including cross-country, downhill, endurance and marathon. Cross-country is the only form so far to be included in the Olympic programme.

Mountain classifications - climbs that feature on the route of a road race are often classified. Classifications range from Category Four (least testing) through to Hors Categorie (beyond classification). The main factors determining the classification awarded to a climb are its length and gradient although where it appears on the route (i.e. near the start or finish) can also be an influence.

NCU – the National Cycling Union, or NCU, oversaw track and circuit racing in Great Britain from 1883. It merged with the British League of Racing Cyclists (see BLRC) in 1959 to form the British Cycling Federation.

Omnium – a multi-discipline track cycling event comprising six races: a Scratch race, an individual pursuit, an elimination race, a time trial, a flying lap and a points race. Points are awarded in each race with the rider with the largest tally at the end of the six races declared the winner. The event entered the Olympic programme in 2012.

Pacing – the practice of riding in the slipstream of an out-rider, or pacer, in order to conserve energy. Pacers most commonly use small motorcycles although riders on tandems and even cars have also been used. While the keirin is the most obvious example of a paced race today, in the past paced road races were commonplace, particularly those that took place over vast distances.

Palmares – the record of results a rider achieves throughout their career.

Parcours – the route of a road race.

Patron – the boss of the bunch. While not a formal appointment, the patron of the peloton is the most respected rider and the one who is listened to most in the inner-workings of a professional peloton.

Pavé – the cobblestone roads that feature in some one-day Classics.

Peloton – the main bunch of riders in a race. Can also be used generally as a collective term for professional road cyclists – e.g. the peloton was not happy with the latest change to the cycle-race calendar.

Prime – an in-race prize awarded to the first rider to pass that point of the race.

Pursuit – a track race where two individuals or teams race against the clock, starting on the opposite side of the track. The aim is to complete the race distance in the quickest time. If one catches the other before the end of the race distance they are declared the winner. Teams comprise four riders with the time taken on the third rider across the finish line.

RAAM – the Race Across America. A 3,000-mile race from California to Maryland run as one continual stage. Racers can compete either individually or in teams.

Race classifications – the UCI classify races according to the type of race (1= one day race, 2= a stage race) and its importance or difficulty. The highest classification of road races is the WorldTour, which includes all three Grand Tours and all the major one-day Classics as well as races such as the Critérium du Dauphiné and Tour of Switzerland. So the Tour de France is classified as 2.UWT. In women's road cycling the highest classification is the World Cup (CDM). Away from the road the Olympic Games and World Championships are the highest categorised races.

Race of truth – a colloquial term for a time-trial – just one person riding against the clock with no team-mates on hand to assist and nowhere to hide.

Randonné – an organised long-distance bicycle ride which is not raced but where times may be recorded.

Rider types – cyclists fall into different categories depending on their speciality. Some road riders are good climbers but aren't as fast as others over a 200m sprint. On the track some riders can sustain a high power output for minutes at a time but don't have the burst of acceleration needed for the sprint events. It often comes down to physiology. The type of body needed to ride to the summit of a 2000m-high mountain three of four times in a single stage is very different to the one needed to contest a mass sprint at the end of a 200km flat race. Also see Grimpeur, Rouleur and Sprinter.

Road racing – races held on closed roads. They may take the form of a single mass-start race where the winner is the first to cross the finish line; a race held over stages (see GC; or a time-trial (see separate entry). Courses can vary from multiple laps of a circuit or run from one town to another and can be designed to feature certain terrain designed to suit a particular type of rider and therefore encourage exciting racing. See Rider Types.

Rouleur – a good all-round rider who doesn't fall into the category of a good climber or sprinter. Often working as a domestique a rouleur is someone who can spend hours at the front of a race driving the pace. Their best chance of a win normally comes from a joining a small escape group and working with the others to keep their advantage intact until the finish line.

Six-day races – a track meeting that lasts for six days. Initially riders rode individually with the winner the rider who completed most laps. The only limit to how long riders spent on the track was their own stamina. Over the years, with the well-being of riders paramount, the format has changed. Today racing usually starts early evening and lasts for six or seven hours, taking in a variety of disciplines with points awarded for each as well as for gaining laps and winning intermediate sprints and in the all-important Madison races (see separate entry). The winning pair is the one which has accumulated the most points at the end of the meet.

Soigneur – the person who cares for a rider throughout a race. Such care will include the giving of massages and the handing out of food during a race.

Sprinter – a type of rider who has the turn of speed needed to excel in the final mass-dash to the line of a road race, or in the match sprint and keirin on the track.

Teamwork – while race wins may be awarded to individuals, cycling, particularly road racing, is a team sport. Teams will designate one or two riders as their leaders for a race and the rest of the team will work for those leaders. That 'work' will include the chasing and marshalling of any breaks that may go, pacing leaders back to the bunch in the event of a mechanical problem, sheltering their leader from the wind, and the fetching and carrying of food and drink. The aim of the team is to deliver their leader into the final moments of the race in as fresh a state as possible, giving them the best opportunity to win.

Time limit (hors-délai) – all riders are expected to finish a road race within a certain percentage of the winning time. The percentage varies depending on the race course (hilly or flat, long or short). If a rider finishes outside of the time limit imposed by the organisers they are thrown off the race.

Time trials – a timed race ridden either individually or in teams. Large differences in times can appear over comparatively short distances, meaning those with eyes on winning races that include time trial stages need to be good riding alone against the clock.

Track racing – races that are held on a track within a velodrome, either inside or outside. Track racing comprises speed and endurance events ridden both individually and in teams. Also see boards, keirin, omnium, pursuit.

UCI – cycling's governing body – stands for the Union Cycliste Internationale, or International Cycling Union.

UVF – France's national cycling federation. Stands for the Union Vélocipédique de France. It later became the FFC - La Fédération française de cyclisme.

WADA – the World Anti-Doping Agency. Established in 1999 as an independent agency to bring consistency to anti-doping regulations and policies. Its Foundation Board include representatives of the International Olympic Committee, National Olympic Committees, Sports Federations, athletes and international governments.

Acknowledgements

A note of thanks...

This book would not have been possible without the support and assistance of a number of people. We'd like to take this opportunity to thank all at Aurum Press who have worked on this project - specifically Robin Harvie, who was instrumental in shaping the book before departing for pastures new, and Jennifer Barr and Lucy Warburton who have expertly guided both of us through the entire process and have had a huge part in the book you now hold in your hands.

We owe a debt of gratitude to everybody at *Boneshaker Magazine*. It was through that wonderful publication that we first worked together and their unique blend of quality writing and great design remains an inspiration. They have always been happy to offer us advice when asked, something for which we are enormously grateful.

We would like to thank our respective families and friends for all of their interest and support - and for their understanding when we disappeared from daily life for months on end (only to be distracted, and with thoughts often elsewhere, when we did occasionally emerge). Special thanks go to Edwin Cruden for the title.

Finally, but most importantly, we would like to thank our wonderful partners who supported us immeasurably throughout the whole experience with enthusiasm and encouragement. Without them this book simply would not exist. Karen and Julia - to both of you, from both of us, thank you.

Giles and Dan, May 2015

Bibliography:
This book draws on a wide range of sources, far too many to list here, but the following are worthy of special mention:
Belbin, Giles, *Mountain Kings: Agony and euphoria on the peaks of the Tour de France*, Punk Publishing, 2013.
Cazenueve, Thierry, Philippe Court and Yves Perret, (eds), *Les Alpes et Le Tour*, Le Dauphiné Libéré Hors-Serie, 2009.
Chany, Pierre and Thierry Cazenueve, *La Fabuleuse Histoire du Tour de France*, Minerva, 2003.
Chany, Pierre, *La Fabuleuse Histoire des Classiques et des Championnats du Monde*, Editions ODI, 1979.
— *La Fabuleuse Histoire du Cyclisme*, Editions ODIL, 1975.
Cossins, Peter, *The Monuments: The Grit and the Glory of Cycling's Greatest One-day Races*, Bloomsbury Publishing Plc, 2014
Howard, Paul, *Sex, Lies and Handlebar Tape: The Remarkable Life of Jacques Anquetil*, Mainstream Publishing, 2011.
McGann, Bill and Carol McGann, *The Story of the Giro d'Italia*, Vol. 1 & 2, McGann Publishing, 2011.
Millar, David, *Racing Through the Dark*, Orion Books, 2011.
Rendell, Matt, *Blazing Saddles*, Quercus, 2007.
Sykes, Herbie, *Maglia Rosa*, Rouleur Books, Bloomsbury Publishing Plc, 2013.
Weidenfeld and Nicolson, *The Official Tour de France Centennial 1903-2003*, Orion Publishing Group, 2003
Woodland, Les, *The Yellow Jersey Companion to the Tour de France*, Yellow Jersey Press, Random House, 2003.
In addition to the above, the archives and back-issues of the following publications were of particular assistance: The Official Reports of the Olympic Games, *La Stampa*, *Le Petit Journal*, *Le Petit Parisien*, *Le Journal de Genève*, *Rouleur*, *Procycling* and *Miroir-Sport*, as well as those of the *Guardian* and the *Telegraph*.